T0339681

YANKS IN THE REDWOODS

Yanks in the Redwoods

Frank H. Baumgardner III

Algora Publishing
New York

Library of Congress Cataloging-in-Publication Data —

Baumgardner, Frank H.
    Yanks in the Redwoods: carving out a life in Northern California / Frank H.
Baumgardner, III.
        p. cm.
    Includes bibliographical references and index.
    ISBN 978-0-87586-801-1 (soft cover: alk. paper) — ISBN 978-0-87586-802-8 (hard
cover: alk. paper) — ISBN 978-0-87586-803-5(ebook) 1. California, Northern—Discovery
and exploration. 2. California, Northern—History—19th century. 3. Frontier and pioneer
life—California, Northern. 4. Land settlement—California, Northern—History—19th
century. I. Title.
    F867.5.B39 2010
    979.4'04—dc22
                            2010034381

Front cover: Postcard of Logger Under a Redwood Tree, Image: © Lake County
Museum/CORBIS, Date Created: ca. 1908–1915, Collection: Corbis Museum

Also by Frank H. Baumgardner:

Killing for Land in Early California
Indian Blood at Round Valley 1856–1863
(Algora Publishing, 2005)

Printed in the United States

"I shall by no means forget my character as a historian to follow the truth step by step, whatever happens, or wherever it may lead me."
—Jonathan Swift, Section IV, Tale of a Tub, 1704

For Emi, Sam, Jack, and all who soon will be taking over from us. In memory of historians Bernard deVoto, Stephen E. Ambrose, Walter Lord, David Herbert Donald as well as local historians, Floyd Barney, Barbara Bull, Jim Nagy, Dorothy Bear, Beth Stebbins, Bonni Gapp, and Nannie Flood Escola. Also to remember James Wargin, Gordon "Skip" West, Phil Snyder, Dick Ruiz, and Howard Heney.

For the forgotten: those whose names nobody now recalls who nevertheless played vital roles in history.

Acknowledgments

Like all writers I owe thanks to many persons who made my work possible. I hope no one will be offended since I cannot list all of you here. First and foremost is my wife, Jeannette, who has stood by me, making useful suggestions, reading rewrites, and listening to tiresome moans and groans. She is always of inestimable value.

Others, Patricia Heinicke, my first copy editor, longtime friend Alice Schilla, who did a final proofreading/edit, as well others, Evelyn McClure, Judy Fisch, Carol Cunningham, Gail West, Alice Smith, Fr. Rod McAulay, Rosemary Manchester, and Robert Winn aided me more than they will ever know. Several museums and their professional curators such as Nancy Freeze, and Carolyn Zeitler of Kelley House Museum, Mendocino, and Russ and Sylvia Bartley of Noyo Hill House, Ft. Bragg, made available priceless manuscripts (for example, copies of the writings of John Work, Jerome Ford, and others). Such curators, including the staff of the Smithsonian Archives, Washington, D.C. can save researchers from weeks of meaningless probing and going up blind alleys. I cannot ever thank them enough. Last, but no means least, thanks to Ms. Ronnie James, Little River and editor of the latest issue of the Mendocino Historical Society's Review. Her knowledge of the specifics of local Little River history- names, events, places- were of inestimable value in preparation for Chapter 13- The Diary of Etta Stevens Pullen and her beloved husband, Wilder. Lastly thanks to Algora Publishing for making a commitment on me.

Frank H. Baumgardner, III
Santa Rosa, California

TABLE OF CONTENTS

PREFACE   1

CHAPTER 1. LEWIS AND CLARK FOLLOW THE COLUMBIA RIVER TO THE PACIFIC,
WITH HELP FROM THE CLATSOP NATION   3

CHAPTER 2. JOHN WORK'S EXPEDITION TO THE NORTH MENDOCINO COAST,
FROM BODEGA BAY TO THE MATTOLE RIVER   11

CHAPTER 3. JESSE APPLEGATE'S JOURNEY ON THE OREGON TRAIL, THE OSAGE RIVER
TO THE WILLAMETTE VALLEY, 1843   19

CHAPTER 4. NORTH COAST EXPLORER/SETTLERS FIND GOLD! GEORGE GIBBS,
OREGON TERRITORY'S FIRST CUSTOMS COLLECTOR, 1850   29
    Ethnologist/Customs Agent George Gibbs Moves to the Far West   32
    Gibbs' Observations of Humboldt Bay area Indians and Their Folkways   40

CHAPTER 5. THE IMPACT OF ANGLO-SAXONS ON EARLY NORTHERN CALIFORNIA
SHIPWRECK OF A BRIG, THE *FROLIC*, JULY 25, 1850   47

CHAPTER 6. COMMISSIONER REDICK MCKEE EXPLORES NORTHWESTERN
CALIFORNIA, AUGUST TO DECEMBER, 1851   51

CHAPTER 7. THE FIRST MILLS ON THE NORTH MENDOCINO COAST   63

CHAPTER 8. OREGON BOUND — 1853   79

CHAPTER 9. FOUNDING OF THE MENDOCINO RESERVATION AND FORT BRAGG,
LT. HORATIO T. GIBSON, U.S. ARMY   93

CHAPTER 10. THE INVESTIGATION OF CALIFORNIA SUPERINTENDENT OF INDIAN
AFFAIRS THOMAS J. HENLEY   105

CHAPTER 11. MENDOCINO COAST SETTLEMENT TAKES HOLD 121

CHAPTER 12. "DOGHOLE" SCHOONERS LINK THE MENDOCINO COAST TO THE WORLD, FORT BRAGG BECOMES A CITY 131

CHAPTER 13. ETTA & WILDER PULLEN, LITTLE RIVER 143

CHAPTER 14. OUT OF THE PAST — A SURVIVOR'S STORY 173

EPILOGUE 183

APPENDICES 187

Appendix I. Gen. Sherman's View of Harry Meiggs, Lumberman and Modern San Francisco's Forgotten Founder 187

Appendix II. Excerpts from the Journal of George Gibbs 188
A. Business data from page 6: 188
B. Gibbs' Notes on Northwestern California Tribes, ca. 1850–52. 189

Appendix III. A Sampling of poetry by Bret Harte. 191

Appendix IV. Depositions relating to Superintendent Henley's Investigation 196

Appendix V. "Doghole" Schooners 220

Appendix VI. Early Little River Families 222

SOURCES 225
Interviews 225
Published Sources: 225
Unpublished sources: 228
GovernmentDocuments: 228

INDEX 231

PREFACE

The settlement of the Pacific Northwest proceeded in fits and starts by diverse groups of settlers with differing origins, strategies and goals. The exploration period of Lewis and Clark and John Work, from 1800 to 1840, yielded to the settlement period of the mid 19th century. That period, in turn, moved into an era of government *laissez-faire* and corporation-dominated development in the late 19th century known as the Gilded Age.

My research for this book builds on decades of study, evolving by 2006 into an initial, specific focus on the "Indians" who had inhabited the Mendocino Reservation. After traveling to the Held-Poage Historical Research Library in Ukiah, the Kelley House Museum in Mendocino, Ft. Bragg, and the Guest House Museum in Ft. Bragg, I realized that there were few records about this short-lived Indian reservation. My research led me to Noyo Hill House located in Ft. Bragg. The early records there, along with those at Kelly House Museum, provided the basis for telling the story of the founding and the early years of the towns of Mendocino and Fort Bragg. Additional research in the Archives of the Smithsonian in Washington, D.C., led me to George Gibbs' journal. Deep amid yellowing papers from Comm. Redick McKee's Expedition (now housed at the Peabody Special Collections Section at Harvard University, which it happens, was Gibbs' alma mater), were a number of crude pencil sketches by George Gibbs. One of these shows a northern California Indian chieftain. In one hand he holds a bow and in the other a war club. Slung over one shoulder is his quiver of arrows. Animal skins cover his groin. What is most interesting about him to me is the expression on his face. Showing absolutely no fear, he calmly faces the oncoming invasion of his world by the white man.

During the first fifty years of the nineteenth century, Indians attempted to accommodate the white immigrants and in numerous cases aided them as manual workers, packers, and guides. After that time, open warfare or genocide was more the rule rather than an exception. Redwood tree (*Sequoia sempervirens*) forests and Indians had coexisted on the north Mendocino coast as well as in coastal areas to the north for thousands of years. By the mid-1850s redwood seedlings that had sprung up during the time of Charlemagne (AD 875) had grown to become more than three hundred feet tall. Groves of giant redwoods thrived along California's thousand-mile coastline. Local Indian tribes, the Mitom Pomo, the Kashaya Pomo of Sonoma County, the Miwok of Marin County, and the coastal Pomo of Kaidu at the Noyo River's outlet to the Pacific, lived in villages beside these giant trees.

To the "Argonauts" and those who arrived by the hundreds from 1850 to 1870, the redwoods seemed to be vast, even inexhaustible. There were so many saw mills operating that by 1875 there was no doubt that the lumber industry would be the dominant industry of the north coast, and it remained so through the nineteenth and twentieth centuries.

There was a change in approach by the white invaders from an earlier individualistic or pioneer phase, 1800 to the late 1840s, to a more rapidly developing corporate period from 1850 to the end of the period covered in this study. This appeared as an almost revolutionary era in which the main actors were company men. Individual mill owners no longer had the capital to keep up with the demand for new technology and heavy equipment. The man vs. man phase rapidly disappeared, almost overnight. In at least one case, a large company took away a tract of timber land that lawfully had been purchased by one man (Mr. Stevens, Etta Stevens Pullen's father). He had bought from an earlier owner. This study will show how many of the most significant decisions, like the purchase of large tracts of timber or the operation of fleets of schooners, weren't made, as the myths often would have us believe, by brave pioneers but in reality by corporate decision makers who were, in most cases, wealthy power brokers or entrepreneurs. Despite the stimulus provided to it by state and federal governmental support, the north Mendocino coast's lumber industry has never been an unmixed success. With the closure of Ft. Bragg's Mill No. 1 in 2002, at the mouth of the Noyo River, a giant mill that produced five hundred thousand board feet of lumber daily from its building in 1885 throughout the twentieth century, the lumber industry is a mere shadow of its former size and its importance to California has faded as well.

CHAPTER 1. LEWIS AND CLARK FOLLOW THE COLUMBIA RIVER TO THE PACIFIC, WITH HELP FROM THE CLATSOP NATION

> We met 4 Canoes of Indians from below, in which there is 26 Indians, one of those canoes is large, and ornamented with Images on the bow & Stern.
>
> That in the Bow [is] the likeness of a Bear and in the Stern the picture of a man.
>
> —Captain William Clark, Journal, Nov. 5, 1805.

The journals of Captains Meriwether Lewis and William Clark represent far more than a log of their expedition to find the sources of the Missouri River and to map the course of the Columbia River. As they traveled, they also laid out the rhetorical path of "manifest destiny" for the rest of the Euro-American population, a few members of which were already on what Bernard deVoto called "the westward march." The nation's third president, President Jefferson, having just succeeded in making the Louisiana Purchase in 1803, conceived of and presented the idea of a journey across the West to his secretary, Captain Meriwether Lewis, of the 1st Infantry. William Clark, a more accomplished frontiersman and cartographer, was contacted and invited to serve in joint command with Capt. Lewis. President Jefferson intended for the Lewis and Clark expedition to obtain information about the West's primary rivers, to study natural resources and begin the study of the climate, geology and plants of the Northwest.

By November 1805, the approximately forty-member party was eagerly anticipating completing their westward trek and, at last, reaching the Pacific Ocean. Still, the winter weather was almost constantly foggy and rainy, which had a profoundly negative effect on everyone's disposition.

November 5th Tuesday 1805

Rained all the after part of last night, rain continues this morning, I slept but very little last night for the noise Kept [up] during the whole of the night by the Swans, Geese white & Grey Brant Ducks &c. on a Small Sand Island close unde the Lard. Side; they were emensely noumerous, and their noise horid. We met 4 Canoes of Indians from below, in which there is 26 Indians, one of those canoes is large, and ornamented with *Images* on the bow & Stern. That in the Bow [is] the likeness of a Bear and in the Stern the picture of a man. The day proved cloudy with rain the greater part of it, we are all wet cold and disagreeable — I killed a grouse which was verry fat, and larger than common. This is the first night which we have been entirely clear of Indians since our arrival on the waters of the Columbia River.[1]

Two days later William Clark noted that they had arrived at the seacoast. "Ocian in view! O! the joy." Unfortunately, he was in error, perhaps due to their over-anticipation or perhaps to the rain. "Tonight's camp is near Pillar Rock and the ocean cannot be seen from there." They moved a bit further on the northern side of the river to Gray's Bay. To put this in perspective: Lewis and Clark's Expedition had begun in mid-May, 1804. By this time, mid-November 1805, the expedition had been going on for about a year and a half.

Two days later, on November 13, 1805, Captain Clark continued writing about a walk he had taken on his own. Clark had struggled his way through "intolerable thickets of small pine, a groth much resembling arrow wood on the Stem of which is thorns." After hiking through three miles or so, he had even more trouble since there were cliffs blocking his way. At this point, in order to complete his hike, he had to pull himself up by grabbing onto bushes.

The Timber on those hills are of the pine species large and tall maney of them more than 200 feet tall and from 8 feet through at the Stump. the rain continuing and weather proved so cloudy that I could not see any distance on my return we dispatched 3 men Colter, Willard and Shannon in the Indian canoe to get around the point if possible an examine the river, and the Bay below for a good harbor for out canoes to lie in Safty &c. The tide at every foot tide came in (*with great swells brakeing against the rocks and Drift trees*) [parentheses and italics those of Clark] with great fury. The rain[s] continue all day, nothing to eate but pounded fish which we keep as a reserve and use in situations of this kind. [2]

Two days later they got some good news. The miserable weather briefly improved. Capt. Lewis returned to the camp. He told them that they might soon be

---

1 Capt. William Clark, "Nov. 5, 1806," Bernard deVoto, Editor, *The Journals of Lewis and Clark*, Foreword by Stephen E. Ambrose (Boston, New York, Mariner Books, Houghton Mifflin Co., 1953). Foreword @ 1997, Ambrose-Tubbs Inc., 277. Capt. Clark's original spelling preserved.

2 *Ibid*. 283. The first editor of the journals, Bernard de Voto, noticed Capt. Clark's mistake.

meeting a party of white traders. They also had an interesting encounter with some Chinnook Indians.

November 14tth Thursday 1805

Rained all the last night without intermition, and this morning winds blows very hard, but our situation is Such that we cannot tell from what point it comes, one of our canoes is much broken by the waves dashing it against the rocks. 5 Indians came up in a canoe, thro' the waves which is verry high and role with great fury. They made signs to us that they saw 3 men we Send down yesterday. only 3 of those Indians landed, the other 2 which was women played off in the waves, which induced me to Suspect that they had taken Something from our men below, at this time one of our men Colter returned, by land and informed us that those Indians had taken his Gigg & basket, I called to the Squars to land and give back the gigg, which they would not doe until a man with a gun, as if he intended to Shute them which they landed, and Colter got his gig & basket

Colter informed us that it was but a Short distance from where we lay around the point to a butifull Sand beech which continued for a long ways, that he had found a good harbor in the mouth of a creek near 2 Indian lodges—that he had proceeded in the canoe as far as he could for the waves, the other two men Willard & Shannon had proceeded on down.[3]

Soon after this some of the men had an unexpected experience with six young Indian women. The incident was described by Capt. Lewis.

Thursday November 21st 1805

A cloudy morning most of the Chinnooks leave our camp and return home, the Wind blew hard from the S. E. which with the addition of the flood tide raised verry high waves which broke with great violence against the shore throwing water into our camp the forepart of this day Cloudy at 12 oClock it began to rain and continud all day moderately. Several Indians Visit us to day of different nations or Bands Some of the *Chiltz* Nation who reside on the Sea Coast near Point Lewis, Several of the *Clatsops* who reside on the Opposite side of the Columbia immediately opposite to us, and a Chief from the Grand rapid to whom we gave a Medal.

An old woman & Wife to a Chief of the *Chinoks* came and made a Camp near ours. She brought with her 6 young Squars (*her daughters & nieces*) I believe for the Purpose of Gratifying the passions of the men of our party and receiving for those indulgences Such small [presents] as She (the old woman) thought proper to accept of.

Those people appear to View Sensuality as a Necessary even, and do not appear to abhor it as a Crime in the unmarried State. The young females are fond of the attention of our men and appear to meet the sincere approbation of their friends and connections, for thus obtaining their favours, the Womin of the Chinnook Nation have handsome

---

3 Capt. Meriwether Lewis, *Ibid.* 283.

faces low and badly made with large legs & thighs which are generally Swelled from a Stopage of the circulation in the feet (which are Small) by maney Strands of Beeds or curious Strings which are drawn tight around the leg above the ankle, their legs are also picked [tattooed] with different figures, I saw on the left arm of a Squar the following letters *J. Bowman,* all those are considered by the natives of this quarter as handsome deckerations, and a woman without those deckorations is Considered as among the lower Class they ware their hair lose hanging over their back and Sholders maney have blue beeds threaded & hung from different parts of their *ears* and about their neck and around their wrists, their dress otherwise is prosisely like that of the Nation of *War ci a cum* as already described.[4]

As long as white explorers or settlers were greatly outnumbered by Indians, interactions tended to be non-threatening. Capt. Clark described how the Indian braves had "robes of *SeaOtter,* Beaver, Elk, Deer, fox, and cat common to this Country." Many men also had blue and red blankets that they probably had traded for with pelts to the Hudson's Bay Company. Some of the Chinnook warriors carried "Guns and powder and Ball." The Chinnook had obtained and knew how to use flintlock muskets that could have been used against Lewis and Clark's party if they had any serious disagreements. The passage is also interesting for it described how many of the squaws had skin problems, "venerious and pustelus disorders. one woman whome I saw at the Creek appeared all over in Scabs and ulcers &c."[5] The Chinnooks were not strangers to guns, even at this early point of time. The men carried beautiful fur robes of "SeaOtter, Elk, Deer, fox" and even cats.

A later entry compares the stature of the Indians of the Northwest with those "of the Missouri."

Monday, January 6th, 1806

The Clatsops, Chinnooks, Killamucks, &c. are very loquacious and inquisitive; they possess good memories and have repeated to us the names capasites of the vessels of many traders and others who have visited the mouth of this river; they are generally low in stature, proportionally small, reather lighter complected and much more illy formed than the Indians of the Missouri and those of our frontier; they are generally cheerful but never gay, with us their conversation generally turns upon the subjects of trade, smoking, eating or their women; about the latter they speak without reserve of their presents, of their every part, and of the most formiliar connection. they do not hold the virtue of their women in high estimation, and will even prostitute their wives and daughters for a fishinghook or a stran of beads. [Here in a footnote the editor deVoto noted, Clark, "The *Chin-nook* womin are lude and carry on sport publickly."] in common with other savage nations they make their women perform every species of domestic

---

4 *Ibid.* 289-90. Unless otherwise stated parentheses are those of the author or editor.
5 *Ibid.* 290.

drudgery, but in almost every species of this drudgery the men also participate.[6]

He had carved a now-famous inscription on December 3 on a large pine tree before they crossed the Columbia: "William Clark December 3rd 1805. By Land from the U.States in 1804 & 1805." After spending a little more time on the northern side of the Columbia's mouth and realizing there was very little game and nothing more to look forward to but cold, miserable weather, the two leaders decided to make their way south and inland where they built Fort Clatsop. With a wry note of chagrin, Clark called the Pacific: "the Great Western Ocian, I cant say Pasific as since I have seen it, it has been the reverse." On Friday, December 27, 1805, Capt. Clark shifted to talking about the work on Ft. Clatsop. He wrote "rained last night as usual and the greater part of this day, the men complete Chimneys & Bunks to day."

Captain Clark noted that a Clatsop chief visited them this same evening, and on the next day various parties went out to hunt and to make salt at "Tillamook Head," at a distance of about twenty miles. Soon after this they began to be plagued by mosquitoes.

> Those Indians gave us, a black root they call *Shan-na-tâh-que* a kind of Licquirish which they rost in embers and call *Cul-ho-mo*, a black berry the size of a Cherry & Dried which they call *Shel-well*—all of which they prise highly and make use of as food to live on, for which bobs, Pice of riben, a pice of Brass, and 2 small fishing hooks, of which they were much pleased, Those roots & berries, are greatfull to our Stomcks as we have nothing to eate but Pore Elk meet, mostly spoiled; & this accident of spoiled meet, is owing to warmth & the repeated rains, which cause the meet to tainte before we can get it from the woods. Musquetors troublesome.[7]

The New Year, 1806, began with Capt. Clark writing about what the Clatsop tribal members told him about the ship traffic they had noted and their unsatisfying contacts with English speaking traders and seaborne hunters on the Oregon Territory coast.

January 1st 1806

> A List of the names of Sundery [*sic*] persons, who visit this part of the Coast for the purpose of trade &c. in large Vestles; all of which speake the English language &c. as the Indians inform us

| Moore | Visit them in a large 4 masted ship. They expect him in 2 moons to trade. |

---

6 *Ibid.* 300-1.

7 *Ibid.* 295-6.

1 Eyd [one-eyed] Skellie	In a large ship, long time gorn.
Youin	In a large Ship, and they expect him in 1 moon to trade with them.
Swepeton	In a large ship, they expect him back in 3 month back to trade
Mackey	In a Ship, they expect him back in 1 or 2 Moons to trade with them.
Meship	In a Ship, the[y] expect him 2 Moons to trade
Jackson	Visit them in a Ship and they expect him back in 3 months to trade
Balch	In a Ship and they expect him in 3 months to trade.
Mr. Haley	Visits them in a Ship & they expect him back to trade with them in 3 Moons to trade. he is the favourite of the Indians (from the number of Presents he gives,) [parentheses of Clark] and has the trade principally with all the tribes.
Washilton	In a Skooner, they expect him in 3 months to return and trade with them — a favorite.
Lemon	In a Slupe, and they expect him in 3 moons to trade with them.
Davidson	Visits this part of the coast and river in a Brig for the purpose of Hunting the Elk returns when he pleases he does not trade any, kills a gread many Elk &c. &c.
Fallawan	In a Ship with guns he fired on & and they doe not know when he will return, well done.

During the next three months there were many more interactions between the small party of white Euro-American explorers and the Clatsops. Lewis and Clark had named their fort after a local tribe of coastal Indians. By 1845 or 1850, it would have seemed odd to name an Army fort or a base after a local Indian tribe; soldiers usually used names of prominent generals or politicians. This was as profound a moment in the three-hundred-year story of Euro-American/Indian contacts in North America as the founding of Jamestown, Virginia, or the meeting of Pocahontas and John Smith. Up until this time the coastal Indians of the Northwest, including those on the Pacific Coast in California, Oregon and Washington, generally had been treated brutally by the mostly English-speaking trading and hunting vessels that stopped along the Washington, Oregon and northern California coast.

Some of Lewis and Clark's men contracted venereal disease from the Indian women and girls. Though there were doubtless one or two later incidents of sexual relations with Indian women, discipline was reinstated by Captain Lewis. The men swore an oath of chastity for the remainder of the expedition. In a journal entry Capt. Lewis mentioned ministering to a man who was down with VD with mercury. He apparently somehow survived both the disease and treatment, but the sick men made slow recoveries. The white men and the Indians gradually became better acquainted, even to the point of definite although necessarily short friendships. Meanwhile the constant rain and heavy fogs, so common to this part of the world, were much in evidence during the winter and spring of 1806.

Once the Lewis and Clark party left the western edge of Euro-American settlement at St. Louis, Missouri, they had no way of communicating or reporting their progress to President Jefferson. Especially as they entered the Shoshone tribe's region in the Rocky Mountains, all contact with anyone in the States was impossible. While it is true that the (1833–1834) early California expedition led by Captain Joseph Walker by chance encountered a Yankee trading vessel, the *Lagoda,* near Monterey, California, just before New Year's Day, 1834, by the end of 1805 Lewis and Clark's party had not met any Yankee ships at the outlet of the Columbia River. The question arises: why didn't President Jefferson seem to care enough about his expedition to send a ship to meet it when the party was due to arrive at the mouth of the Columbia River?

At this point Capt. Lewis noted that Sacagawea, the now famous Shoshone wife of guide Toussaint Charbonneau, insisted that she be allowed to accompany her husband, "Charbono," so that she also could see the Pacific Ocean. Capt. Lewis continued this entry and noted the Indians' cooperative attitude between the sexes when it came to "subsistence" and their treatment of the aged. Capt. Lewis granted her request. Meanwhile the main point, as far as the explorers were concerned, was that now they were running out of goods for barter.

Fort Clatsop, the small fort constructed south of the Columbia River's mouth, consisted of an outer square stockade and seven small buildings or cabins within. It also included a parade ground. The group's stay at Fort Clatsop finally was reaching its end by mid-March. Despite occasional illnesses among a few of the men, their "pirogues" were almost all ready to go. On March 17th, 1806, Capt. Clark remarked as he gave up his uniform coat to one of the Clatsop Indians in trade for a canoe,

> I think the U'States are indebted to me another Uniform coat for that of which I have disposed of on this occasion was but little worn. we yet want another canoe, and as the Clatsops will not sell us one at a price we can afford to give we will take one from them in lue of the six Elk which they stole from us in the winter.[8]

---

8 *Ibid.* 330.

When there was a need for it, theft was not ruled out in order to obtain what was needed for the mission to proceed.

Their party would endure more hardships during the long journey back East to civilization. This journey began in the Northwest in March and did not end until almost the end of November. On November 25, 1806, the Lewis and Clark Expedition ended in St. Louis. Capt. Clark noted,

> had all of our skins &c. suned and stored away in a storeroom of Mr. Caddy Choteau. payed some visits of form, to the gentlemen of St. Louis. in the evening a dinner & Ball.[9]

One by one, the first thirty years of the nineteenth century passed. Fed by increasing contacts with Euro-American trappers, traders, then settlers, the Indian populations of the Northwest were devastated by disease epidemics. The Clapsops, Chinnooks, and Killamucks, as well as many other tribes of the early California coastal regions, such as the Pomo, Yuki, Shasta, Yurok, Ohlone, and many more, suffered as yet untold losses numbering in the tens, perhaps even hundreds of thousands. In the meantime, Americans of all backgrounds, races and religions were on the move.

---

9 *Ibid.* 478. Regarding the names of the tribes of Washington and northern California see Appendix II for Deputy Customs Collector George Gibbs' observations in 1851-3.

CHAPTER 2. JOHN WORK'S EXPEDITION TO THE NORTH MENDOCINO COAST, FROM BODEGA BAY TO THE MATTOLE RIVER

> You will find the road ahead of you passable for the next hundred miles. However, be prepared to being surprised by many deep gullies along the way.

—Peter Kostromitinoff, Ft. Ross's Acting Governor, April, 1833.

Twenty-seven years after Captain Clark made his final entry to the *Journal* in St. Louis, another exploration party looking for beaver departed northward from the tiny settlement of Bodega Bay, which is about seventy miles north of San Francisco. John Work (his actual Irish surname was "Wark," while his name is spelled "Work" in his diary preserved at Bancroft Library) had been appointed leader of the "Southern Brigade of the Hudson Bay Company." Work's exploratory party in the spring of 1833 was made up of sixty-three participants: nineteen Indians and forty-four whites. No Indian tribal name was listed by Work in his diary. The whites, many of whom were French-Canadian, also included a few women, partners or wives of some of the men. The Hudson Bay Company wanted to know if it was worth the additional costs of equipping trappers to trap throughout northwestern California. Before eventually returning to Oregon, Work's troupe passed in a lengthy zigzag across the gently rolling hills and rugged mountainous terrain of Mendocino County, first going almost directly north up the coast to the outlet of the Mattole River and then ending up in Lake County, about a hundred miles as the crow flies to the southeast of the coast. After leaving Bodega it passed by the Russian settlement at Fort Ross, up the Mendocino coast to the mouth of the Mattole River. There Work divided his party in two. One half continued northward to return to Oregon as Work's half proceeded in a south-easterly direction to the shores of Clear Lake. Along the way some Redwood Valley Pomo Indians wearing war paint threatened and might have killed a detachment of Work's men. The whites carefully withdrew to avoid being slaughtered. Eventually Work's party returned to Astoria via a different route.

Born in 1792 in Londonderry, a suburb of Dublin, Ireland, John Work went to work for the Hudson Bay Company in 1814. In 1832 Work chose those who would participate as members of the Southern Brigade. Beginning perhaps as early as January, 1833 near present-day Portland, Oregon, the party followed the Columbia River to Walla Walla, where horses awaited them. The group turned south to Goose Lake along its eastern shore until the Pitt River was reached.[10]

A depression in the Cascade Range enabled Work's party to reach the headwaters of Cow Creek, and they followed it through the foothills to reach the Cow River.

After following it for over a hundred miles, the party turned southward, passing along the edge of Goose Lake. They once more followed Cow Creek until reaching the headwaters of the Sacramento River. Following the Sacramento southwest, they skirted San Francisco Bay to the coast near Bodega Bay. They followed the Pacific Coast northward carefully examining each river and stream for possible evidence of beavers. At the end of March the expedition was in the northernmost Mexican coastal outpost at Bodega Bay. By mid-April, 1833, they had reached the southernmost post of Russia's North American settlements, Fort Ross. It was located about eight miles north of the mouth of the Russian River. The primary reason the Russians established a fort this far south was to produce food for the larger Russian outpost of Sitka, Alaska. It was established also to hunt fur seals; a group of Aleut Indians harpooned the seals for their valuable skins. Primarily manned by just over two hundred Russians, this fort sat high up on a broad plateau about one hundred fifty yards from the sea. Steep ravines on the south and west helped to protect it from would-be invaders. Constructed of eight-inch thick redwood logs, fifteen-feet long and driven three feet in the ground, the quad-shaped fortress was an imposing sight. Each side of the fort was two hundred fifty to three hundred feet long, The Russians had over one thousand sheep, one thousand horses, and two thousand cattle.

The Russians constructed bidarkas out of the skins of sea lions—small, light weight canoe-like boats that could slice quickly through the Pacific's swells, al-

---

10 About the same time in January 1833, a party of Euro-American and French Canadian trappers had been passing the winter shooting buffalo on the headwaters of the Arkansas River. One night a large raiding party of fifty Crow Indians stole nine of their horses. Kit Carson described how the horses eventually were retrieved along with the killing of some of the Crows. Carson claimed they killed nine Indians. A Cheyenne fellow trapper named Black Whiteman who reported the number killed as just two refuted this number. At any rate, although the two parties never met, both Work and Carson eventually would play important roles, albeit in very different regions of the state, in the settlement of California.

lowing them to go after the seals. The fort had begun to lose its purpose since about 1818 when the population of the fur seals began declining. The Russians worked now as mechanics, farmers or soldiers. They also produced leather and dried beef at Fort Ross.

As Work's party approached Fort Ross, a fierce-looking party of Russians came out to greet them. John Work spoke first. "Our two great nations are not at war. My party will not disturb your fields, your settlement, or your fort. We simply ask for safe passage and will leave your territory in only one or two days."[11] Work was a man of few words. He knew the Russians were a proud people who might not stand still for long listening to intruders. Work said a silent prayer as he stood face to face speaking to the lead Russian. He had no way of knowing how many soldiers might be standing behind the fort's tall stockade, ready to open fire.

After at first objecting that Work's path would pass too near his fort, Peter Kostromitinoff, who would serve at Fort Ross from 1829 to 1836, calmly replied, "Since there is no other way, I will allow your party to pass tomorrow. Make your camp where you are now but come to dinner as my guest tonight." Work must have heaved a silent sigh of relief. He appointed his second-in-command, Michelle, to take over command of the expedition as he chose two others in his party to accompany him to dinner at the fort.

The Russians welcomed the commander of the party of French-Canadian trappers and mountain men with a dinner that began with an exchange of toasts with the Russians.[12] They feasted on roasted salmon, venison, elk meat and duck at Fort Ross. While the actual governor of the Russian American Trading Company was Baron F. F. Wrangell, the acting commander, Governor Kostromitinoff, spoke only a few words of French. Work spoke no Russian. Their conversation necessarily was limited. Work made his apologies and took his leave as soon as he could after the main dish of salmon was consumed. Perhaps he thought he was fortunate that his party didn't have to do battle with the tough-looking Russian-born soldiers whom he encountered entering and leaving the fort.

The next day was a Friday. Work's Southern Brigade traveled five miles northward across sand dunes and a deep canyon. Gov. Kostromitinoff once again hosted the leader of the party for dinner. Over a roast pig he confided to Work, "You will find the road ahead of you passable for the next hundred miles. However, be prepared to be surprised by many deep gullies along the way." This terse two-sentence prediction turned out to be accurate, if disappointing.

---

11 Diary of John Work, 1833, Bancroft Library, University of California at Berkeley, copy at Noyo Hill House, Ft. Bragg, CA.

12 *Ibid.,* 4. A copy at Noyo Hill House, Ft. Bragg, CA. id. The diary consists of ten single spaced pages with annotations by an unknown archivist.

The exploratory party continued north through today's Gualala, crossing from the present-day Sonoma/Mendocino County Line to Point Arena and the Garcia River. After several mishaps in which tidal surges swept horses out to sea, as well as successful hunts for elk and deer, on Tuesday, April 30th, the group reached Big River. Soon after they reached the southern bank of the Noyo River. A group of between twenty-five and thirty bold coastal Mittom Pomo Indian braves suddenly materialized, like phantoms, out of the thin coastal fog. Most of them carried bows, long arrows, and short stone knives. They acted as if they had not seen horses before. Each was clad in just a small rabbit skin blanket; to Work, they looked like the Indians they had seen earlier when they rode across the San Joaquin Valley. The tribe's cooperative ways surprised everyone in the party. These gentle, peaceable Pomos helped them to construct rafts on which they placed their baggage. They swam their horses and floated their goods over to the north side of the Noyo. Once again Work was relieved that there had not been a conflict. The Indians assisted in the hard work of making their way through dense trees that lined both banks of the river.

One of the members of the party, S. L. Larocque, had split up with his partner. While the diary doesn't include details, apparently the woman left to return to "the Mission." This might have been Fort Ross, perhaps even Sonoma. According to other members who observed his behavior, Larocque had been "like a fool and not knowing what to do with himself." Larocque told at least one or two other party members to look after his horses while he departed to look for his wife. On April 29, S.L. Larocque took off on his personal mission. Exactly one week later, at Shelter Cove, Mr. and Mrs. Larocque rejoined the party. The couple had made up.

John Work's party focused on looking for beaver, or, at the very least, evidence that furry mammals were present in any of the northern California streams or estuaries that empty into the Pacific. Although the party's hunters shot numerous other animals, like elk, antelope, and deer, neither beaver nor any telltale signs of their presence could be found. They continued to press northward about twenty-five miles until reaching the outlet of the Mattole River just above Cape Mendocino.

Trappers, in what people back East called 'the Far West,' more often than not acted together in parties like the Work Expedition of 1833. All were welcome to any beaver pelts they could trap on their own, purchase, or obtain by bartering with other trappers or Indians. Mendocino County, California was far south of the areas in Canada, Washington and Oregon where they were used to working. Since they were not successful in finding any California waterways rich in beaver, they decided to return and concentrate their efforts further north.

On May 11 the party progressed about ten miles northeast along a branch of the Eel River. At first the going was very rough. Later that day they encountered more hilly terrain. They killed "a few deer" and also saw a "large party of Indians." Work commented, "probably they look upon all strangers as enemies."[13] On May 12, as they were running low on ammunition, Work split his party in two. They had been finding only deer to kill and "it requires a great deal [of ammunition] to feed so many people."[14] They were between present day Briceland and Garberville. Michelle and half of the party continued northward along the coast. Work and the rest of the group made their way southeastward through dense groves of redwoods and pleasant valleys toward Clear Lake. They passed directly across the middle of Mendocino County.

Monday, May 13, 1833

Fine weather. Separated the people this morning, I with my party cut across a steep hill and ascended the fork on which we encamped 11 miles S.E. The road very rugged the forepart of the day afterwards it was more level but through thick woods. Michelle & party came on a place the same road, and will have to take to the E. or N. E. & a better country. Michelle's party amounts to 30 Men, 17 whites and 13 Indians and my party amounts to 22 Men, 27 Whites & 6 Indians.

Tuesday, May 14, 1833

Frost in the morning, showry afternoon. Continued our journey to the little fork and across a height of land to another small fork which falls into a river that runs toward the N. W. [Eel River] along this side of the snowy Mountains. The road very hilly and rugged, but the woods pretty clear & not much encumbered with underwood [underbrush]—fortunately we find good feeding for the horses.—We marched about 12 Miles S. E. today. Michelle and company are encamped a little on this side of our last station here they expect to be able to strike along the Mountain to the N. E. There are a great many Indians in the mountains, a party of forty came to our camp in the evening, a few of them had bows & arrows & spears the others were only armed with stones. They do not appear ill disposed at least when the people are all together, they are afraid of the horses. 5 deer killed.[15]

The Indians that Work met "in the mountains" were less afraid of contact with white people than the coastal Indians, who were either a branch of the Pomo or Yuki. This party of forty natives boldly entered Work's camp in the evening. They were armed only with a few bows and arrows with some carrying only stones. It seemed obvious these Indians had had less contact with whites and with rifles or guns than the Clatsops or Chinnooks of Oregon had had. On May 15 two large parties of Indians appeared in camp although they were not very communicative about either the road ahead or about the presence of beaver.

---

13 *Ibid.,* 7.

14 *Ibid.,* 8.

15 *Ibid.,* 9.

Thursday, May 16, 1833

Sharp frost in the night, fine weather during the day. Continued our journey over another range of rugged hills and down a small fork which runs to the S. E. 12 miles S. E, For a woody rugged hilly country the road good. Encamped where there is good feeding for the horses on the north side of a hill pretty clear of wood, on the S. side of the hills where there is little wood the grass is already becoming dry and burnt up with the sun. We were not aware of any Indians being near us when we encamped, in a short time a number of them came to us from a large village which is a short way below us. The hunters killed some deer they are very numerous about here. 6 deer and 1 bear killed.[16]

Friday, May 17, 1833

Fine weather, very warm until toward evening when a breeze of wind sprang up & rendered the heat more supportable. Continued our journey 10 miles S. E. down the river. The road good. Here we found the tracks of our people when they passed this way when they were sent after the Americans in March last [March, 1832]. This is considered to be the Russian river which falls into the sea a little to the southward of the Russian Establishment [Work was at the headwaters of Russian River]. Some beaver are supposed to be in the lower part of this river, I arranged a party of the men to pass that way & endeavour to take what beaver are in it while with the rest of the people and families I proceed to the valley by the shortest route I can.— — Late last night after all hands were in bed an Umquah Indian arrived from Michel's [Michelle's] camp, it seems he had a quarrel with the man he was with, A. Carson [?] and came off and left him. He states that had got within sight of a river which one of his Indians recognized as a fork of the Sorty [*sic* sp. Sasty or Shasta?]. — 7 deer killed.[17]

As often typical this time of year in northern California, the days were warm. Each day seemed hotter than the one before. Now they moved inland. On Saturday, May 18, the road was very difficult and "very severe on the horses." They saw more deer and bear tracks. Their hunters killed two deer and a bear. The following day they reached the head of Clear Lake. "There are a band of Indians encamped a little below us." Again it was "very warm weather."[18] On Tuesday, May 21, they encountered a very large herd of elk but were not able to get close enough to kill any. In the passage continued below, Work describes how a group of his men nearly got into a nasty fight with Indians in Redwood Valley.

In the evening the men who were sent off on the 18th returned. about midday yesterday at the entrance of an apparently fine valley [Redwood Valley] they were met by an immense number of Indians all armed with bows & spears with their faces blackened and war caps of

---

16 *Ibid.,* 9.

17 *Ibid.,* 9.

18 Ibid., 10.

feathers on their heads & raised such a hideous war yell, and had such a hostile appearance, (indeed, they fired 3 arrows, at them.) — that the men did not deem it prudent to advance but turned about & retreated, while the Indians were endeavouring to surround them. The situation the Indians had chosen was among woods and long grass & bushes and was unfavorable for acting on horseback. The men considered themselves fortunate in getting safe off. They had before this passed several large villages without being molested, or the Indians in any way ill disposed, here they saw no village nor women but only armed men, of which there were great numbers advancing from every direction below. On their return they lost 3 horses one belonging to J. Cornoyer, one to L. Boisvant, & one to G. R. Rocque, the horses it seems took fright & ran off and were not gone after with sufficient promptness, so that night came on and they could not be found afterwards. The horses seems to have been lost by negligence. We know no motive the Indians could have for coming in such a hostile number. They had got no provocation. They are probably a very numerous party of very ill disposed scoundrels who are always committing depredations on the Spaniards and Russians, and whom their people frequently attempt to punish, where fore they probably look upon all whites as enemies. I had hoped that a few beaver would have been caught by this party, but they have failed, the country had a fine appearance when they turned back but it is likely the distance to the sea was not great, the river also was not large & on account of such numbers of Indians it is probable not many beaver would have been found.[19]

Work ended his diary at this point.

John Work was the first Euro-American to explore what is now Mendocino County from the coast to Clearlake. Throughout his diary of the adventures of his sixty-three member Southern Brigade from Bodega Bay to Shelter Cove including the Redwood Valley, there was no mention by Work of seeing beaver. In 1833, demand for beaver pelts was still high for coats, shawls, drapes, and especially for men's hats in England and throughout northern Europe. Once his superiors at the Hudson Bay Company's headquarters at Portland and Vancouver (and also London) had had a chance to read this diary, California was destined to remain a low priority for colonization by Great Britain. Many other parts of America such as Canada, the West Indies, even Guatemala, seemed to hold out the promise of far greater return than this backward northern outpost of Mexico called Alta California.

As for the beaver, this unique little furry animal's primary habitat extended only as far south as northern Oregon. Judging from the fact that the Hudson Bay Company sent no more expensive-to-equip exploration parties to northern California, we can assume the directors of this trading company reacted by letting

---

19 See the diary of John Wark (Work), Bancroft Library, a copy at Noyo Hill House, Ft. Bragg, CA. The diary consists of ten single spaced pages with annotations by an unknown archivist.

workers go and "downsizing" in the effort to salvage remaining business with the goal of preserving the existence of the company.

The members of John Work's exploratory party on the coast of Mendocino County and his employers couldn't have known that by 1845 changes in fashion throughout the so-called "civilized Western world," including the East Coast of the United States and most of the capitals of the leading western powers — Germany, France, Holland, Spain, Switzerland, Great Britain, and Russia — ended the demand for beaver pelts.

Northern California's Native Americans in the 1830s continued trying to live as they had for centuries before. They had not developed agriculture since nature provided everything needed to survive. Except for the introduction of epidemic diseases to which they had almost no immunity, the Indians seemingly had no reason to either fear or to admire the invading hordes of predominantly Caucasian immigrants to their homelands. It would soon become clear to the few Euro-American settlers that the Indians wanted to be left alone. In the few contacts they had with whites, the Indians quickly suffered more than their share of hardships and humiliation. A pattern of mistreatment was set.

About eighteen years later, in 1851, another generation of the same tribe encountered by Work would sign one of the first treaties agreeing to relocate onto a reservation. The treaty was written by the Euro-American Commissioner Redick McKee. Commissioner McKee's exploratory party, composed of about the same number of participants as Work's plus a herd of cattle, and mules as well as horses, began in Clear Lake, backtracked to northern Sonoma County before marching northwestward following the Russian River and one of the main branches of Eel River to Humboldt Bay. McKee's party also explored up the Klamath River and into the Sacramento Valley to Shasta Mountain and then departed by ship from Humboldt Bay in December 1851.

The treaties offered by McKee were rendered meaningless when Congress failed to ratify them. Development of reservations continued, with diminishing funds provided by Congress and poorly administered under the Office of Indian Affairs. Eventually the larger reservations were consolidated, co-mingling the tribes, some of which had been enemies. There they languished in poverty for many years.

CHAPTER 3. JESSE APPLEGATE'S JOURNEY ON THE OREGON TRAIL, THE OSAGE RIVER TO THE WILLAMETTE VALLEY, 1843

> John East, a good, honest man, also from Missouri, who was walking and driving his team, was told that we were crossing the Missouri line, whereupon, he turned about facing the east, pulled off his slouched hat, and, waving it above his head and said, 'Farewell to America!'...
>
> —"Recollections of My Childhood," Jesse Applegate, 1914.

The movement of the American people across the Great Plains, beginning in the early 1840s and continuing until after 1860, was one of longest and most profound migrations, not just in American history, but also in human history. During the spring of 1843, the third year of service to the nation of the tenth president, John Tyler, two hundred eighty-eight people made one of the first journeys along the Oregon Trail from the Caw River in Missouri to the Willamette Valley in southwestern Oregon.

One of these was a bright, nine-year-old boy named Jesse Applegate. His uncle, also named Jesse Applegate, led a group of Euro-American settlers in Oregon on a trail blazing expedition that laid out the famous Applegate Trail by which many immigrants found their way across the Rocky Mountains and across northeastern California into Oregon.

Jesse A. Applegate's father, Lindsay, was from Lexington, Kentucky. Jesse's mother was born and raised in eastern Tennessee. Several aunts and uncles, whose names weren't included in the train's roster, accompanied Jesse and his mother and father on this journey across the Great Plains that took place ten years after John Work's expedition through rugged coastal Mendocino County.

In 1914, when he was nearly eighty, Applegate published his memoir. He may be forgiven for not recalling the exact date that the party set out in the train of wagons bound for Oregon in 1843. He did however recall that early in the trek they reached a place that was called 'Harmony Mission,' which had a Caw Indian settlement nearby:

> The day we started on our journey to Oregon, I do not remember, but before we reached the Caw River [in Missouri] I can call to mind Harmony Mission and Grand River, as being the name of a place and river on or near our route. We came up on the south side of the Caw River and camped below and near an Indian town of the Caw tribe. There were huts and cabins, ranging along the river on either side of a street. It was said those Indians grew corn, beans, and pumpkins.[20]

The Caws cautioned the travelers about the hostile nature of two particular tribes, the Cheyennes and Pawnees. Jesse said the Caws simply called them "bad Indians."[21]

Not long after they departed from Harmony Mission,

> One afternoon, when the sun seemed to be about three hours high, and we were traveling along at an ox-team gait, over a level prairie, John East, a good, honest man, also from Missouri, who was walking and driving his team, was told that we were crossing the Missouri line, whereupon, he turned about facing the east, pulled off his slouched hat, and, waving it above his head said, 'Farewell to America!'[22]

After they had been at least a week on the trail across southern Nebraska,

> It seems to me now that the next point of note on the route was Fort Bridger... I saw several very pretty squaws with cheeks painted red, wearing beaded moccasins and beautiful red leggings, fringed along the outer seams. Some of them had papooses almost white and very pretty. Some were wives of white men at the fort, and some belonged to the great war party I saw there mustering to fight the Blackfeet. As I remember this army of Sioux warriors, they were all mounted on nice horses, bucks and squaws all painted about the face, and armed with bows and arrows encased in quivers slung at the back. Some had spears, some war clubs, but no guns, or if any, very few. This war party, as I see the picture now, looking back sixty years, marching or halting in close array, covered several acres of prairie. It was a gay and savage looking host, and sometimes when a squadron of those warriors would break away from the main body and come toward us shouting the war whoop, urging their ponies at full speed, I thought it a grand display indeed, although I fancied I could feel the hair rise on my head. Several of the Amazons of this war party visited our encampment. They were dressed and painted and armed like the men. Some of them

---

20 Jesse Applegate, *Recollections of My Boyhood*, Roseburg, Oregon, Press of Review Publishers, Co., 1914, 12. In SODA (Southern Oregon Digital Archives), assessed December, 2007-January 8, 2008.

21 *Ibid.*, 12, 13.

22 *Ibid.*, 13.

were very fine of figure, had pretty faces, and eyes as soft and bright as the antelopes on those wild plains. They were all young women, and as I thought made love to our young men with their eyes like city damsels, but in the excitement of battle I suppose they became very furies and those lovely eyes flashed fire. Their small, shapely hands and small feet clad in beaded moccasins were admired even by our women, and I fear our men, bold as they were, were almost captured already by those lovely warriors.[23]

Difficulty in starting campfires was one of several basic survival challenges faced by immigrants to southern Oregon and northern California, like the Applegate family in 1843 and Stanley Taylor ten years later.

It seems that matches were not in use when we crossed the plains, for I remember that to get fire at times a man would rub a cotton rag in powder and shoot it out if a musket, or put it in the pan of a flintlock gun, and then explode the powder in the pan.[24]

This kind of challenge was perhaps easier to deal with than the fear of the unknown presented by the tales of the "bad Indians."

One day, as the train was slowly tramping along over a wide plain, a party of horsemen appeared in our front about a mile from us, coming down a little hill toward us. A man of our party was riding a quarter of a mile in advance of the train when those horsemen came in sight, and he, supposing them to be a party of hostile Indian, came galloping back, lashing his horse with his hat, which he carried in his right hand, and shouting at the top of his voice, 'Injuns! Injuns! Corral! Corral! Corral.' The corral was soon formed and all in readiness to do battle, but there was some excitement and confusion, I was at that time in the little red wagon with mother, and I noticed she had a bright brass pistol in her hand. I did not know before that she had a pistol. I looked at her face and I thought she was a little pale but not scared. They were mountain men or trappers, so the train was soon on the march again.[25]

The train had passed over the greater part of the Oregon Trail that consisted of prairie land to enter more rugged country, the foothills of the Rocky Mountains. Before they actually confronted any mountains an accident occurred that might have ended in Jesse's death. While riding along in a wagon driven by his former teacher George Beale, Jesse attempted to swing a six-foot long ox whip. The effort to crack the whip pulled him forward. While Beale had dozed off and was unaware, Jesse was yanked off of the wagon. He fell forward under the wheels and was run over. He was badly bruised, aching in body as well as pride, but didn't inform his mother—who nevertheless was not fooled.[26]

---

23 *Ibid.,* 17, 18.

24 *Ibid.,* 19, 20.

25 *Ibid.,* 21.

26 *Ibid.,* 30, 31, 32. After his description of his painful back injury, Jesse stated that none of the Applegates saw George Beale again after they arrived in Oregon until they were

The wagon train had to continue rolling as if nothing unusual had happened. They were nearing the Sweetwater River, with its beautifully peaceful green banks and shallow blue water, when they met a party of famous observers, the Frémont party.

> There was a soda spring or pool between our camps, and Fremont's men were having a high time drinking soda water. They were so noisy that I suspected they had liquor stronger than soda water mixed with the water. Fremont had a cannon, the first I had ever seen, a six-pounder, they said, and made of bright shining brass. It was resting on a low carriage, which was standing between our camp and Fremont's, and near the soda spring... After Fremont's men had been drinking soda water from that spring, and enjoying it greatly nearly a whole day, one of our party fished out an enormous frog from the pool, almost as large as a young papoose, and falling to pieces with rottenness. Soon after this discovery we noticed that the hilarity at the Fremont tent soon ceased. I thought Fremont was a very fine looking young man. In fact his party was pretty well dressed, and jolly fellows.[27]

Everyday rigors of the trek continued. Jesse recalled "breaking" roads through brush, and the boys that walked behind the wagons having to sit down frequently to pull thorns of prickly pear out of their toes.

After their seemingly endless trek across the dry flatlands, the train was about to pass over one of the most perilous parts of their journey, a narrow ledge called "the Devil's Backbone."[28]

Like the Israelites at the Red Sea, the faint of heart among them may have wished to turn back.

> ...it is a very narrow ridge with a gorge a thousand feet deep on the left hand and a sheer precipice on the right down to Snake River, which looked like it might be a mile or more away. Indeed, it was so far away that it looked like a ribbon not more than four inches wide. The danger was so great that no one rode in the wagons... But we passed it in safety, and again were slowly tramping along over a broad and level expanse of sage brush and greasewood.[29]

They were now making their way through the rugged eastern Rocky Mountains. Jesse's family and possibly one or two others had split up from the others. As they entered Idaho, one of the men in their party killed a threatening grizzly. After their harrowing passage on the Devil's Backbone, some Snake Indians appeared and surrounded the train. For a moment it appeared that the "savages," as they called them, would overwhelm them.

---

living in Salem. Beale and another man named Baker murdered a third man named Delaney. Both Baker and Beale were hanged for their crime.

27 *Ibid.*, 30, 31.

28 *Ibid.*, 27.

29 *Ibid.*, 26, 27.

They were in such great numbers and crowded so closely about the wagons and teams that we could not move on. But they were very friendly and we learned in some way that they were visiting us to see white women and children, for they had never seen any before. They peered into all the wagons from the ends and both sides, and caught hold of the wagon covers on the sides and raised them so they could look in. There was a host of them around the wagon I was in, lifting the sides of the cover and peeping in at mother and us children. We were not afraid of them for they all looked pleasant and much interest-ed. Some were squaws, riding astride of saddles which had very high horns before and behind. The women's saddles were decorated with large headed brass tacks, and long flowing fringes. Some of the squaws had infants encased in sacks made of dressed hide of some kind, with a board attached so as to fit on and support the back of the child. They looked like cocoons of some kinds of insects and were swinging from the front horn of the saddle, like a holster pistol. There was nothing to be seen of the papoose but its little chubby face. While they were crowding about our wagon, a squaw, with a youngster hanging to her saddle bow was trying to get a peep into the wagon when a horse-man swung his horse against the child, which commenced crying. This drew forth such a volley of Snake lingo that the offender appeared very suddenly to lose all interest in the show and got away from there in a hurry.[30]

The two groups parted on an amicable basis. Another encounter demon-strated the vast cultural gap between Jesse's people and the ancient ways of the Snakes.

When we arrived at Boise River...the kids found 'white beads in ant hills.' We picked up many of them, but while searching for more presently came to a place where the ground was white with them and looking up discovered that we were under a broad platform raised on posts seven or eight feet high, and that the platform above our heads was thickly strewn above with the decayed corpses of the dead bodies [that] were yet rolled up in blankets and robes. Some had been torn into fragments by carrion crows and other scavenger birds, and skulls and other bony parts of the body lay bleaching in the sun; a few had fallen to the ground. After this ghastly find we did not tarry long, for the shades of evening were now creeping along the ground, and the Bannock, Shoshone, Crow, or Blackfoot spooks may have been already congregating to hold their nightly 'wake' at this Golgotha.[31]

Without knowing what they were doing and without their parents' knowl-edge, white children had stumbled upon a sacred Indian burial site. They quickly returned to camp.

About October 15, 1843, the wagon train safely reached Fort Walla Walla. This fort in western Washington had been built by and at this time was still maintained by the British-Canadian firm, The Hudson Bay Company. As at both

30 *Ibid.,* 27, 28.

31 *Ibid.,* 26, 27.

Ft. Laramie and Ft. Bridger, a Native American group had established a camp near Ft. Walla Walla. Inevitably, the white children began to play with native youngsters. In one instance, what may have begun as a game ended badly for one young man. Playtime degenerated into a nasty incident that might have led to a battle or worse. Some of the older white boys began a tussle. In a mean act, one of them grabbed a burning branch from a fire. He walked up behind the Indian boy and deliberately burned his shoulder with it. The other white boys quickly separated the belligerent from the Indian boy.

After the white children had returned to the fort, the Indians were justifiably angry with all of the whites.

> Probably the next day the commander of the fort, McKinley, visited our camp and remained quite a while. I understand that afterwards he invited, or rather advised, us to sleep in the fort, as the Indians were not well disposed toward us. I remember sleeping in this fort after this.

The trip down the Columbia River began smoothly enough. Once the party was almost at the outlet of the Columbia at Astoria near the Pacific Ocean, they were able to disembark from their homemade boats. These boats provided the family with some much-needed funds to buy other necessities and to prepare to begin their lives in the Willamette Valley, Oregon. They were near the end of their long voyage when tragedy befell them. One of the boats the Applegate group was using to navigate the Willamette River capsized. Not only were valuable supplies lost, but due in part to the fact that his mother had forbidden him to learn how to swim, young Edward, Uncle Jesse's son, drowned. It was a tragedy that both Jesses never forgot.

The family lived for the six years, until 1849, in the Willamette Valley before moving eastward across the Calopooia Mountain Range to the Yoncalla Valley. This was in the Umpqua Tribal Indian country.

> In the course of three or four years [1846–1849] after we began life in the wilderness of Salt Creek, we had pastures fenced, grain fields and gardens, small apple and peach orchards grown from the seed, comfortable log cabins, barns and other outhouses and quite a number of cattle, horses, hogs and chickens. We had grain growing and in store and vegetables in abundance. But many things we had always considered necessities were not to be had in the wilderness where we lived. Coffee, tea and sugar were among these... [32]

While still living along Salt Creek along the Willamette, the family planted maple trees. Soon they made their own maple syrup and the children enjoyed some candy. As the canvas from their wagons eventually was used up, they completely ran out of material to make clothing. As Jesse noted,

> The skin of the deer, when tanned by the Indians, was soft and pliable and was used by the pioneers. Coats and trousers of buckskin

---

32 *Ibid.,* 61.

were worn, but I confess to a prejudice against buckskin. In a climate where it never rains a buckskin suit might be comfortable, but in the climate where we lived, such garments proved wretchedly disagreeable. Trousers, after frequent wettings and dryings would assume a fixed shape that admitted of no reformation.[33]

Jesse's aunt Melinda carried a "wool card." Using this, along with her spinning wheel, she made a number of garments out of wolf hair from the wolves they killed. Jesse's uncle Charles had a sweater made out of wolf hair. It was an ingenious solution to the clothing problem.

Necessity demanded very plain attire among the first settlers and custom sanctioned it. Buttons for these coats were made of pewter cast in the moulds cut in blocks of soapstone. Old spoons, plates, and other pieces of worn out table ware that had seen service around many a camp fire on the plains and in the mountains were used for this purpose. Garments were sometimes made of the wool-like hair of the wolf....[34]

Their experiences on the frontier had brought the family closer together. The rigors of surviving in the wilderness dictated that everyone in the family had to contribute something. Jesse's older brother Elisha was particularly apt at carpentry. Following a set of plans he had carried with him from Missouri, he constructed a number of log structures that served them all well.

During 1849, Uncle Jesse and Jesse's father Lindsay tried prospecting for gold at the Rogue River but didn't succeed. Along with a group of others from Oregon, Uncle Jesse and Lindsay ended up stranded in San Francisco. Temporarily without transportation back to Oregon, the self-described "Oregon men" chartered one of the ships that had been anchored in San Francisco Bay. In the following description his nephew told of their experience once at sea:

We often heard father tell the thrilling story of the dreary voyage in winter weather, of how for weeks the little craft was buffeted by chilling winds until the sails and ropes were covered with ice, and the passengers were half starved and half frozen. Of how they were tyrannized over by a heartless captain and crew until they believed they were in the hands of pirates whose purpose was to starve them to death and throw them overboard in order to gain possession of the gold they had accumulated in the mines. Of course the Oregon men would not stand this. They organized a rebellion and took the ship. The captain and crew were put on short rations, along with the other men, and were required to make the mouth of the Columbia River in as short a time as possible. This they did landing the Oregon party at the old pioneer town of Astoria.[35]

---

33 *Ibid.*, 80.

34 *Ibid.*, Chapter III, 80.

35 *Ibid.*, 90.

In 1850, the family moved away from the Willamette River. The moved east-ward and began living in the Umpqua Valley, closer to California. In the follow-ing entry Jesse described how they fared.

We had lived in the Willamette Valley seven years when father and my uncles decided to move to the Umpqua country [1850] ... Our first dwelling was built of logs, but in about two years [1852] after we set-tled in the valley a frame house was built... After we were comfortably located, father built a flouring mill on a small stream not far from our dwelling. With the knowledge acquired from his old book on mechan-ics, Brother Elisha was able to do all the reckoning necessary for the mill. This was the first mill for grinding grain built south of the Kala-pooya mountains.

A half mile from our house was an Indian village... There lived a small tribe called the Yangoler or Yoncalla Indians... Our grist mill was only a few paces from this village and the footpath used by the Indians passed near the door of the mill. They were frequently in and about the mill and looked upon it as a marvelous thing.[36]

Indians from the village were frequent visitors at our home. One day when a number were there I was reading in a small book which was illustrated. I read from the book and showed some of the pictures to the Indians, expecting them to be greatly surprised, but they were not, and it appeared from what they said to me and to one another that they had seen 'paper that talked,' as they expressed it, or had some information in regard to books. This discovery aroused my curiosity and led to the following tradition, which I gathered after much labor and many interviews with the Indians. Suniyowhiynoof was a man, a foreigner, of what nationality I could not learn, who came to the tribe from they knew not where. He was a doctor or priest [shaman] and healed the sick, but I could not learn anything about his methods. He had a book or books which he read and he showed the Indians pic-

---

36 *Ibid.*, 90. What follows is Jesse's account of the Indians' creation myth: "The Indian's theory of the origin of the red man is interesting. I first heard this tradition from the lips of a venerable Chemomochot priest or doctor, sixty or more years ago, and I have never found an Indian who was able to add a word to it. All the priests or 'medicine men,' and I believe, all the people knew this much of their origin. This is the tradition: 'In the beginning was a mountain, and on the mountain top was a table of stone. On this table was a deposit of some kind of matter jelly-like in consistence—we would call it protoplasm—and out of this protoplastic [protoplasmic] mass grew a living being in the form of, and was, a woman. She held in her arms a male child, and when she was fully grown she descended, carrying the child on her bosom, to the base of the mountain, where the two were joined by a wolf. The woman placed the boy astride on the wolf's back and passed a strap around the child and over the wolf's head above his eyes.' This ends the story of the beginning of the red man. It ends abruptly with the group of three persons: Snowats, Isukaw, and Quartux (woman, boy and wolf) [parentheses of the author]. Some of the Indians believed that when a man died he became the same as a clod of earth or kahte (a stone). Others seemed to believe in the transmigration of souls. I recall a number of times when an Indian, pointing to a wolf which was often seen near the village, suggested that Quartux was some person, naming someone who had recently died. They regarded the wolf as a sacred animal."

tures of a good country up in the heavens. He told them good people would go to this country after death.

Eventually Suniyowhiynoof was attacked by unknown enemies who "left his body filled with arrows."[37]

There was another local Indian called "Lolokee" [meaning 'fire nose,' as his 'nose was almost as red as fire'].[38] Lolokee was such a powerful medicine man that supposedly he once charmed a rattlesnake to straighten himself out and to lie still so that Lolokee and his friends could safely pass. Lolokee was a shaman of the Yangolers Tribe.

One of the last entries in Jesse's memoir tells the story of Chief Halo, chief of Yangoler Tribe, who made a brave stand in the face of almost certain death. After the Applegate family had lived for awhile in the Umpqua Valley, they became friends with Chief Halo. Unlike some of his tribe members who opposed white settlement, the chief told the family that he admired their work in tilling the soil. He sometimes traded with the Applegates. When Chief Halo began to build a new hut or house in 1856, they provided him with some rails in order to fence in a plot of his land.

Soon after an Indian agent appeared and assembled many Indians to a meeting:

> The promise of houses, farms and agricultural implements and a yearly food supply to be given them on the reservation appealed strongly to the majority of the Indians. Of course the agent spoke to the Indians through an interpreter, and the Indians answered through the same medium. Chief Halo said, 'I will not go to a strange land.' This was not reported to the agent. When the tribe arrived on the reservation without the chief the agent was troubled, and came to our house to get father to go with him to visit the chief. We boys went with them. When Halo saw us coming he came out of his house and stood with his back against a large oak tree that grew near the door. We approached in our usual friendly fashion, but the chief was sullen and silent. He had lost faith in the white man. The agent said, 'Tell the old Indian he must go to the reservation with the other people, that I have come for him.' The chief understood and answered defiantly, 'Wake nika klatawa,' that is, 'I will not go.' The agent drew his revolver and pointed it at the Indian when the chief bared his breast, 'crying in his own tongue as he did so, 'Shoot! It is good I die here at home. My father died here, his grave is here. 'Tis good I die here and am buried here. Halo is not a coward. I will not go.' 'Shall I shoot him' said the agent. 'No,' cried father, his voice hoarse with indignation. The chief, standing with his back against the giant oak tree, had defied the United States. We returned home leaving the brave old man in peace. Father and my uncles protected the old chieftain and his family and they were allowed to remain in their old home. I have read histories of Oregon, volumes of memoirs and many tales of the early days, but have never

---

37 *Ibid.,* 95.

38 *Ibid.,* 96.

found anything relating to Chief Halo. He was a character worthy to be remembered. Should coming generations learn to know him as he was, they will see a noble figure standing with face uplifted and eyes wide open with wonder and delight to behold the coming of civilization. This noblest and last sachem of the natives of the Umpqua Valley has slept with his fathers 'Lo these many years.' And his people, where are they? Their war songs, and their songs of exultation and lamentation these hills and valleys will hear no more.

In the summer of 1853 the Rogue River Valley Indians swept down upon the straggling settlements, in Southern Oregon, murdering the inhabitants, burning homes and carrying away captives. There was a call for volunteers and father organized a company or detachment known as 'Captain Lindsay Applegate's company of mounted volunteers.' Brother Elisha was then twenty-one years of age. I was seventeen, and we both enlisted for the war. The tribe inhabiting the Rogue River Valley was small and has been estimated at eight hundred people; less than half were warriors. This tribe was divided into small bands or tribes under sub-chiefs. Chief John, as he was called by the whites, the head chief of all these tribes, their great war chief. A treaty was made with these Indians in September, 1853, at our encampment, which was between the upper Table Rock and Rogue River. After the treaty had been made Chief John and his son visited our camp. The son was about my age, only a boy. We had many interesting talks together, and I liked and admired the young chief.[39]

Throughout Washington, Oregon, and northern California in the 1850s natives were faced with the same life-or-death decision Chief Halo had to make. Should they resist and simply accept being gunned down by the whites or should they accept moving onto an uncertain future at a reservation?

Jesse Applegate's rite of passage to manhood began early in the year 1843 and took him from a log cabin beside the Osage River in Missouri across North America to southern Oregon Territory by way of an early Oregon Trail. Near the end of his life, Jesse realized he and his family had earned a special place in the settlement of Oregon and northern California and Oregon. Completing his memoir in 1914, he noted that most of the persons who had been on the wagon train with him were gone, and the railroad age was well underway. Indeed, the railroad was itself would soon give way to the automobile age.

---

39 *Ibid.*, 96, 97, 98.

CHAPTER 4. NORTH COAST EXPLORER/SETTLERS FIND GOLD! GEORGE GIBBS, OREGON TERRITORY'S FIRST CUSTOMS COLLECTOR, 1850

Amt of lumber exported from Humboldt Bay up to December 1, 1852.

Say 50 cargoes piles before custom house was established.

—George Gibbs' Journal #1

Prior to either Spanish or Anglo-European settlement, the Miwok Tribe lived in northern California's coastal region, from the Golden Gate north through the Tomales area to present day Bodega Bay. In the 1800s, unlike today, Tomales Bay reached inland to the town of Tomales. The Miwoks may have originated in central California areas as far east as the Yosemite Valley. The Indian tribes or tribelets throughout Marin and Sonoma Counties were, anthropologically-speaking, Miwok, Meewok, or Licatuit, but each occupied small areas and spoke different dialects. Certain words were so common that everyone who lived in this part of northern California understood them. The Tomales (or *Tomalles*) Indians were active fishermen and divers who brought home plenty of succulent seafood, crabs, mollusks, and abalone.

When twenty-seven-year-old whaling ship sailor, William Richardson, asked for the captain's permission to leave the *Orion* in San Francisco in 1822, he unknowingly was helping to start an Anglo-Saxon takeover of the region. Walking in the Presidio he encountered a young Hispanic woman, Maria Antonia Martinez, who fell in love with the handsome sailor. She vowed she would marry this man, Richardson. Marry him she did, and together they had three children while Richardson carved out a permanent name for himself in California history. Adept as a carpenter, Richardson applied for Mexican citizenship and converted to Catholicism. He immediately began building a sailing vessel that he manned with Indians. Selling San Francisco produce to both the Russians in Sitka and the Mexicans in Los Angeles, Richardson with his hard work and pluck eventually won notice by Governor Figueroa. In 1835 the governor granted Richardson's wish to begin a commercial town of Yerba Buena on the San Francisco Bay. During the same year author Richard Henry Dana described Richardson as the only non-Mexican in San Francisco.

Richardson returned with his family to the Bay Area in 1838 when the governor set aside Rancho Sausalito that included Stinson Beach, the present day town of Sausalito, and Muir Woods. Richardson's Bay was named for him. Relevant to this study, Richardson also received the Albion Grant that included a ten-mile Mendocino coastal stretch from the town of Manchester near Pt. Arena to Mendocino including the Albion and Little Rivers. Later on, William A. Richardson, along with Henry Meiggs, was responsible for inducing Jerome Ford to explore the redwood country. After the end of the Civil War the Richardson family lost almost the entire Albion Grant through prolonged and expensive lawsuits.

One of the most influential early landowners who set forth from San Francisco was Jean Jacques Vioget. Vioget was French-Swiss; he was born in 1799. Vioget was a seaman who never gave up sailing ships, making many trips to various Pacific ports, especially Honolulu, Hawaii. He arrived in San Francisco in 1837 as the captain of the *Delmira*. Vioget plotted the first map of San Francisco in 1830–40. After building one of the first houses there and becoming a naturalized Mexican citizen, Vioget worked as a saloonkeeper and trader. He acquired a gambling hall and bar and the Portsmouth House, one of the first hotels. Vioget served as judge of election. Turning from his properties back to the sea, Vioget hired a barkeep to replace him at the saloon. In 1846 Vioget sailed to Honolulu as a crewman on the *Don Quixote*. He piloted another ship, the *Euphemia*, back to the City in 1847.

While Jon Sutter employed him as a surveyor to plot out a map of the Helvetia Grant near Sacramento, Vioget had trouble getting Sutter to pay for his work. Later, as the captain of the ship *Clarita*, he carried Gov. Micheltorena to Mexico. In 1848, apparently, he was rewarded with the Blucher Rancho Grant, a huge six-league (27,192-acre) stretch of land on the present-day Marin/Sonoma County Line.

Some California settlers left wives and families at home and never returned. For example, Capt. Stephen Smith, who ran one of the first northern California saw mills at Bodega, bought the Blucher Rancho from Vioget but mortgaged half of it. When the captain died, an extended lawsuit revealed the existence in Baltimore of Smith's first wife and a family.

Thomas Wood was an English seaman who sailed the California coast. His ship touched land at Tomales Bay in 1841. For some reason, he decided to jump ship. He soon learned to ride and so patterned himself after the Spanish horsemen that he changed his name from Tom Wood to Tom Vaquero. He met friendly Licatuit (Licitiut), the North Bay's Meewok or Tomales Indians. The word Miwok (or Meewok) meant "people." Soon he set up a small trading post at Wood's Point where he traded with French ships that often called there. The French were looking for abalone shells for the Paris jewelers' market. Wood built himself a cabin and soon had piles of abalone shells as high as the roof.

Riding home one night after attending a fandango at a nearby rancheria, Tom suddenly encountered a gigantic grizzly bear. Pulling his *riata* from his saddle and forgetting that he'd left his gun at home, Tom decided to have some fun. He lassoed the bear and wrapped the other end of the rope around the horn of his saddle.

For the first hour or so he alternately pulled and drove the bear closer to his cabin.

Gradually the bear's strength wore down his horse's stamina so that the bear began to shorten the rope. Soon the horse and rider would be close enough to the bear for him to tear them apart. At last using his knife Vaquero severed the rope and succeeded in getting home safely. Next day he rode out in search of the grizzly with the short rope around its neck. He never found him and on his deathbed 1876 he told the story of the only Californian who got the best of him.

During the late 1850s, using the timbers he retrieved from a shipwreck (either of the *Cambridge* or *Oxford*), Tom Vaquero built himself a large house. Since he was the spokesman and leader of Indians living in Tomales, Vaquero let out contracts for their labor digging potatoes and harvesting grain when farming became common during the 1850s and 1860s. Later he married an adopted daughter of James Black, another settler.

John Keyes, who was born in 1824 in Northern Ireland, arrived in San Francisco in 1849. Keyes traveled through Sonoma, Petaluma, and Tomales Bay to Bodega Bay to Captain Stephen Smith's home. Along the way Keyes had met another man, Alexander Noble, who became his partner in a scheme to grow potatoes. Later the potato was nicknamed the "Bodega Red" potato. Potatoes were one of a number of farm products that played a significant role in the growth and development of northern California. Before the lumber industry became dominant, crops like the potato, grain, fruits and vegetables gave many settlers a living.

Hearing a rumor that others coming cross country wanted to stake out claims to Tomales, in September, 1850, Noble and Keyes built a shanty beside their tent on the west end of the estuary. Alexander Noble soon sold out his half stake in order to move to the southern states.

Just as the War with Mexico was ending in 1848, an unlikely person made the first discovery of gold in California. This discovery almost instantaneously changed the course of American history and greatly speeded up the process that unfolded under the banner of "manifest destiny."

By the mid-1840s a tiny minority of California immigrants, men like Thomas O. Larkin in Monterey and John A. Sutter, at his compound in north central California, Sutter's Fort, had become powerful and wealthy. In early 1848 John Sutter dispatched James W. Marshall, a carpenter in his employ, to take a crew of men up into the High Sierras to build a new saw mill on the South Fork of the American River. After his work crew made up of whites and Indians had erected the frame of the new mill, Marshall diverted water to flow from the river into a channel to provide the power that would cut the wood. James Marshall probably had no thought of finding gold, but early one morning late in January of 1848, he did. Possibly he was thinking of nothing more than completing his work and reporting back to his boss that he'd finished the job. Perhaps he was just killing time when he glanced at the water in the mill's trace. There he glimpsed a shiny object reflecting the bright California sunlight.

The mill happened to be located near an old Nisenan (Southern Maidu) Indian village they called "Callooma." The name was eventually Anglicized to "Coloma." On the way back to report his find to his boss, Marshall found more gold nuggets in a ravine in the foothills of the Sierra and at a place later called Mormon Island. Once he was safely back at Sutter's compound, Marshall handed over some of the nuggets to Sutter, who quickly confirmed that they were gold. At first Sutter tried to keep the news secret but inevitably word got out. Once it reached San Francisco, the news spread as quickly as a California forest fire, igniting the California Gold Rush. Whole crews of seamen on ships deserted in a mad rush to get to High Sierra gold country.

Typical of most miners in early California, Marshall never really prospered from his discovery of Sierra gold. Throughout his life Marshall was hounded and frequently held up and robbed by unscrupulous thieves and gold seekers. Sadly, this son of a New Jersey carriage-maker died alone and almost penniless.

ETHNOLOGIST/CUSTOMS AGENT GIBBS MOVES TO THE FAR WEST

Born in New York in 1813, George Gibbs might have lived a life similar to many other 49ers' except for the fact that he chose to pursue lifelong interests in science, zoology and botany, including also the Indians of the Northwest and their languages. In so doing, he gave up all thought of enriching himself or leaving a fortune for others to enjoy. While details about his early life are lacking, Gibbs had family members who introduced him to George McClellan. He probably began college at Harvard about the time John Work returned from his expedition through northern California. In 1838 Gibbs graduated from Harvard with a law degree. Instead of pursuing a lucrative career practicing law, Gibbs chose to join the immigrants in the California Gold Rush. It must have been obvious to his fellow students and professors that Gibbs had unusual strength of character and determination as well as above average intelligence. Gibbs' literary interests led him to eventually become a librarian for the American Ethnological Society.

Arriving in California in 1848, Gibbs began noting reports in his journal, recording stories and news he heard or gathered about exploration parties, including the names of ships that traded with early settlers and carried most of the explorers of the northern California and the Northwest, especially of the Humboldt Bay region. As well as recording the first real history of Eureka and Humboldt Bay, Gibbs focused his attention on California Indians: names and locations of villages, folkways, customs including their dialects and languages.[40] While in Astoria, Oregon, in 1852 Gibbs served as deputy customs collector of the Port of Astoria and was responsible for assessing customs duties. Astoria rests on the southern bank of the Columbia River just a few short miles from the Pacific, not far from where Lewis and Clark had located Ft. Clatsop in 1806. At the time both the present states of Washington and Oregon were considered as one entity, the Oregon Territory. Oregon separately entered the Union in 1859, with Washington following, not until 1889.

For some reason Gibbs happened to be in Sonoma, California, during the summer of 1851. "Colonel M'Kee," as Gibbs called the Indian Commissioner Redick McKee, hired Gibbs to be the primary interpreter and record-keeper for the McKee Expedition through northwestern California that was launched in the fall of 1851.

At the conclusion of this expedition to seek out and sign treaties with northern California's many tribes or tribelets, Gibbs returned to his work as customs collector. Later he became a member of the Indian Commission in Oregon. In 1853 George McClellan, his old family friend, hired Gibbs to work on the Northern Railroad Survey. A self-trained geologist and botanist, Gibbs also collected specimens of local species of plants and animals that became part of the Smithsonian Institution's collections. While in the Willamette Valley in southern Oregon, he also studied the Native American languages and compiled valuable dictionaries of Indian tongues. As can be seen from a few examples of his maps from the Klamath and Trinity Rivers in northwestern California, he made the first accurate map of the Willamette Valley. In the 1860s he was a member of the northwestern boundary survey team. His scientific observations have survived. They are on record at the Smithsonian Institution's Archives in Washington, D.C. After retiring and until his passing in 1873, Gibbs studied Native American languages at the Smithsonian Institute in Washington, D.C.

---

40 According to notes by eminent anthropologist Robert Heizer in 1972, Gibbs later went to Oregon at

first as a member of the Mounted Rifle Regiment.

There are two of Gibbs' journals together with a set of 1860 botany notes, "Notes on Forest Growth in Washington Territory, ca. 1860," at the Smithsonian Institution's Archives. The first journal is about four-and-a-half inches tall and three-and-a-half wide. It is bound in thin brown leather. It contains pages that have long since become loose. The journal, wherein Gibbs made notes on whatever interested him, is basically a history of the founding and early years of white settlement at Humboldt Bay.

On the first page of his journal (which is unnumbered) Gibbs wrote:

> Athr,
>
> George Gibbs
>
> Astoria[41]

Next was the following list of nineteen Euro-American names.

> Charles McDermit, Yreka
>
> Moses Dusenberg, Peoria, Ill.
>
> Wm. M. Bercan, Union
>
> Geo: W. Ellsworth, Orleans Bar
>
> Geo: N. Whitmore, Orleans Bar
>
> F. N. McKinney, }
>
> Maj. Theor. F. Rowe } Scotts bar
>
> Geo: W. Taggert }
>
> Chas. Liscom   }
>
> I.L. Read   }
>
> A. K. Murdock   } (These four, Union)
>
> W. L. Landsbury } Sonoma
>
> Benj. Kelsey   }
>
> Chas. Sebring
>
> Horatio Cushing, Trinidad
>
> Norman Dupern, Humboldt.
>
> C.D. Moore, HappyCamp,
>
>   (about pine tree sugar)
>
> George Peters for map of the Trinity
>
> Walter McDonald[42]

---

41 See George Gibbs' Journal, Astoria, Oregon, Oregon Territory, 1850–1853, Smithsonian Archives, Capital Gallery Building, Washington, DC.

42 *Ibid.,* "3," journal pages were unnumbered.

It is not clear why he listed these nineteen names and not others. Perhaps the purpose of this part of this first of the two journals that he kept during the 1850s was that he might better recall a person's exact name when it came time for him to write a required periodic report for his superiors in Washington, D.C. What made this journal unique was that a few individuals, such as Charles Sebring, Charles Liscom or Benjamin Kelsey, for example, who were scouts for parties of exploration, were recalled along with the part each one played in the early development of Humboldt Bay and northern California. More specifically, Charles Sebring was the scout first for Bernardo Nordheimer and later for the famous Redick McKee Expedition of 1851.

After noting the earliest pathfinders and others most important to the settlement of the Humboldt Bay area, Gibbs started his narrative, which followed, in no strict chronological order. Instead Customs Agent Gibbs wrote in an elliptical, nineteenth century style that was especially remarkable due to his usually clearly legible handwriting and dedication to preserving the truth about who were the first explorers in California's extreme northwestern corner and what they did to further knowledge of Humboldt Bay and the outlets of the most important rivers such as the Trinity River, the Klamath River, and others such as the Madd River. Gibbs paid special attention to detail since accuracy was so important in his reports about California trade to the Treasury Department in Washington, D.C.

Before he was promoted to Collector of Customs for the port of Astoria, Oregon Territory, he had acted in the same role for Humboldt Bay for the towns of Eureka, Trinidad, Union, and Bucksport. Perhaps his proficient performance was what caught the attention of his superiors leading to this next position. In a following page he noted the number of vessels (including scows, schooners, brigs, and other ships) in 1851 and 1852. They totaled sixty-nine vessels at Humboldt Bay.

The next three pages of the journal are blank; then there is a page of data on the lumber mills and ship traffic at Humboldt Bay (see Appendix II for details).

Three mills had begun constant operations near Eureka producing two million board feet of lumber per month from 1851 to the end of 1852. Lumber production did not start on the north Mendocino coast until at least three years later so that Humboldt Bay produced more lumber products at this time. It was only about five years after this when the Fort Bragg/Mendocino region's production began to approach that of the Humboldt Bay.

Gibbs' next entries described how five different parties separately explored flat areas near the shore of Humboldt Bay. Passengers from three ships, the brig *Emily Farnham*, the *Eclipse*, and the *James R. Whitney*, began settling Humboldt Bay in June, 1850. Several other ships, including also the *Schrokeinder* [sp?] and the *Susan Wardler* also took part in the initial settlements at Humboldt Bay.

An earlier voyage by the *Paragon* ended in a shipwreck at Point St. George. Charles Liscom and a few other men arrived in a whaleboat from the *Paragon*. Another early party, called the Josiah Griggs party, included Jonas Southard, Lewis K. Wood, Van Duzan, Isaac Wilson, Charles Sebring, Davis A. Buck and Truesdale. A third party, led by John W. Whaley, left San Francisco on May 7, 1850, reached the Humboldt Bay on June 22. Indians were very numerous at this time around the bay, and some made off with Whaley's cattle although the members arrived safely. A man with the surname Carnes led another party from Sonoma. This party included Benjamin Kelsey and W. L. Lundsbury. It "laid out Bucksport and Union," while others founded Eureka, which became the largest town.

The number and origins of schooners and brigs that followed the less successful voyage of the unfortunate *Paragon* illustrated that there was great interest in Humboldt Bay and the rivers that terminate in this region. Ships like the *Eclipse* also made frequent calls to Fort Bragg, Mendocino and Little River later throughout the nineteenth century. Although they hailed from many European nations as well as from the East Coast, the captains of many, if not most, of these ships were Scandinavian-born. Local Indians like the one Customs Collector Gibbs referred to as "Blue Jacket," whose tribe unfortunately he did not record, played a key role in locating the termination of many rivers and streams, such as where the "Trinity and South Fork" joined. By May, 1850, Kelsey, Liscom and a few others had cut a trail from the bay to this spot.

"A few days before" the date a second party from San Francisco landed, "Shaw, Major Graham and a few others" from a schooner, the *Laura Virginia*, pitched two tents at the site of Trinidad. The San Francisco party on board the *Galinda Nordius* consisted of forty men. Another ship, the *Cameo* also preceded those from the *Galinda*. The *Cameo* had launched two boats, one going up the coast and another to seek the outlet of the Trinity. The first boat with five men aboard capsized at the mouth of the Madd River with three of the men drowning. A fourth ship, the *Caranos Parangus*, on its way south from Paragon Bay, also launched a long boat that swamped, resulting in the loss of four others.

> This party did not mention discovery [of] the mouth of the Klamath or Trinity as they then thought it, until after their arrival at Trinidad, when they disclosed it, and invited the *Galinda* party to join them in marking a location. Nordheimer, Euniou, Stinchfield, went up with them. They located on the island and two days after the *Laura Virginia* came in. This was in the middle of May. The *Sierra Nevada Edwards* in, also interio[r], both landed passengers & provisions. Nordheimer party located on the island, the *Sierra Nevada*'s on the south side of the river at "Klamath City.' Both places were laid off for towns.

At first it was gold, not lumber, that interested most of the whites. A man from the *Caranos Parangus* departed "from Wolf's bar 1½ miles below Gullion's & reported good diggings there." However it wasn't until November 1850 that the North Fork of the Eel River was discovered by a party from "Scott's bar."

Gibbs noted how many suffered from serious hunger. The price of food sky-rocketed in March 1851 as the new settlements were left stranded clinging to the coast when a late snowstorm closed all the passes from the interior. Mule trains carried the only reliable supply of food and other necessities and none were able to get through until the summer.

One of the earliest settlers of the Humboldt Bay, a man frequently mentioned by Gibbs, was Bernardo Nordheimer. In the following summary, Gibbs elaborated on him and other early settlers. As Gibbs described these early explorers, some were drowned when their longboats turned over. Death from accidents or from an occasional Indian attack seemingly was around every turn on a trail or bend in a river or stream.

> Nordheimer's party kept the discovery of Gold Bluff secret for a while, when despairing [author wrote the word "anything" and un-derlined it here] of making anything of it themselves. About Feb., 1851, the celebrated Gold Bluff find broke out at San Francisco & a large party went up & took possession of the place.

> A few days after N's [Nordheimer's?] first arrival at Trinidad a party of Oregon French who had wintered on the Trinity came in and in-formed them how far it was to the mines. A good many miners had wintered there. These men sold their horses and a party started to cut a trail to the Trinity. On their first arrival at Trinidad they found a tree with Griggs name, the date of his visit & the latitude & longitude on it. This was afterward cut down.[43]

Gibbs included almost all of the towns listed as founded by early explorers, most of whom arrived not overland, but onboard ships that frequently stopped at Humboldt Bay. Trinidad, Eureka, and Klamath ("Klamath City") were communities that originated in that way. Some faded away, others continued to thrive and remain today. What makes Gibbs' journal account important is that he actually had the names of the individual men and women involved. Few if any partici-pants recorded events in such complete detail. Almost simultaneously to Bernar-do Nordheimers and the others, George W. Taggert arrived on the Trinity River from Redding. Gibbs placed the date as "say February, 1850." Vance and about thirty others who had wintered there accompanied Taggert. Gibbs also credited "Moore, McDermot & Taggart" with going down to the "forks" and then reaching the "mouth of the Trinity, May 12, 1850." Recognition for this discovery might also be shared with other white settlers from Oregon who came during 1850.

While he may have made discoveries of gold of his own, George Taggert pro-vided invaluable help to the miners and prospectors who did. As we see in the following two paragraphs from the Journal

> After the burning of the Writspek ranches he [Taggert] moved to the mouth of the Salmon & while the miners dug there went back to Trinidad for provisions, when news from the Salmon river was re-ceived as before mentioned.

---

43 *Ibid.*, 5, 6, 7.

Van Dusen [Van Duzen], of Griggs party was the first to explore the Klamath, in the Spring of 1850, in May. They crossed below Serrazoin & turned off below the forks. His trail is the one still known as the Serrazoin trail. He lost his animals by the Indians[.] Dancing Bill and Dad Wilson were with him. Van Dusen had returned from Sonoma with the Kelsey party. He raised a second train of animals after the loss of the first, probably as at the springs & came down the Trinity. Was Captain of the Company that burnt the Writspek ranches [Indian houses?]. Taggart packed back & forward to Salmon during the fall of 1850. In the Spring of 1851 he took the first train up the Klamath of provisions & mining, located Wingates and Wood's bars and mined & packed on Klamath during the Summer of 1851 and at Happy Camp during the winter.[44]

Located approximately one hundred twenty five miles northeast of Eureka, Happy Camp recently had witnessed some gold strikes. Miners never minded pulling up stakes and traveling to possible new discoveries. Many were nearly oblivious to distances and thus were drawn to wherever the latest findings were. George Taggart certainly was no exception.

Gibbs described a contest with prize money that was set up in order to promote trail blazing and the building of better routes from older inland towns like Sonoma to the Pacific coast. The winner sometimes really did not merit the prize:

A.J. Huesti left Sonoma with a company of 17 persons May 1, 1850, taking nine yoke of cattle and 3 wagons. He brought the wagons to within 40 miles of Humboldt bay & to save something to eat, they abandoned them and packed out their oxen. Their route was substantially the same as McKee's, up Russian R. & down Eel R. They left Eel River at the Cañon just above the mouth of the South fork, & disbanded there[.] Brown went down to the Bay, the rest to the mines. From Eel River he pursued an easterly course, crossed 3 branches of Eel River and Mad River crossed the latter above Nipple mountain took up the divide between East fork of Mad River and Redwood & then on the main divide between Redwood and Willow Creek, or ['as' was written and lined out by Gibbs] they called it Sonoma fork of Trinity. They struck the Trinity at the mouth of the South fork about the close of June and walked Big Bar July 4th. This expedition was occasioned by the reward of $3000 offered to anyone who should take wagons from Sonoma to Trinity river, which, of ['cour' written at the end of the line by Gibbs and lined out] course was not earned.[45]

This description was followed by the date "1852." At this point Customs Collector Gibbs began to recount some of the harrowing murders of whites and their retaliatory attacks upon Indians.

Two young men by the name of Cooper were living on Eel River, going out to meet a sick brother who was coming in on the trail from the Trinity early in November were killed by the Indians on Yager

44 *Ibid.*, 7, 8, 9.

45 *Ibid.* 9, 10.

Creek, running into S. fork of Trinity. The murder was known among the Klamath Indians before the news reached their friends. One of their hats being found, a party went out from Eel river & found their bodies much mutilated....The murder of the Negro on the Bald Hills during the past summer was traced to the Lagoon Indians near Trinidad. An Indian of the Trinity living at the ferry offered to take the Whites at once to the place & point out the murderer.[46]

The journal continues with a description of the founding of Eureka by passengers on board the *Ryerson*. Gibbs stated "Walter Van Dyke came in *Bark Tarquin, Vincent*, in the fall of 1850 to the mouth of Klamath River." A settlement was started but later abandoned as impractical. In his next passage Gibbs wrote of a geological description by Mr. Van Dyke, whom Gibbs credited with being the first to discover gold close to the beach at Gold Bluff.

In his next paragraph Gibbs described how the Tompkin's Ferry massacre began with a "premeditated" murder of "Bender," a "packer." This took place near the end of June, 1851, and Indians also killed the "elder Blackburn." The following passage described what life was like for some white settlers. The passage concluded with one of Gibbs' surmises about "a white boy" who angered male Indians by making disparaging remarks about the Indian women.

> The ferry house consisted of a cloth house or large tent in front of a small clapboard building. In the former were three men. In the latter the younger Blackburn & his wife slept. Early in the morning the Indians cut open the Sail house and killed the three men. A noise one of them made awakened Blackburn who went to the door where an Indian jumped at him and he had just time to get back and bolt the door. They then commenced hurling stones to break in the house and attempted to fire it. Blackburn had two guns and his wife loaded for him to fire. he fired 20 rounds and as was believed killed 7 Indians. Two of them came with a brand swinging it. One he shot when the other took it up and he killed him also. This struck them with a panic and they drew back. About 8 o'clock they hauled off. The squaws [?'tried'] to get his wife by telling her that it was all quiet. About 10 A.M. a pack train came up and relieved them. The Indians expressed great admiration of the conduct of the woman. It is difficult to tell what was the real motive of the act. It is generally alleged to have arisen from the conduct of a boy who had made a practice of insulting the women.[47]

In this account the Tompkins ferry massacre appeared to be a senseless act of violence that served nobody's true interests. Without a record of the Indians' side of the story we will never know the cause of the murders.

Indians supposedly killed three more white men, Skink, Cushing and Walker, in 1850 and in June, 1851. As was usually the case an "expedition," really, a posse was raised "at Trinidad by McMahan" which rode out but could not find the

---

46 *Ibid.* 10, 11.

47 *Ibid.* 12.

guilty Indians, despite the fact that a Trinity Indian had a pistol that had belonged to Walker. The man who owned and operated the ferry, Tompkins, told the party that he wanted to deal with the Indians in his own way. The posse then gave up and returned to Trinidad but not before it found another body, that of "Dr. Higgenbottom in a gulch leading into Redwood Creek."

It appeared that white bodies were turning up frequently but few Indians were found to be responsible. The more reports there were of settlers' murders, the greater the rage among whites who demanded government intervention or the formation of posses to take the law into their own hands. The reports in Gibbs' journal were reinforced by news reports among local frontier newspapers. The reports reached a crescendo by the mid-1850s. Small wonder then that militia units massacred Indian warriors in retaliation without regard to guilt or innocence.

GIBBS' OBSERVATIONS OF HUMBOLDT BAY AREA INDIANS AND THEIR FOLKWAYS

There are several unique descriptions by Customs Collector Gibbs characterizing Indian life such as how the tribes made a drink from manzanita berries. Whites reported to Gibbs "it tasted like cider."

> The Indians on the Salmon are almost all extinct. There are none on the North fork, on the South only one. Small band & on the main river but one down to Woolley's Creek.
>
> The upper Salmon Indians belong to the Shasta tribe, that is from the forks up, though on the Sough fork they are connected with the Trinity Indians as the passage is a short one over and they intermarry.
>
> Below the forks they belong to the Arra Arras. The remains of houses and their own report show very considerable numbers here at the former fusion.
>
> I noticed a drink at the head of the South fork of Salmon in use among the Indians made from the berries of the manzanita. It was acid, but whether from the natural taste of the fruit or formulation I did not learn—The men said it tasted like cider. Says the Klamath Indians keep a sort of record. They indicate their age by a notch cut for every moon. [48]

He also referred to the Indians' keeping track of numbers:

> [t]he men they have killed by a red mark. The number of their wives by a black one. During life this is kept in his private basket in the lodge. After death it is placed in a sort of case woven from a particular plant & hidden in a hollow tree, on a hill over the village with others of the tribe. If the Indian dying has a canoe, they split it up & place a part over his grave. The dead one if 'waked' three nights & a fire kept burning over the grave. The medicine man digs the grave with a wooden instrument [here Gibbs wrote '& will not use iron for the purpose' and lined it out] in fashioning which no iron has been used.

---

48 *Ibid.,* 13, Gibbs headed these passages with the names "Driscell" and "Wm. N. Bercaw."

Making it difficult to interpret the correct meaning for these mysterious lines about sacred burial practices, Gibbs concluded this subject by noting that he thought "some of the above doubtful." Customs Collector Gibbs sketched three maps included here below. A sample page of his journal precedes the first map that he sketched.

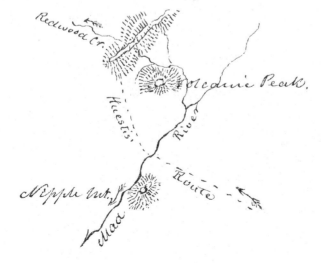

Names & Positions of Ark-Arra vill-ages. Note – The Weitspeks give different na-mes to these, probably translations. 106 houses

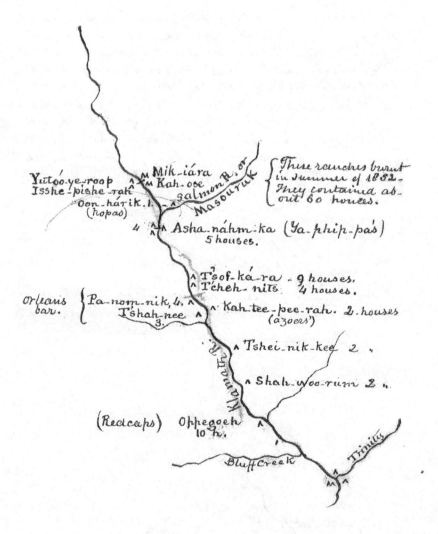

Yutoo-ye-roop
Isshe-pishe-rah
Oon-hárik. 1.
(hopas)

Mik-iára
Kah-ose

Salmon R. or
Masoutuk

{ These ranches burnt
in summer of 1852 –
They contained ab-
out 60 houses.

4   Asha-náhm-ka (Ya-phip-pas)
5 houses.

Tsof-ká-ra – 9 houses.
Tcheh-nits   4 houses.

Orleans
bar.   { Pa-nom-nik, 4.
Tshah-nee
3.

Kah-tee-pee-rah. 2. houses
(azoers')

Tshei-nik-kee   2 ,,

Shah-woo-rum   2 ,,

(Redcaps)   Ohpegoch
10 h.

Klamath

Bluff Creek

Trinity

Names & Positions of the "Ho-pah" or Lower Trinity villages.
– 99 houses –

South Fork

Perry

▲ Weitspek 3 houses

Waug-ulle-wutle-kauh, ▲ 1 house

Willow Cr.

Waug-ulle-watl, ▲ 3 houses

o-Hopah-pahw

✗ Seh-ach-pe-ya 4 houses.

Trinity R.

✗ Wauch-ta, 6 houses.

Peht-sau-an ▲ 9 houses.

Kahtetl 28 houses. ▲▲

Olle-hotl ▲ 10 houses

Ople-goh ▲ 20 houses

Eh-grertsh ▲ 6 houses

Okenope ▲ 9 houses

Klamath R.

Klamath R.

Referring to the map above, Gibbs first listed ninety-nine houses. On the next page, in Gibbs' words, were the "Names & Positions of Arr-Arra villages. Note-the Weitspeks give different names to these, probably translations. 106 houses." The final sketched map illustrated the "Names and Positions of lower Klamath ranches." Except for one ranch name, "Otche-pah," there were no other notations. Gibbs' map clearly laid out the Trinity River's course.

Almost at the very end of the journal Gibbs wrote,

Humboldt Bay Indians

The yellow butterfly they call Scruwauk, apparently meaning & Spirit; they believe with the souls of the dead children animate them. These are often seen hovering around graves. They wash the bodies of the dead and bury them with them.

The women delude themselves during menstruation. The first occur-rence in a girl is attended by the visit of all the squaws, who swim with her. They bathe frequently during the period in cold water. When pregnant if delivery is difficult or retarded they steam the parts with certain herbs, & they bathe their breasts with a concoction of roots to facilitate milking. They have certain superstitious observances relative to the partaking of food by women analogous to those of the Chinooks respecting salmon. Do not allow them to cut venison or Elk meat when menstruating but the game should be driven away. Certain parts of the animal alone are also allotted to women. The men tattoo to some extent and mark the number of enemies they have slain by scars on& the breast. The women tattoo the underjaw or on the Klamath & occasionally other parts. The coloring matter which is of a blue or greenish tinge they obtain by burning strips of redwood under moist-ened stones from which they obtain the soot or black. The men occupy themselves in long furrows when unsuccessful in gambling. The game usually played, is made with six small [indecipherable] sticks about four inches in length, all but one of which is marked with rings. These are wrapped up by the players in a little bag & after being waved & tossed about for awhile are torn into two parcels the object being as in the Chinook game of 'Hand' to guess in which the unmarked stick is. The game is called toop-stick. A losing gambler sacrifices himself with a flint, secludes himself from the band for a few days & bathes. The tallies or counters vary in number according to agreement. They are called Péh shwah, the game sticks Poh-kah-wa-rihl.

On the last page, Customs Collector Gibbs ends his journal with a list of six-teen more names, fifteen men and one woman. Included were some of the most famous military officers in northern California and Oregon Territory history, including Major Henry M. Wessel[l]s, who commanded the mounted troops (at this time mounted soldiers were termed dragoons by the U.S. Army) on the Mckee Expedition of 1851:

A. G. Morrison Sacramento

R. S. Williamson Lt Top Eng

G. N Derby

Lt. Chas. P. Stone Ordnance

Dr. Jas S. Griffin U.S.A.

Maj. Henry M. Wessels 2nd Inf.

Lt. Thos. Wright, 2nd Inf.

Lt. Col. Jos. Hooker

Col. W. W. Loring. U. S. Rifles

Lt. Theodore Talbot.

Mrs. Alonzo A. Skinner

Dr. Joseph Leidy. Ac. Nat. Sci., Philadelphia

Barker Burnell, Sonoma

Dr. Arthur B. Stout, Washn. St., San Francisco, betw. Dupont and Stockton

Maj. Hiram Leonard, Paym.

Maj. Albert Smith

There are similarities between the Lewis and Clark journal, John Work's diary, southern Oregon settler Jesse Applegate's memoir, and Custom Collector George Gibbs' journal that set these four recordings apart from later works. In a few cases Indians were represented as equal participants along with individual white men. As the nineteenth century wore on, however, and greater and greater numbers of Euro-American, Asian, South American, Kanaka (Hawaii natives in early California), and other ethnic groups immigrated and contributed to northern California's story, white–Indian communications as well as trusting, close relationships between individuals gradually became less and less mutually beneficial. Conflicts between the predominantly white settler community and Indians increased. Almost imperceptibly at first, but to an increasing degree after 1850, Indians were marginalized.

CHAPTER 5. THE IMPACT OF ANGLO-SAXONS ON EARLY NORTHERN CALIFORNIA

SHIPWRECK OF A BRIG, THE *FROLIC*, JULY 25, 1850

News of the wreck of a San Francisco bound brig filled with valuable cargo hit the papers in late summer, 1850. The news brought attention to the north coast and consequently to its huge lumber resources drawing entrepreneurs.

The shipwreck of the *Frolic*, a clipper ship that had been in almost constant use from 1845 to 1850 shuttling opium from India to China, occurred on July 25, 1850. The captain, Edward Horatio Faucon, had been portrayed by the young novelist Richard Henry Dana (*Two Years Before the Mast*), who had served under him. By the time the *Frolic* was built in 1844, Capt. Faucon had managed to buy one-fifth ownership in the ship he would sail as her captain.

Professor Emeritus Thomas N. Layton in his 1997 book, *The Voyage of the Frolic New England Merchants and the Opium Trade*, noted that exporting the opium from Indian ports became a highly profitable enterprise. The first trading company to exploit the opium trade was the Scottish firm of Jardine, Matheson & Company. James Matheson and William Jardine co-founded the company in 1827. This company's timing could not have been better; its directors could reinvest their growing opium trade profits back into their fleet of sailing merchant ships.

By 1850 the big trading firms had begun trying to sell off their unprofitable clipper ships like the *Frolic* in order to replace them with steam ships. In part as a test of using the older ships to carry Chinese-made products to ports in California, the Heards, New England opium traders, sent the *Eveline*, a ship similar to the

Frolic, to San Francisco in 1849. The voyage was highly profitable so the Heards thought they would try again with the *Frolic*.

Reading the handwriting on the wall regarding the future of clipper ships in the opium trade, Captain Faucon sold his one-fifth share in the *Frolic* by the start of 1850. By April 1850 John Heard and Capt. Faucon had nearly completed purchasing goods like silk and art works, porcelain, bottles of ale, and other items that were cheap in China but expensive in San Francisco. They tried to hire more Chinese coolies who would sail the ship for almost nothing and once on shore were willing to work in San Francisco at lower than the going labor rate. There were three Chinese sailors, a cook, a carpenter and a steward on board the *Frolic*.

As Dr. Layton's work recalled, the silks alone were worth $31,000. There were many more miscellaneous items, including ivory fans, flatware with ivory and mother-of-pearl handles, combs, umbrellas, measuring rods, games with engraved shell counters, and tens of thousands of porcelain beads, probably intended for trade to California Indians. Some of these items are preserved at the Kelly House Museum in Mendocino. The manifest also included a prefabricated house to be constructed and sold once the ship reached San Francisco.

The *Frolic* sailed from Hong Kong on the morning of June 10 1850. The journey started out well enough. It was on the evening of their forty-fifth day at sea that the captain left the deck, turning over the ship to his first mate. At 9:10 P.M. First Mate Deutcher saw breakers where they should not be, according to their faulty chart. Captain Faucon no doubt was shocked. The ship was about to strike a large rock just south of Point Cabrillo on the north Mendocino coast.

The situation was hopeless. Captain Faucon ordered the *Frolic*'s two boats lowered, with one officer in charge of each. Most of the men climbed into the boats. Inexplicably, two Chinese, one Lascar, and three Malays refused to leave the sinking vessel. Capt. Faucon and his men made it safely to shore. Almost as soon as the ship started to sink, Mittom Pomo Indians, a local tribelet of the North Pomo, saw what was happening and began to salvage cargo from the stranded vessel.

On July 29 at 5 p.m., the ship's survivors landed at a ranch where they were given beef and milk. This rancho was probably the one that later was called "the German rancho," about four miles north of Fort Ross, owned by Henry Hegeler and two partners. The next day Faucon reached Fort Ross, where he spent the night at the home of William Benitz, owner of the settlement. Faucon traveled on to Bodega the following morning and passed the night with Captain Stephen Smith, who operated a steam-powered saw mill there.

On Sunday, August 4, ten days after the wreck, Captain Faucon arrived at San Francisco. Within hours he gave an interview to a reporter from the city's largest newspaper, the *Daily Alta Californian*. The following day, August 5, 1850, an article titled "Shipwreck and Loss of Life," gave a brief report about the loss of the *Frolic*.

Capt. Faucon, estimating the *Frolic*'s cargo would have brought a two hundred percent profit over invoice, calculated the loss at $150,000.

Less than a year later some of the camphor chests were resting in George Parker Armstrong's home in the Ukiah Valley. A number of fortunate Indian women had fine quality Chinese silk to fashion into shawls and skirts. A sword, also supposedly from the *Frolic*, became the prized possession of the Jerome Ford family in the coastal village of Mendocino. The New England ship's cargo had been intended for auction to the highest bidders, miners with gold nuggets to spare, or for others including Indians who might be interested in goods from China such as art work, furniture, large urns, umbrellas as well as beer and ale.

In a twist of fate, much of the clipper's cargo ended up first in the Mitom Pomos' summer settlement of Buldam on Big River and later at Taklit village near present day Willits. Some items also found their way to white settler George Parker Armstrong's cabin just north of Ukiah. Many years later a granddaughter of Jerome Ford remembered playing with a Chinese sword that had also been part of the ship's cargo.

It must have seemed like a blessing to the coastal or Mitom Pomos to be able to carry off chest after chest of salvage when the *Frolic* sank. The irony was that publicity from the shipwreck led to a flood of settlers that eventually destroyed the Indian way of life.

CHAPTER 6. COMMISSIONER REDICK MCKEE EXPLORES NORTHWESTERN CALIFORNIA, AUGUST TO DECEMBER, 1851

> You will mix with us by marriage; your blood will run in our veins, and will spread with us over this great island.
>
> —Pres. Thomas Jefferson in the White House to a delegation of New England Indians from three different tribes, Dec. 21, 1808.

The fall of 1850 was a difficult time to be alive in America. The nation was racked by serious, poorly understood, epidemic diseases including cholera, small-pox, diphtheria, as well as malnutrition, poor hygiene, VD. Infections incurred during childbirth or accidents claimed thousands of lives yearly. Most Americans eked out meager existences as farmers working small plots of land with poor soil under difficult climatic conditions. After a series of bloody victorious battles dur-ing the Mexican War, the nation paused for a few short years to enjoy a period of hard-earned relative peace, if not prosperity. Change was in the air. During the summer of 1850 the unexpected death of the beloved President Zachary Taylor thrust Vice President Millard Fillmore into the presidency. Fillmore would prove to be a very able leader and president.

In that same autumn of 1850 under President Fillmore's tutelage and with the consent of Congress, the national government, with almost no knowledge of what it might be getting into, began an effort to make peace treaties with the California Indian tribes. This was a time before the Indian reservation system had become an accepted national policy. Most Americans, especially those who moved westward as the frontier moved, opposed any treaties with Native Ameri-cans. While many of the parties involved no doubt had good intentions, the overall record of the era led to the tragic deaths of uncounted thousands of innocent Native Americans as well as a considerable number of Anglo-Americans.

There was hardly a more unlikely choice to lead a Far Western expedition to locate and attempt to make treaties with northern California Indians than the fifty-year-old West Virginia businessman Redick McKee. McKee was born on December 7, 1800, in the rugged Allegheny Mountains of southern Pennsylvania. He was the son of a Scot-Irish immigrant. His adult life began at about age seventeen teaching school. A deeply religious young man, he taught the Christian (Protestant, Presbyterian) faith to his students using a sandbox to sketch out the letters of the alphabet. He was a lifelong Christian and dedicated educator, although at times somewhat didactic and what many today would view as priggish.

By 1820 he settled down in the town of Wheeling, which was then a part of Virginia (since the Civil War, West Virginia). There he bought a small glassworks. By concentrating on producing high quality glassware, his company grew and became profitable. Eventually The Virginia Works, Knox & McKee, Wheeling, built up a large clientele that included customers all the way from New Mexico to New York.

With his wife Eliza, McKee raised five children. One of his sons, John, graduated from Harvard. Redick McKee served a term as a councilman on the Wheeling city council. Until 1850 most of his work had been as a businessman. He was the founder and developer of a successful glass company. He had held a few slaves as personal servants but wasn't a particularly wealthy man. His most recent biographer, Ray Raphael, was not able to find out why McKee happened to be chosen in October 1850 to be a special federal Indian Commissioners to California. California became a state in December 1850. John agreed to accompany his father on his 1851 expedition to northern California. John's diary was a key source of information about the tribes throughout northern California.

By Congress' final great pre-Civil War compromise, the Compromise of 1850, California entered the Union as the thirty-first State. To Washington D.C. insiders California was a strange and forbidding place, a territory that until recently had been unknown to most Euro-Americans especially the residents of the states east of the Mississippi River. Up to this time it had been just another neglected northern territory of Mexico, a foreign Spanish-speaking nation.

Eastern Indian tribes had been force-marched west of the Mississippi River. Few Americans could communicate with Indians living west of the Rocky Mountains since, unlike Plains tribes, California Indians didn't use sign language. The general purpose of the three Indian commissioners' mission was to meet with local chiefs in order to make treaties binding the Indians to relocate to a system of reservations. Behind the idea of reservations was the concept of making the Indians into farmers able to grow and sell farm products much as white settlers did. While initially each reservation was to include a small detachment of regular soldiers to keep order, the Office of Indian Affairs wanted every reservation to become economically independent, supported by sales of crops.

Congress, through the Acting Commissioner of Indian Affairs, A.S. Loughery, gave a vague set of instructions to the commissioners. They were supposed to get all the information possible with regard to ways of all the tribes within California. Having learned about the Indian ways, they were to meet and form a united course of action. Somehow the Indians were to be made to see that their interests matched those of the government. All the tribes could then be united. Lacking any precedent, McKee and the other commissioners had to figure out on their own how best to accomplish their goal of locating, communicating with, and inducing the numerous California tribes to enter into treaties. Later the commissioners were to achieve the relocation of the Indians from their homelands onto reservations, again with no instructions provided.

Further, just how the commissioners were expected to convince recent California immigrants, mostly rough and tumble white settlers, whether farmers or miners, to give up land for Indian reservations in the soon-to-be-admitted state, was left unaddressed. Further, the commissioners were supposed to enlist the leaders of all the Indian tribes to sign treaties giving away their traditional homelands. And at first, there were no funds allocated to buy the mules, horses, cattle and the equipment needed to conduct expeditions across hundreds of miles of unexplored, rugged California terrain. As a result McKee and his son John had to cool their heels in San Francisco from February to July 1851, before they finally laid hands on the five thousand dollars for the needed equipment and supplies for their trip. This unusual mission through the northern California wilderness would last just a few days more than five months, from mid-August to just before the end of 1851.

As was explained by historian Ray Raphael, the natives of northern California must have thought that McKee's expedition was a bizarre and scary sight. Included in the McKee party were approximately seventy white men, including thirty-six dragoons (cavalry soldiers) with the remainder being drovers, a cook, a commissary, interpreters, McKee's immediate subordinates, and others. There were also 160 head of cattle and 140 horses and mules. Besides himself and his son John, McKee also employed as his secretary, George Gibbs, as well as the commander of a cavalry unit, Major H. (Henry) H. Wessells. Thus there were four recorders: Maj. Wessells, John McKee, Redick McKee, and George Gibbs. Unlike the Lewis and Clark Expedition and the trek along the coast of John Work in 1833, this journey inland included not a single woman.

Departing from San Francisco on August 11, 1851 they passed through the small settlement at Santa Rosa. They progressed northeast to Clear Lake, where they negotiated a treaty with a Pomo tribelet. Next they traveled north through the rugged terrain of the Mayacama Mountains and central Mendocino County.

They encountered various tribelets of Native Americans on their way in a north-westerly direction to the Humboldt Bay area, west to the Shasta region, and back at last to the Humboldt Bay by December 1851. Since almost all of the Indians they encountered refused to even speak with them, they successfully negotiated less than five actual treaties.

McKee gave the Clear Lake Indians the following short speech

> Brothers, listen to my talk. We come among you as friends to learn the cause of your troubles, if you have any, and your condition generally. What I say comes straight from the heart, and there shall be no crook in my path, nor fork in my tongue. I come from the Great Father, the President, at Washington, the most powerful and richest chief on this continent, and anything I may do in his name will be final and binding upon you, if he approves. That Great Father, my chief, has conquered this country, and you are his children now, and subject in all things to him...The President has learned that his red children in California are at war with the whites and among themselves, are very poor and ignorant, and he has sent three commissioners among them to inquire into their condition.[49]

Commissioner McKee, former schoolteacher and glass merchant, had his first success in reaching his Clear Lake audience with this speech. Nowhere else in northern California was the expedition able to reach as many Indians with its message. In just two other instances did he induce any Indians to sign treaties. Commissioner McKee listed estimated population totals for three separate northern California areas: twelve hundred for the valleys near Sonoma and along the Russian River, one thousand for the hills, mountains, and area around Clear Lake, and eight hundred for the coastal area from Fort Ross to the San Francisco Bay. It was an ominous sign when the chief of the Kan-no-meahs, whom Comm. McKee described as living on "Fitch's ranch," changed his mind about signing the treaty "being unwilling to consent to a removal."[50]

The McKee party discovered that during spiritual observances as the members of a certain tribe participated in a dance, certain kinds of fish and fowl couldn't be eaten. Some dances invoking spirits of revered tribal members who were long dead could go on night and day over many days. Another nearly universal custom was refraining from eating any bear meat since bears were thought to be inhabited by souls of dead Indians. According to a conversation that Comm. McKee had with George Parker Armstrong, Armstrong was married to an Indian woman who believed in a deity she referred to as "Big Head." According to the native tradition, whenever Big Head became angry there would be a storm. A thunderstorm meant he was especially displeased. Many tribes along the Russian River had been influenced by Spanish missions, so that Christian doctrine co-mingled

---

49 Ray Raphael, *Little White Father Redick McKee on the California Frontier* (Eureka, CA, Humboldt County Historical Society, 1993), 33.

50 *Ibid.*, 222-223. Fitch's mountain is near the town of Healdsburg, CA.

with native beliefs. Christian beliefs are to this day comingled with native ideas in some parts of the Southwest, Mexico and elsewhere in Latin America.

Gibbs noted that the northwestern California Indians subsisted on acorn meal, acorns, the roots of certain plants and pinole. Pinole is defined as "US flour made from parched cornflour mixed with sweet flour made of mesquite beans, sugar and spice. Its origin is from Latin America, Sp., from Nahuatl *pinoli*."[51] Unlike Euro-American fishermen, who preferred using hooks and poles or nets, they employed weirs, which are basket-size cages made from the strongest stems of certain plants with an open end, in order to capture fish from rivers and streams or salmon from the Russian, Mattole, Eel, or Klamath Rivers.

Perhaps Clear Lake Indians were more open to the party's overtures than others since they had been attacked and slaughtered at the bloody battle on Clear Lake's Island only a year before in the fall of 1850. Comm. McKee and a few others of his party may have eaten some acorn bread and pinole bread either at Clear Lake or at Armstrong's cabin. Commissioner McKee probably handed over several cattle and perhaps a horse or two to help the Clear Lake tribes make up their minds to sign the treaty. Maybe Commissioner McKee was having beginner's luck. At any rate as Raphael, noted,

> The party made a treaty with the tribes [McKee termed them 'the Sah-nel, Yukai [Yuki or Ukiah?] Pomo, and Masu-ta-kaya.' at Clear Lake and marched towards the northwest. Soon it arrived in the heart of some of the most rugged country on the California frontier, the home of grizzly bears and towering redwoods.[52]

This treaty ("Treaty O") was Comm. McKee's first successful negotiation with northern California Indians. He estimated the total number represented by these four tribes as "one-thousand-forty-two souls." At that early point it appeared that his mission was headed for real success. Before long, however, he would start to encounter two problems that eventually prevented him from this: each tribe spoke a different dialect, and many tribes simply either turned tail completely at the sight of the strange party of whites or sent in one or two chiefs or intermediaries to accept the cattle or other presents from McKee but then refused to talk about making a treaty. Speaking through an interpreter in either the language spoken by the Clear Lake tribes or in Spanish, Commissioner McKee usually could make his "Brothers, ... I speak with a straight tongue" speech to enough of them so that some of them at least could understand what he was trying to tell them. However the interpreter often couldn't understand the Indians' replies.

---

51 *Concise Oxford English Dictionary*, (Oxford University Press, Oxford, England, (eleventh edition), 2004), 1089.

52 Ibid., 41.

On the morning of August 23, 1851, the party broke camp and headed upriver [Russian River]. Having heard tales of the rough trail ahead, the men loaded all their provisions onto mules and sent the wagons back to Sonoma. Later that day, near the present site of Ukiah, they passed the thatched log home of George Parker Armstrong, the last abode of a white man they would see for almost 150 miles. After crossing the Ukiah Valley, they headed up the divide between the Russian and Eel rivers, where they encountered 'some stupendous mountains.'[53]

While there is no accurate record of their conversation, McKee and his companions must have been happy to pause in their trek at the comfortable Ukiah home that was Armstrong's. Surrounded by salvage from the wreck of the *Frolic*, including very large china jars, camphor trunks, and many lacquered pieces, McKee and his host must have had much to talk about. Armstrong obtained these items from the Mitom Pomo braves, or possibly their wives, who first had plundered the ship. However they got there, certainly these were not the usual belongings of a white settler far away from the civilized world in the wilderness of northern California.

Bears were considered to be at the very least semi-spiritual beings by most Far Western Indian tribes. They believed the souls of dead relations lived in the bear skins and heads of the largest animals such as the grizzly, brown and black bear and were manifested during ceremonial dances and rituals. According to McKee, he met with a large group of one hundred twenty-seven men, one hundred forty-seven women, and one hundred-six children. The men had strong legs and large muscular chests yet short arms. They were all of smaller stature than white men. Almost all had ears pierced by pieces of wood or sticks. While some had bows and arrows, only one carried an obsidian-tipped spear. He estimated their total as between four hundred fifty and four hundred seventy-five.

From this point in the Ukiah Valley onward, the going became a great deal tougher for McKee's expedition. On August 24 Thomas Sebring (or Seabring), their main guide, met the McKee party. Near present day city of Ukiah, McKee's party made a two-day stop. The Indians here were what archeologists would term southern Pomo. McKee said they left their rancherias and hid in the mountains in order to avoid contact with the all white party. The arrival of a group of white men who represented no immediate threat but wanted to talk with them was something these Indians had never experienced before. While they were perhaps used to being fired on by settler or trapping parties of white men, McKee didn't want to take something from them (in the short run) but instead wanted to barter with them and to give away cattle as gifts. Certainly, such a thing was unheard of.

After crossing the Ukiah Valley, McKee's group of soldiers and civilians traveled up the Russian and Eel rivers, where they encountered some "stupendous

53 *Ibid.* 49.

mountains," the daunting Mayacama Mountains. Later, writing from Humboldt Bay, McKee noted that this was a real turning point on the trip

> The first seventy or eighty miles, up the valleys of Sonoma creek and Russian river, were accomplished with but little comparative difficulty; but from the time we left Russian river at its source, and commenced crossing what our guide [Thomas Seabring or Sebring] called the divide between the Russian and Eel rivers, we had, for about one hundred miles, a succession of hills, mountains, gulches, gorges, and canons, such as are not to be found east of the Rocky mountains, and but seldom even in California and Oregon.[54]

Despite the fact that Comm. McKee hadn't seen much of California or Oregon, other members of his party had. Perhaps he was relying on their tales. The Mayacama Mountain range is one of the most impressive mountain chains in the West. It came as a surprise after the relative lowlands above the Russian River in southern Mendocino and northern Sonoma Counties. As they began to encounter rougher and rougher terrain, they resumed moving to the northwest. Commissioner McKee ordered all their supplies transferred from their four wagons to the mules and horses. He sent the wagons back as they left Ukiah and sought out the source of the Russian River.

As noted, prior to becoming the commissioner's chief scribe, George Gibbs had been a scout and an interpreter in Oregon and northern California. The entries in his daily journal or log of the McKee Expedition are reminiscent of writings of Mark Twain, Bret Harte, and other newsmen. The party crossed the Russian River. They had entered a large tract of land owned by the *Californio* Señor Feliz. Like other recipients of huge land grants from the Mexican government, Sr. Feliz had received the large ranch upon his promise to settle and develop the land in a constructive manner. As had been the Mexican government's practice before the Mexican War, a number of fortunate Hispanic- and Euro-Americans were given titles for huge tracts in all parts of California. The grants were a kind of trust given with the condition working ranches should be set up. Just south of Ukiah, when the McKee party arrived at his rancho, Sr. Feliz received them with warm hospitality, according to George Gibbs,

> [the usual] Spanish courtesy, and insisted in turn upon everyone sitting down upon the only chair in the establishment. A more attractive spot for us were [was] a pile of tule under the shed, where were seated the two daughters and the daughter-in-law of the host, with a visitor, eating water-melons. The ladies were all tolerably pretty women, and their plump figures shadowed forth agreeably beneath the thin folds of a chemisetts [sic sp. chemisettes] and petticoat which constituted their costume.[55]

---

54 McKee to (Commissioner of Indian Affairs) Lea, Sept. 12, 1851, in *Sen. Exec. Doc. 4, Serial 688*, as quoted by Raphael, *ibid.* 181.

55 George Gibbs, *Journal*, Raphael, op. cit. 114.

On August 28 Comm. McKee wrote that his party had lost its way as it began to cross the Mayacama Mountains. It ended up in a completely unknown mountain cul-de-sac. The party got lost more than once after that, either in redwood forests or in mountain ravines. The rugged terrain northwest of Round Valley consists of incredibly steep canyons, steep defiles, and breathtakingly beautiful scenery. Despite their missteps by August 29 they had arrived at "a creek" near or in Round Valley. As the party paused to observe the Sabbath on the last day of August 1851, McKee noted that they were in a valley called "Ba-tem-da-kai," on what they thought was the South Fork of the Eel River. Actually they were near present day Willits, about to enter more relatively level open land.

Despite their being lost on occasion, guide Thomas Sebring had been doing his job well. The party was back to proceeding along in a reasonably good groove, making fairly decent time. Good trail time would have been five to eight miles a day through such rugged terrain and up to ten to fourteen through level or gently rolling land.

Whenever Indians actually entered his camp Commissioner McKee handed out presents. But even with all of his gestures of good will he couldn't bring the Indians to the treaty-signing stage. Seemingly friendly Indians would accept gifts and appear to be settled down to sleep peacefully for a night in their camp. Yet at daybreak they could not be found, and McKee's gifts were gone with them. Comm. McKee must have felt frustrated at the lack of progress by December 1851 at Humboldt Bay as the party awaited a ship to take them back south to San Francisco. Part of the problem stemmed from the fact that very few northern California Indians had ever even heard of the "great chief at Washington." How could McKee's "great father" speech have made an impact on them, when it could only have been translated in a form that was barely understandable to them?

On Auguse 21st the commissioner compared the Indians' appearance with the description made earlier by the well known western scout and explorer, Jedediah Smith.

> In general appearance they resembled the Indians in the upper valley. They pluck their beards, and some of them tattoo. Many had their hair cut short, but others wore it turned up in a bunch in front, or occasionally on the back of the head. The practice of cutting the hair, so unusual among American Indians, is referred to by Jedediah S. Smith, one of the most adventurous of the whole class of fur traders, who, during his various expeditions, constructed a map of Oregon and California. An entry upon this, designates the tribes living on the west of the Sacramento range as the 'Short-haired Indians.' The average height of these men was not over five feet four or five inches. They were lightly built, with no superfluous flesh, but with very deep chests and sinewy legs. Their expression was mild and pleasant, and vastly better than

their reputation warranted. We saw no women, and the proposal to bring them in, at once excited their fear and distrust.[56]

There were wide variations among California tribes with regard to their physique, hairstyle, and manner of tattooing. That they were protective of their women was not surprising since most white men were disrespectful to Indian women. Commissioner McKee made a rare and, for him, poetic attempt at describing the natural majesty and beauty of Northern California. He also noted the temperature of a hot sulfur spring.

> I took the opportunity of to-day's halt, to ascend the hills on the eastern side of the valley. The view from this point was beautiful, the stream winding in serpentine form along the margin of the plain, fringed with oaks and firs, and the long slopes beyond diversified with forest and prairie. To the east rose heavy ranges of mountains, and deep gap indicated another valley, supposed to be the source of the main fork or [of] Eel river. Returning to camp, Mr. Sebring pointed out a sulphur spring, the water of which was very strongly impregnated. The temperature proved to be 70 degrees, while that of the air was 68 degrees.[57]

Following this short stay beside the spring, in his next letters to Commissioner Lea, the Commissioner of Indian Affairs, Comm. McKee noted how one of their horses was lost,

> Saturday, August 30th– Here they lost their lead white mare that broke her neck after a fall down a hill. Our course continued northward, up high grassy hills, and then over the wooded table-land, which forms the western side of the valley....

> Trees were mixed fir and oak. A few Indians visited us, and were directed to call in the adjacent tribes. The distance traveled to-day was four miles.

> Sunday, Aug. 31st– Quite a number of Indians were assembled and presents distributed, but no treaty attempted; for our Clear Lake interpreter, although able to comprehend them, could not explain freely in turn. Their language, however, is clearly of the same family as that of the tribes at the head of Russian river, and those last encountered. The total number in the vicinity, as near as could be ascertained, was about six hundred souls.[58]

As has been well documented by his biographer Ray Raphael, Commissioner McKee had vague ideas about Indians and what was possible for his expedition to accomplish. Many of his observations were repetitious. Unable to communicate clearly what his goals were, almost all of his efforts to make actual treaties

56 See Commissioner McKee's journal, August 21, 1850, *Ibid.* 230-231.

57 Chad L. Hoopes, *Lure of the Humboldt Bay Region,* "Journal of Redick McKee of the Expedition," 231.

58 Raphael, *ibid.* 231.

were useless. For the commissioner, thousands of miles from his wife, family, and home town, the experience must have been extremely disappointing. While Raphael's attitude toward McKee is in many ways smug and disdainful, it does not seem warranted, given the hardships McKee's party faced, and, especially also, given the fact that the Indians were fearful of the motives and the intentions of all white men in this period.

Certainly almost every action by white men, whether they happened to be settlers, explorers, or soldiers, was hurtful in some way to the Indians, and almost all white men were armed. Some whites took potshots at them at almost every opportunity. While describing his hunting trips through Mendocino County Special Agent J. Ross Browne noted that the group took "target practice" at Indians they came across on the trail. There was also the fact that white men usually made social contact with them for the purpose of having sex with one of their women or to barter for goods like beaver pelts, or to obtain needed directions; then often cheated them when it came to paying the agreed amount.

The Indians impressed Maj. Wessels, the officer in charge of the dragoons, even less than they did George Gibbs, Commissioner McKee, or his son John. Maj. Wessels was openly contemptuous of the Indians and warned that newcomers or white settlers, who might have to pass through this rugged northern California region should be extremely watchful. Maj. Wessels believed that all the Indians had a "thievish" nature. It was a common observation by whites about western Indian individuals.

Furthermore,

> Our camp was freely visited by [the] inhabitants, and with them another fruitless effort was made to form a treaty. They could not be made to understand the obligations of a contract, and were very suspicious of our design.[59]

During the latter part of the exploration Commissioner McKee thought it would be a good idea to establish a reservation in the extreme northwestern section of California. After this the Klamath Reservation and later the Hoopa (or Hupa) Reservation were founded.

The expedition arrived at the Humboldt Bay. Here Commissioner McKee made the following entry in his journal, describing the northern California fog that had become a frequent problem for the explorers. They were experiencing such magnificent scenery that the entire party had trouble concentrating on their primary tasks of trying to locate, to communicate with the Indians and note their responses and appearance and, secondly, to make treaties of removal with them.

In the following entry Gibbs wrote:

> Sept. 8th– The trail here crossed the river, and, skirting a grove of redwoods, ascended the mountains beyond. This timber had now re-

---

59 *Ibid.*, Maj. Wessels, *Sen. Exec. Doc. 76, Serial 906*, 61.

appeared, and was abundant in the bottoms, often attaining a gigantic size. Higher on the hills the fir and oak prevailed. The mountain sides and tops were generally very rich, and, where not the only open country was upon these high slopes; the valleys, if the narrow bottoms can be so called, being generally filled with forest. Reaching the top of the ascent we found the fog so dense that the advance party had stopped; and we were compelled to halt for about an hour. From this the trail descended to the foot of the Bear Butte, a high serrated crest, which forms a conspicuous landmark for many miles, and is even visible from the Bald Mountains, between Humboldt Bay and the Klamath.... During the day we met a party of half a dozen Indians, and induced them to stop.

They were exceedingly pleased with the small presents given them, but could not be prevailed upon to accompany us into camp. Two or three of them were of larger stature than usual, and one was really a fine looking young fellow. They wore the deer-skin robe over the right shoulder, and carried the common short bow, backed with sinew, and arrows pointed with stone, both tolerably well made. With all these Indians the arrow-points are fastened into a short piece of wood, which in turn is fixed, though but loosely, into the shaft. They had also, suspended around the neck, small nets, neatly made after the fashion of the common game-bag; the twine which was very even, being of course their own work....

As it was already evening, and the march had been the most laborious we had yet made, we had no opportunity of seeking further. It had drizzled a good part of the day, and the night was still wet. Our estimated distance was fifteen miles.[60]

Notes such as these are the only record of the McKee Expedition. Probably the most detail oriented writer, Gibbs brought us face to face with a northern California Indian brave. Although a "fine looking fellow," his weapons were crude compared to the firearms the whites possessed at this time. Such sketches made by George Gibbs in his role as ethnologist brought to life California Indians as individuals, not merely stereotypical "digger Indians."[61] Part of the mission, as had been spelled out in the fall of 1850 in Acting Commissioner Loughery's instructions to McKee and the other two federal treaty commissioners, was the injunction to learn what were the customs and problems of the tribes in faraway California. These instructions may have struck some as expressing an earnest quest for knowledge and an honest desire to make life easier for the California Indians, but it also effectively meant finding their weak points and gaining a stronger hand in negotiations. And the acting commissioner's instructions were very vague.

---

60 Gibbs' *Journal*, as quoted by Raphael, *op. cit.* 235-236.

61 The stereotype described California Indians, as conceived by the majority of "white men," as a kind of subhuman species living like apes completely lacking in normal intelligence and in the what most whites thought of as the arts of civilization.

Given the vast gulf that existed between white people and Indians in every section of the United States during the mid-nineteenth century and the general lack of education that prevailed, it was incredible that Commissioner McKee and his party returned from their expedition without firing a shot in anger at anyone. Except for the loss of a few of their lead animals, they completed their journey. Results from both modern and contemporary perspectives were disappointing. Statewide, just eighteen treaties were signed. While some more tribes might have been willing to sign, only a few agreed to relocate onto reservations. When public opposition to the treaties mounted, Congress refused to ratify any of them placing the Indians' future in great risk. However, one positive result came in 1864 when Congress established the Hoopa Indian Reservation southeast of Eureka.

The record Comm. McKee left may not have been all that it could have been. As McKee's biographer, Ray Raphael, demonstrated, because of his own prejudices and narrowness of mind, Comm. McKee made numerous mistakes. Yet to do all that Congress asked in its 1850 instructions to the Indian commissioners would have taken superhuman powers of tact and forethought. Next to the ignorance of nearly every federal government official and decision maker, Commissioner Redick McKee through his mission into the wilderness of Northern California completed his journey without losing a single man and few livestock. Later Commissioner McKee returned to California to argue the case for establishing Indian reservations before the public through the press and by making numerous speeches to the California Legislature. In part, through these later considerable efforts as well as others by many men and women of good will, the federal government came to establish the Klamath, Mendocino, Nome Lackee, Nome Cult (Round Valley) and Hoopa Reservations.

CHAPTER 7. THE FIRST MILLS ON THE NORTH MENDOCINO COAST

Question:

"Prior to the contact period [ca. 1830s] when white trappers, traders, and settlers began to settle here, which tribe, or tribes, was the primary residents of the north Mendocino coast? In other words, around here?"

Answer:

"All I know is our area's....I don't know who lived on the Sonoma coast or whatever. They were the coastal Natives, the coastal Indians, so they were given that name: people. My husband, who is deceased, said they were called 'Come-a-lon Pō'-mo,' which means 'coastal person.'

"And they got the name 'Pomo' when some white man came along and they heard the word, 'Puh-mo' and changed it to 'Pō'-mo.' When they were goin' 'Puh-mo' or ... 'Uh-mo,' which was 'a person' or another — you know — a being."

—Author's interview with Mrs. Harriet Rhoades, Pomo tribe member, Ft. Bragg, CA, January, 2008.

At about the same time, the early spring of 1851, when Commissioner Redick McKee and his party were laying plans for their northern adventure, another journey began, in part also an exploration and an attempt to induce the Indians to the idea of relocating onto other remote California areas designated by the federal government, "reservations." Henry Meiggs and one of Bodega's original settlers, Captain Steven Smith, had dispatched Meiggs' employee, an experienced lumberman named Jerome Ford, to salvage the wreck of the *Frolic*. Neither the visionary San Francisco contractor/builder Harry Meiggs nor Jerome Ford could have known that even when Ford's journey began there was little cargo left to find at the brig's shipwreck site, Cabrillo Point. What he did find after arriving on the north Mendocino coast, was hundreds of thousands of acres of redwood and Douglas fir trees which would yield fortunes for a few.

Henry Meiggs immigrated to San Francisco in 1848, the same year gold was discovered. Employing Yankee ingenuity along with business shrewdness and sheer will, the contractor Henry (Harry) Meiggs accomplished far more than most of the 49ers. Mr. Meiggs began his career employing others to build an extensive wharf on the northern tip of the San Francisco peninsula. Meiggs' Wharf extended eastward like an outstretched arm calling for progress into San Francisco Bay. Cutting timber in the East Bay in Contra Costa and Alameda Counties, Meiggs' lumberjacks, probably composed of Euro-Americans, Hawaiian-born jacks (so-called "Kanakas") and Australians, connected logs into great floating platforms and moved them across the San Francisco Bay to a saw mill he erected there. Soon he was making money simultaneously in the lumber business and by buying and selling real estate, selling redwood lumber for houses and businesses, and through charging others to use his wharf.

One year after Meiggs' arrival on the West Coast, a twenty-eight-year-old Jerome B. Ford traveled west from New York City to San Francisco on board the *Boston*. Born in Grand Isles, Vermont in 1821, the son of Robert and Martha Davidson Ford, Jerome had been orphaned at an early age and raised by his mother's relatives in Waterford, Vermont and Windsor, Connecticut. Once in California, Ford took a position working for Meiggs and Stephen Smith at Bodega Ranch California, near the coast of Sonoma County. Making use of saw mill equipment that the *Boston* carried to California, Ford and others erected a small mill. About the same time that others, for example, Jasper O'Farrell, started other mills in what is now northern Sonoma County. In 1849 Ford accepted a position as manager with a new lumber operation, financially backed by Meiggs and Smith, at Bodega Ranch.

Ford met another early California immigrant named E.C. (Edward) Williams. During the spring of 1850 Williams either owned, or managed for Harry Meiggs, a lumber yard that was close to the land's end of Meiggs Wharf in San Francisco.[62] According to Mr. Williams about that time, he noticed a large pile of lumber that had potential for use as a building material. At the time lumber for building had to be shipped all the way to California, around the Horn from either New England or Europe. Williams stated that he was the one Meiggs sent north up to Smith's ranch near Bodega to start a lumber mill. Whether it was primarily Williams or Jerome Ford who was most responsible, a mill went into production there that produced eight to ten thousand board feet per twelve hour day. Mr. Meiggs bought the mill and operated it successfully, but began to realize that to

---

62 E.C. Williams' article (memoir), "Start of the Redwood Industry," *Pioneer Western Lumberman*, San Francisco, July 12, 1912, at the Noyo Hill House on July 12, 2007.

satisfy his building plans in San Francisco he would need a mill, or mills, with much greater production capacity.

In 1851, Meiggs dispatched Williams on a journey back East to New York and Connecticut to buy the saw mill machinery that would be needed to establish the Mendocino Lumber Company.[63] This included a series of sash saws, a boiler and a steam engine. Williams originally thought he would buy all of the needed machinery from a factory in southern New York State. When he arrived on the East Coast, Williams discovered that he could get a boiler and engine for less from a company in Norwich, Connecticut. But when the machinery nearly was completed, at the last minute Williams saw that they would have to alter the specifications of the boiler and various gears to drive the saw blades. Because Long Island Sound happened to be frozen, he made use of the recently invented telegraph to order the necessary changes in time. During the early spring of 1852 the ship carrying the equipment departed the East Coast bound for California. Mr. Williams returned to San Francisco and began laying plans to return to the north Mendocino coast.

In August 1850, after the news of the *Frolic*'s demise had spread around the City by the Bay, Harry Meiggs decided it might be worthwhile to send one of his brightest employees up the coast from Bodega to view the wreck and see if any-thing could be salvaged from it. Ford made his way from Sonoma by a mule pack train northward to Big River. There he borrowed a small log boat from resident William Kasten. According to one version of the story, Kasten guided Ford to a high point along Big River that Ford knew would make an ideal spot for a lumber mill. Although by this time it was far too late for him to find anything of value from the *Frolic* shipwreck, Ford noticed many thick groves of redwoods which he realized would be an almost limitless source of raw material for saw mills.

In his first two diary entries, Ford ended his involvement with Meiggs' Bo-dega Bay lumber mill and began turning his eyes northward to the Mendocino County coast.

> Monday, February 16, 1852- L.P. Hanson took the mills at Bodega to Manufacture Lumber by the M (thousand) [Lumber mills were rated according to how many thousands of board feet they produced per day.].

> Monday, April 5, 1852—Left the Sch *Fogonoy* for the North Coast in search of a mill sight in Company Cap: [Captain] Kisssomes [?] Dr. Knight's....Mr. E. C. [Edward C.] Williams joins us at Bodega.[64]

---

63 Meiggs, Williams and Ford co-founded the California Lumber Company at Big River in 1852. When Meiggs left the country, the name of the company was changed to the Mendocino Lumber Company.

64 See Jerome B. Ford's diary, 3, Kelley House Museum, Mendocino, CA.

According to Ford's associate, E.C. Williams, when the ship carrying the new saw mill machinery from back East arrived in San Francisco, Meiggs leased the *Ontario*, his pick out of the numerous deserted ships floating bereft of their erstwhile crews in the Bay. For the mid-nineteenth century, the *Ontario* was a large ship, between five and six hundred tons. In early June 1852, the *Ontario*, under the command of Capt. David Lansing, sailed out of the Golden Gate bound for the north Mendocino coast.

Unfortunately two years of his diary (1851 and 1853) have been lost. Jerome Ford did not make daily entries but used his diary to record dates, significant events, many figures, and, rarely, for brief business notations. For example when traveling he recorded the length of a voyage, speed of the vessel he was on, and sometimes specific details like the cost of his ticket.

Many believe that E.C. Williams challenged and won a shooting match against Capt. John C. Frémont's famous scout Kit Carson.[65] Williams and Ford share the credit, along with Harry Meiggs, for founding the Mendocino Lumber Company and Mendocino. On June 8, 1852, Ford sailed from San Francisco bound for the "new mill site" he called "Bull Don River," Upon reaching Sonoma he witnessed a gunfight,

> Tuesday, June 8, San Francisco– Left this [San Francisco] at 5 P.M. on steamer *Antelope* for Benicia. – Bound north to new mill sight ("Bull Don River"). Ship "Ontario" is bought and is to leave in a few days for the above Port with 40 men & provisions. Stopped at American Hotel- Benicia

> Wednesday, June 9– Left at 8 a.m. in stage for Sonoma and Napa Arrived at Sonoma at 4 o'clock p.m. put up at Union Hotel– Hyatt shot Waterman at 1 o'clock– ball took effect in the face & Broke out a few teeth.

> Thursday, June 10– Left Sonoma with horse and stage accompanying me with some of my things which I could not will pack. Arrived at Capt. Smith 6 o'clock making 6 hours time. Stayed at the mill over one day.

> Friday, June 11– Have visited Capt. Smith today so my time has been taken up preparing for the morrow. Have 2 horses and 1 pack mule and 5 yoke of oxen to take up. Have hired Mr. Warner who will accompany me. Also G. C. Smith part way.[66]

---

65 Christopher (Kit) Carson was a famous hero of the Old West. He was born in Missouri in 1810. He was an orphan who lived by his wits and became a scout. He guided Capt. John C. Frémont on his exploratory journeys from the Mississippi River to the West Coast across the Great Plains.

66 *Ibid.* A bit later in his diary Ford referred to buying a timber tract from someone he referred to as "the blacksmith" that he termed "Bull Don." This might have been "Buldam," which was also the name of the coastal Indian tribe that had removed the *Frolic's* cargo the previous year.

After taking weeks to prepare for his journey into the wilderness of northern Sonoma and Mendocino Counties, Ford felt considerably relieved finally to be able to make his departure. With a newly-won hat from someone named Phelps resting squarely upon his head, Jerome Ford set out on the trail toward the Russian River and then into the wilds of Mendocino County.

> Saturday, June 12 Have got off at last [at] 11 o'clock—arrived at R. [Russian] River at 3 o'clock found "Gassier" [Garcia] with party bound north of his rancho.

> Crossed the river in company with him. Found it almost impassable. Our pack mule left us immediately after packing him again. Cross back and lost him with all of our provisions. Blankets etc– gone home.[67]

Jerome Ford's travel through the rugged wilderness of the Mendocino coast was somewhat similar to that of John Work's of 1833. In some ways Work's party had been more fortunate than Ford's since the occasional loss of a horse or a mule was not enough to make a difference to a large, well equipped expedition. To the young pioneer, Ford, the loss of his pack mule "with all of our provisions, blankets, etc." must have been costly indeed. His mishaps and misfortunes while on the trail were not unlike those of J. Ross Browne and countless other early California hunters and settlers in that, once they left the relatively predictable confines of a town or city, they were left almost entirely to their own devices.

Despite the loss of his lead pack mule, Mr. Ford continued on his journey, almost reaching the remains of Fort Ross as well as the Gualala River. There he nearly met with a similar disaster when another mule tried running off to go "home." Ford had to pass the cold night of Sunday June 13 with only "sweat cloths for blankets." About ten o'clock he arrived at "Walhalah" (Gualala). He described "a beautiful Tambien [? I liked it too!]—vegetables green peas, potatoes..." On the following day Ford came close to "being precipitated down hundreds of feet" as he had to catch himself from falling as he followed the treacherous "road" beside the Pacific Ocean. Finally at about nine o'clock they "arrived at Gassier [Garcia] Rancho" There he recorded that he "bought the blacksmith claim on 'Bull Don' for one hundred dollars.[68]

Apparently Meiggs' support allowed him the liberty to buy a valuable land claim on the Garcia Rancho. On Tuesday, June 15 proceeding again near the ocean he "passed down one of the steepest hills I ever attempted to go down [Mal Paso]" before spending the night at "Navata [Navarro] house." That night there was nothing to eat. It was "very foggy all day and evening." They swam their horses across the outlet of the Navarro River. He noticed that it might be a good landing for small ships and that several had been wrecked there. Two days later, on June 17, when he reached the outlet of the Big River, Ford stayed in a house

---

67 *Ibid.*

68 *Ibid.*

that stood on the property he referred to that he'd purchased from a blacksmith. Ford did not name him. Because their livestock were so tired from their journey, they tethered them on the south bank, crossed Big River, future site of the town of Mendocino, on June 17, and returned to guide their oxen, mules and horses across the following morning.

Thinking ahead to when his saw mill would be up and running, on Friday June 18 Ford noted "the Harbor is a very large bay." It was the first possible site north of Bodega Bay for a port. Ford also noted that there were six settlers: "Warner, Caston (Kaston), myself and 3 Germans." The three "Germans" Ford met could have been members of the Hegenmeyer family. The following day, June 19, Ford explored as far north as Ten Mile River, which he stated was "a very pretty harbor and still waters making up the river a good entrance into the river for any vessels drawing 6 ft. water" and "very beautiful sands adjoining the bay." The following day, Sunday June 20, Ford apparently returned from Ten Mile River to Big River. There he "went up the river today about a mile." That afternoon he was joined by "'the Blacksmith,' George James, Frank Greenwood, and others." A schooner belonging to Capt. Richardson arrived the same day that had sailed from San Francisco "twenty days before." Richardson's ship made the voyage hoping to load "wood & lumber." A smaller schooner, "'King & Company,' exploring, hunting, etc." also arrived.

Ford turned his attention to preparing his own abode at Big River,

> Monday, June 21—Today have been cleaning out house arranging berth, etc. Employed Indians—have 5 here at work. "Casper" arrived from "Ross" & stopped all night. The Germans have been down to Richardson's after their groceries.[69]

The Indians were members of the Northern Pomo or Coastal Pomo (Buldam) tribe. While hiring them for casual labor didn't strike Jerome Ford as significant, this was the first recorded instance in this region of whites employing the services of natives to help them get settled. It wouldn't be the last; but in 1856 the Indians were forced to live on the Mendocino Reservation.

For approximately one week in June 1852 Mr. Ford explored Mendocino, the Fort Bragg area, and the region close to Ten Mile River, a large coastal area. He was buying up the claims that held large stands of Douglas fir and redwood. These early timber claims were the basis of his Mendocino mill from the 1850s and throughout the nineteenth century.

For the next two days Ford hunted deer and elk in the hills just east of the seacoast. On Thursday, June 24 he and some of his men paddled a canoe "up the (Big) river about fifteen miles." There he noted "great quantities of fine Timber." After a night spent at the German camp, he returned to his hut or house on the coast with "a bad headache." There he encountered a man named "Thomson of

---

69 *Ibid.*

Pine Grove [present day Sebastopol?]" who departed for the "Gassler [Garcia] Rancho" to the south. Ford split wood all day Friday, June 25. On Saturday "all hands hunting."

Ford had brought some saw mill machinery up with his oxen teams but couldn't complete constructing of the mill until the *Ontario* arrived from San Francisco. On Sunday June 27 he wrote a letter to "my friend Clarence Gilchrest of San Fr....." He also sent Meiggs some dispatches on board the "sch. Sovering" [*schooner Sovereign*] which was scheduled to leave on Wednesday. On Monday June 28 he was "employed: splitting rails. Have the Blacksmith Indian Big George." Besides a few more men from "Thomson party" that had come up from Sausalito there was another group of three who came up from "Duncan & Hendy's Ranch near Fort Ross" on Monday. He paused to finish writing his letter to Gilchrist in San Francisco that he entrusted to a "hombre from S.H.D. Ranch who stayed with us last night." That same day, Tuesday, June 29, Ford wrote, "Have been looking this eve. to see if I could see the ship as the sun set clear[.] I could see a long way seawards but nothing in sight."

Ford and his men had to be fed. He killed a large buck on Wednesday, June 30. Ford was looking at the banks of Big River for the best possible saw mill site. As noted above Meiggs' company, the California Lumber Mills Company, with Ford's coworker E. C. Williams in the lead, had chartered an abandoned ship, the *Ontario*, in San Francisco Bay. As the days of June 1852 slowly passed, tossed to and fro out in the Pacific Ocean, the passengers and crew aboard the *Ontario* were uneasy as they became aware that the ship's hull had begun to leak. They were being tossed about by huge swells, well out beyond the Golden Gate. During the months that the ship had been floating idle in San Francisco, the calking between planks in the hull had begun to give way. As the ship began to encounter rougher seas, it appeared that the ship might sink. The seamen asked for and received extra pay to man the pumps so that eventually it safely reached Mendocino.

The ship arrived during early July, 1852. Indians and some of Ford's men worked to unload the machinery. They set it up at the first mill site that Ford had selected. Once this task was complete, Capt. Lansing decided the ship was no longer sea worthy. It was abandoned on the shore at Big River. Laborers filled the hull with soil and rock. For a short time it appeared the ship might be used as the base of a wharf. However in time this project was abandoned; the *Ontario*'s upper section including the deck separated and floated out to sea. A storm eventually broke apart the hull, although some wreckage remained on the beach for many months.

Ford, with Meiggs' financial and business connections in San Francisco during the rest of 1852 and 1853, started producing lumber. Ford and Williams had co-founded the California Lumber Mill Company in Mendocino. Williams noted the original millwright proved to be unequal to the task of getting the mill up and running at what Meiggs and Ford had hoped for: 60,000-board-feet-a-day capacity. Meiggs hired another millwright in San Francisco, but there was a considerable delay. Ford noted that he and his men had to use an old sail for a roof. At the same time they were shingling a new "cook room." Due to a full moon on October 27 and heavy seas Ford thought it was too dangerous for a ship to enter the harbor. On the last day of October and the first in November heavy surf disassembled most of what remained of the *Ontario*. On November 1, Ford noted that just "the bow" remained on the beach.

At "7 o'clock" Wednesday, November 3 Ford left Mendocino on his return with "T. Clark" to San Francisco. After crossing the mouths of the Albion and Navarro Rivers and on the same day Ford "met Mr. Anson & party with 12 yoke oxen for mill north of Sand Beach." Thursday, November 4 they got away early. Ford noted seeing "about 100 vultures and an enormous great Grisley." The bear "did not show signs of fear and with great reluctance gave us the road." On the same day they passed Garcia's Ranch and ran into one of the Hegenmeyers. On Friday, November 5, they were nearly at Gualala and "arrived at Hendy's at 5." Here they "met Capt. Lansing "and put up there." "Weather very fine, wind soft, clear," a typically beautiful, north coast fall day. On November 7 Ford reached the mill site near Bodega: "Mill idle. Everything looks very gloomey [sic sp. gloomy] and sad." Ford continued to head south passing through Petaluma. Since he just missed the "vessel bound for the city" (San Francisco), he was diverted to Sonoma. He "arrived at Sonoma at 7 o'clock eve. "[70]

The first complete year of operation of the mill, 1853, was difficult for everyone who worked for the company. Mr. Williams' memoir told how many of the men gave short notice of quitting. This meant the mill ceased operations until replacement workers were found. Rough trails and difficult fords across wide bodies of water like San Pablo Bay or the Russian River meant that the trip up from San Francisco to the north Mendocino coast took at least ten days. If the trip had to be made in the winter months or even late fall or early spring, heavy rains made any progress difficult if not impossible. Ship traffic up to Mendocino often was sporadic and costly. The only place reliable workers could be found was in San Francisco. Once hired workers had to make the tedious journey through rugged terrain up the coast to Mendocino. In the meantime Indians and white workers had to fend independently for themselves for weeks until the Mendocino Lumber Company mill resumed operations. It is likely that each community fell back into old patterns of separate communal lives during the down time at the mill. In addition to problems posed by the loss of key employees, in 1853 the winter rains started early before a roof had been constructed covering the mill and its valuable

---

70 *Ibid.,* While it was destroyed at least once by fire, the mill continued in operation throughout the nineteenth century. It eventually became part of the Union Lumber Company. The November 7 entry was the last one for 1852.

machinery. Years later Williams had recurrent nightmares about being aroused from deep slumber by heavy, pouring rain.

The Mendocino Lumber Company was incorporated in 1853. Harry Meiggs, perhaps along with some financial backing from a German named Silem, put up most of the funds to start up the mill. When he needed financial backing for further real estate moves in the Bay Area, Meiggs borrowed heavily from bankers on the value of the mill, about $100,000. Although not a great deal of capital in to-day's dollars, in the mid-1850s this was a much more considerable sum of money. According to Mr. Williams, Meiggs used his stock in the Mendocino Lumber Company as collateral to obtain loans from San Francisco bankers. Using the money thus obtained from firms like Godeffrey, Silem & Company, Mr. Meiggs financed large construction jobs he had planned to improve San Francisco docks, hotels and other ventures. He also sold a huge contract to the financier W.N. Thompson agreeing to deliver two million feet of redwood lumber from the Mendocino mill. During the late fall of 1854 the business boom in San Francisco suddenly collapsed. In the financial crash that followed Harry Meiggs had to either declare public bankruptcy or leave the Bay Area. He decided to do the latter, chartered a ship for himself and his family, and left San Francisco during the early winter of 1854. He sailed to South America, leaving all of his financial dealings and his creditors in California in the lurch.

Although he later remade his fortune by building railroads in Chile and Peru, Meiggs did not pay off all of his loans. To his credit as a contractor and engineer, Meiggs' Peruvian construction company later laid the roadbeds and constructed railroads across the Andes Mountains and through the Amazon, connecting Lima and other cities in Peru with towns and cities throughout the continent of South America. Eventually, before he died, Harry Meiggs returned to San Francisco. He made good on some of his old loans. In the meantime the Mendocino Lumber Company mill had to close for a number of years. When it reopened new machinery produced fifty thousand board feet per day. In 1872 the company was co-owned, free and clear, by E.C. Williams and Jerome Ford.

Jerome Ford and E.C. Williams weren't the only men to establish a lumber mill on the north Mendocino coast. It soon had numerous competitors at Little River, Salmon Creek, the Albion River, and in Caspar, between Mendocino and Ft. Bragg. Only three of the five Hegenmeyer brothers' names are known, George, Gebhardt, and John B. According to Beth Stebbins's study, "*Saw Mills on the Noyo*," (1986), in the spring of 1853 George and Gebhardt Hegenmeyer built a saw mill three miles from the mouth of the Noyo River. Their brother John acquired a preemption, or the right to build a mill, on a tract of timber further up the river. Their mill was planned to produce lumber at the rate of six thousand board feet a day while the Ford-Williams mill on Big River had increased production to about one hundred thousand board feet a day.

Very few of the first and eventually most successful saw mills on the north Mendocino coast were stand-alone, one man companies. William A. Richardson financed the Hegenmeyers' mill, which started out with every hope of succeeding. In February, 1853 just as his mill was nearly completed and the new machinery was to be installed, George Hegenmeyer had to travel to San Francisco to hire mill workers. His brother Gebhardt left the Hegenmeyer house temporarily empty. A group of renegade Indians took over the house driving a few workmen away and stole everything except for three guns. Obviously establishing a saw mill on one's own was difficult.

On the other hand by the start of 1854 no one doubted that Jerome B. Ford was a success. His lumber business produced a larger profit each year. Ford, along with E.C. Williams and William Kelley, co-owned a profitable business based on seemingly inexhaustible supplies of redwood and Douglas fir trees. In fact he had almost everything a man could possibly want with the exception of one essentially important thing: a wife with whom he could share his life and his success and who also might bear him children. Having come to the Golden State with just the clothes on his back, he could be proud of his accomplishments. Ford left the thriving saw mill located approximately one hundred seventy miles north of San Francisco to embark on a mission to return to Connecticut.

While many details of Jerome Ford's childhood are lacking, he had met and fallen in love earlier with his future wife's older sister. Unfortunately, this older sister became ill and passed away. Martha Haves, his future bride, had cared for her sister in the latter stage of her illness. Miss Hayes and Jerome became friendly when both were growing up near Hartford, Connecticut. Ford and his future wife Martha kept up a long distance relationship by corresponding through letters during the early 1850s.

In February, 1854, Ford's journey began in San Francisco. If Mr. Ford had decided to have a drink at the "after salon in [the] Promenade deck," his prospective trip back east might well have been over almost before it began.

> Thurs. February 16, 1854– Went on board *Steamer Uncle Sam* bound for Panama at 9 o'clock am. found they postponed sailing till noon–. Went on board again at 11 & 3 o'clock we got underway—in steering from wharf we ran into a ship which carried away our after salon in Promenade deck—at 5 o'clock outside of Heads passed a clipper ship on the Bow.[71]

He barely escaped being badly injured or worse in this collision. After its mishap leaving San Francisco the ship made very good time as it headed south along the California coast. Some ships in this era employed both sails and steam power as propulsion. He also noted that there were a large number of passengers,

---

71 See Diary of Jerome B. Ford, 3, Kelley House Museum, Mendocino, CA.

"four hundred-eighty passengers" on board. After crossing the Isthmus of Panama, Ford arrived first in New York and then in Connecticut.

On March 20 he attended church at Lunenberg, Connecticut. Soon after that he bought two tickets, for himself and his bride Martha, to return to Panama on the *North Star* and then back on the *Uncle Sam* to San Francisco. There were no details in Mr. Ford's diary notes concerning his courtship. At the same time, April 28, 1854, a hard rain began to fall.

> Wednesday May 3 — Married at one o'clock today [Ford's bride's name was Martha Hayes.] Started for Htfo [Hartford] & arrived at five – on way to New York at one at night.[72]

Unfortunately the young groom left nothing in his diary about his bride, her appearance, or the presence of important friends, family, and guests during the ceremony. There is no record of how her family felt regarding the young lady's imminent departure for the faraway West Coast. On Friday, May 5, the Fords boarded the *North Star*. On May 13 they arrived at 3 A.M. in Aspinwall, Panama. By May 15 they were at the Aspinwall House, a hotel in Panama. There Ford met Wilhelm Silem, "W.H. Thompson & others."[73] According to Ford's diary there were eight hundred passengers on board the ship that sailed from Panama on May 18 bound for San Francisco. Due to bad weather and the need for fuel the ship made a stop, "for wood," at Monterey, California's original capital when it was a Mexican province.[74]

By the middle of 1854 the nucleus of Mendocino City had arrived on the north Mendocino coast: the four co-founders of the first Big River mill and thus the community of Mendocino City, Jerome Ford, E.C. Williams, Capt. David C. Lansing, and Henry Meiggs. San Francisco, as well as other California cities and towns, and Oregon also needed a steady, reliable, cheap supply of lumber.

Martha and Jerome arrived and made their home in tiny Mendocino. He resumed management of the lumber mill. Like most California settlers, the Fords were also part time farmers and his entries concern feeding their animals. On "Wednesday, November 23," he added, "F. Helt 872 ft. lumber." Ford recorded the length of time "Frank Denildt," one of the workers, had worked at the mill. A shocking entry on December 13 concerned the murder of "Walter D. Minterrn [Mintern?] shot dead by 8 Balls from the Hand of Franklin Sneither."[75] There is no further discussion about the crime or a possible trial in this case. Ford's notes range in content from prosaic to profound, from keeping tabs of mill worker's hours, the amounts of lumber milled and shipped, to this local, unexplained murder.

---

72 *Ibid.*, 6.

73 *Ibid.*, 6.

74 *Ibid.*, 7.

75 *Ibid.* 6.

There were also entries regarding markets for north coast lumber. Three days later Ford's entry revealed a new market. Due to bad weather and the need for fuel the ship made a stop at Monterey, California's capital at the time.[76] The stop included the purchase of redwood "rough lumber and siding" produced at the Mendocino mill.

On Saturday, December 16, an entry read,

Cargo *San Hendrick* for Sydney, August 1855[77]

Siding	38758
Rough lumber	41407
Tsl	62785

Interestingly, the "August, 1855 Sydney destination" meant that ship was scheduled to make several other ports of call before it reached Australia. The December 16th entry was the last one for the year 1854.

There is an approximately four-month gap in the diary. Then Martha Ford wrote the following poignant entry on May 3, 1855. It was the first anniversary of her marriage to Jerome Ford.

> One year ago today we were married, left home — and all friends to seek <u>another home</u> in <u>this land</u> to henceforth—share each others joys & sorrows—May we as we journey on through life find each successive year the happiest we have ever spent as I now feel this to have been, and we indeed become 'one in heart and in mind' and may we so live that when the fleeting years have passed away — Our Heavenly Father will welcome us to our Eternal Home.[78]

By this time Martha and Jerome Ford were leading citizens of the town of Mendocino, California. In a subsequent note the mill founder recorded the arrival of another of the community's leading figures, the former shipbuilder, William Kelley (1821-1895) and his wife on the *Schooner Manfred* on May 29, 1855, along with "forty or fifty" other men.[79] The Kelleys arrived at Mendocino City during the summer of 1855. Kelley was born November 2, 1821 in the small town of Morrell, Prince Edward Island, Canada. As the elder child in a large family, he was expected to make his own way in the world. After working a short time in Eastport,

---

76 *Ibid.,* 7.

77 *Ibid.,* 8.

78 *Ibid.,* 9.

79 *Ibid.,* 10.

Maine, he took a crewman's position on a ship sailing to Bermuda. He served in various capacities on board ships. William and a brother, James, started across the Isthmus of Panama in 1850. Like many of the Argonauts of the Gold Rush era who took the trans-isthmian route to the west coast, both men contracted the deadly tropical disease, cholera.

William Kelley was forced to watch as his brother sickened and died. To the doctor who was treating the Kelley brothers and several other travelers at the same time, William said, "You neglected my brother, and if you neglect me I will pay nothing, for my money is out of reach; but if you save me, I will pay you well."[80] William Kelley survived his bout with cholera. After arriving in San Francisco with about two thousand dollars to his name, he realized that the sprawling, raucous city by the bay did not appeal to him. He moved across San Francisco Bay to the town of Benicia, where he applied himself to the same trade his father Peter had worked in, shipbuilding. A few years later William Kelley started over again, this time as the ship's carpenter on board the Schooner *Manfred* from San Francisco to Mendocino in 1855.

After arriving on the north Mendocino coast, he used what remained of his funds to buy the house that is now the home of one of the foremost historical museums in Mendocino County. After that, Kelley continued to prosper both through carpentry as well as buying and selling real estate. He eventually became one of the town's prime movers and shakers, one who was credited with building hospitals, the Baptist Church, and schools. William Kelley's sister Abigail arrived in Mendocino a few years after him. Captain Samuel Blair was another California immigrant who in 1850 had arrived from Northern Ireland. Blair, who was of Scottish descent, married Abigail in 1861. Together, the couple and Captain Blair's partner, Alexander McCallum, established the Glen Blair Lumber Company on Pudding Creek north of Fort Bragg. Lumber families tended to intermarry. William and Eliza's firstborn, Emma Shirley (Daisy), was courted by numerous suitors before marrying Alexander McCallum. William gave the couple the lot on Albion Street from the Kelley House that still is called McCallum House, which the couple built in 1882.

As the 1850s passed, the local settler population of the region grew in complexity and diversity as well as numbers. When Mendocino City's pioneer lumberman E.C. Williams concluded his remarkable memoir in 1921, he wanted to set the record straight and react to a recent San Francisco court's action dissolving his beloved Mendocino Lumber Company. An eloquent writer, Williams stated his case in the following two paragraphs. Note that by about 1867 (or 1868) the mill had produced, shipped, and sold enough redwood lumber to fully reimburse all the creditors of Mr. Meiggs' schemes of the early 1850s. It was a significant achievement.

---

80 See "William Henry Kelley," *Mendocino Historical Review*, Vol. II, No. 2, Spring, 1975, 3-5.

In 1857 or '58 the Mendocino mill shipped to Sydney 100,000 feet, mostly surfaced and T&G clear boards, consigned to correspondents of Godeffroy Brothers of Hamburg. They paid freight and all subsequent charges of storage, fire insurance, etc., and some ten or twelve years later sent the mill a statement closing the account showing a debit balance of something less than $50 against the shipment, which they under the circumstances, generously remitted....

In closing these reminiscences the writer is glad to think that the hardships and trials of the pioneers in the business are passed and to congratulate the present lumbermen upon the certainty that while prices may have their ups and downs, No. 3 redwood boards will never again sell for $7 and $8, or thick rough clear to average 30 inches wide for $15 or $16, as was the case in the last years of the last century and the first of the present one. That chapter in the redwood industry is closed—and so are these reminiscences.[81]

Starting in 1857 and 1858, another lumber baron, Alexander Wentworth MacPherson, emerged. MacPherson was the man for whom the major present-day north-south street, "McPherson Street," was named. In 1879 in its incorporation Carl Stewart named the primary streets of the City of Fort Bragg. During the latter half of the 1860s McPherson's Noyo Lumber Company grew into the one of the largest company on the north Mendocino coast. After the turn of the nineteenth century this company was reorganized into the Union Lumber Company. In the 1920s C.R. Johnson multiplied the assets of the company, with thousands of employees into one of the largest lumber corporations in California.

The year 1865 had been a profitable one for the Mendocino Lumber Company on Big River as well as the lumber industry on the north Mendocino coast in general. Jerome Ford wrote a letter of advice to the son of friends in Illinois. The letter, which Ford penned on December 26, 1865, was written to Jerome Kendall, whom he had briefly visited in Illinois when Kendall was only two years old. In his letter Ford omitted mentioning the Indian laborers who had helped him build his lodging and the structure of the Mendocino Lumber Company. Ford's letter was an answer to one that Jerome Kendall had written him. It outlined the history of Ford's experience as a pioneer in the lumber business. Ford reported to Kendall that he and his wife, Martha, had had two sons, Charles and Chester, for whom Ford had high hopes. He cautioned the younger man that in Ford's opinion, young men in California grew up too fast and tended to be overly boastful about their property. Ford recounted going "around the Horn" with stops in Rio de Janeiro and Chile before arriving in San Francisco on December 19, 1849. Unlike others who were distracted or tempted by the Gold Rush, Ford remained true to his goal of becoming a West Coast lumberman by continuing onto Bodega. While the first winter wasn't successful, by the spring of 1850 he, along

---

81 *Ibid.* E. (Edward) C. Williams' article.

with a man named Hanks, had established a saw mill capable of producing ten thousand board feet of lumber per day.

Back when Ford ran the Bodega saw mill he found that early shipments of lumber to Sacramento turned out to be unprofitable since the costs of shipping the lumber exceeded the price received. However, as Ford explained in this letter to Jerome Kendall, he stuck with it. Once he'd established the mill in Mendocino, it produced thirteen million board feet per year or, in dollars, "about two hundred and fifty thousand dollars per year." Meanwhile Mr. Hanks, who got discouraged, gave up, and returned to Connecticut, got hardly anything for all his efforts in California. Ford ended his letter by encouraging young Kendall:

> Be steady and faithful and you will never want a friend, and you will be prospered. I was thrown out onto the world an orphan boy, and how wonderfully I have been prospered, and had I not ought to be thankful to so kind a providence? I hope we shall all live to see each other. I hope to have good news from you all. Remember me to Mr. and Mrs. Ranlett if you meet them. They are good people. Much love to your father and mother and the same to yourself. You will please let your people read this as I shall not write them just at present. Write often and let me know how you all are. Family all well and send love.

> I am yours truly,

> Jerome B. Ford[82]

What makes this letter significant are the specific details Mr. Ford included about his first lumber mill at Bodega and his friend, simply named "Hanks." In many ways Hanks was a typical California emigrant since he left the territory and returned to "old Connecticut." Interestingly the so-called "honest boy Schoolteacher" that Mr. Hanks vouched for ended up selling the valuable shipload of lumber for less than it cost to ship! Obviously Mr. Ford's saw mill lost out, one dollar per thousand board foot of lumber, on the transaction. Thus sadly for him the entire product of this whole year was lost, along with three thousand dollars of Mr. Ford's personal savings. No wonder he did not want to return to Bodega. However, Jerome Ford wasn't a man who did not learn from his own business mistakes. His fortunes soon mended.

In spite of his early difficulties in the lumber business, the letter went on to add that the Mendocino Lumber Company boasted of a profit in 1865 of two hundred sixty thousand dollars. Nevertheless they revealed a great deal indeed about the beliefs Mr. Ford held about raising his own two sons, Chester and Charles. Recall that Jerome Ford had been orphaned at an early age. Perhaps more than many he valued people like the Kendalls and Ranletts. The letter is a remarkable

---

82 Jerome Ford letter, Dec. 26, 1865 to Jerome Kendall, Princeton, Illinois, Kelley House Museum, Mendocino, CA.

snapshot of the mid-1860s revealing the great degree of development that had taken place in only a little over ten years.

John Work, Jerome Ford, and numerous others employed many Indians in various roles in the discovery and early settlements, as guides, boatmen, builders, or manual laborers. They were the only true natives of the north Mendocino coast. At first, when they received anything at all other than possibly a bite to eat in return for their labor, Indians were paid only half of whatever the white laborers received and sometimes were cheated out of being paid at all. Jerome Ford's diary contained two entries referring to Indians with whom he had very brief contacts and whom he employed. One was the case of "Big George the Blacksmith," who helped build Ford's first mill. In other words, the Indians' hard physical labor as well as their loyalty to a few lumber families such as the Fords or the MacPhersons played a key role in the early development of the northern Mendocino coast community.

From 1856 up until about 1868, California Indians from many tribes or triberlets in Sonoma and Mendocino Counties lived together at the Mendocino Reservation. While this story remains murky and poorly understood, it was a vitally important one. Equally significant was the story of the ships that carried the lumber to worldwide markets.

CHAPTER 8. OREGON BOUND — 1853

The commerce of the country is carried on upon pack mules, and so mild are the winters that the 'packets' expect to sleep and live in the open air in all seasons, even without tents.

—S.H. Taylor, Oregon Bound 1853, Jacksonville, Oregon Territory, December 17, 1853.

While the term Manifest Destiny may have originated before with the New York City newspaper, the *Journal*, actual westward movement of pioneer wagon trains bound for destinations in Washington, Oregon or California began in earnest about the year 1840 or 1841. George R. Stewart in his *The California Trail 1841–1859* (1962), wrote that in 1853 some 15,219 people were counted at Fort Kearny, one of the starting points of the wagon trains. While estimates from over a hundred years can be erroneous, taking in account all those trains, like the Taylor Company that passed through Council Bluffs, Iowa, in 1853, the total rose to twenty thousand emigrants. It was one of the most profound movements of a people in world history.

Weather determined when each wagon train left assembly points, usually Independence, MO or Council Bluff, IA. Most waited until late April so that the spring grass in southern Nebraska could grow greener and be ready for their livestock. In order to escape being caught by heavy snowfalls in a High Sierra pass, the trains had to cross the Sierras by the middle of November. This was a fairly narrow window of opportunity.

Beginning in the 1840s, train after train of wagons, handcarts, and livestock driven by adventurers of all descriptions began making the long journey east to west across the Great Plains of the continent. Many who remained home learned about the travels and travails of the more adventurous by reading newspapers or magazines. A few professional writers, women and men like Stanley (S.H.) Taylor took on the job of telling their fellow countrymen about how to prepare for the journey. The following letter first appeared in the *Watertown [Wisconsin] Chronicle*, July 6, 1853. It was written just over a month and half earlier by a former Watertown resident who would soon become a member of a wagon train bound for southern Oregon. The newspaper editor, whom Taylor addressed as "Friend Hadley," shortened the author's name to "S. H. Taylor."

Council Bluffs City, May 24, 1853

Friend Hadley—

Yesterday the 23rd, after 47 days, mostly on one of the worst roads in the world, we arrived at this place, and with about 300 people, and 1000 head of cattle, kept back and dammed up by floods and broken bridges, "sat down before the town."

It [Council Bluffs, Iowa] is built of log cabins, one story high, on both sides of a street running about 60 rods down the bottom of a ra-vine..... There are perhaps a half dozen two story buildings in the place, all devoted to gaming, the only business that can afford to live in them.

The correspondent, at this time near the end of May 1853, had heard that about ten thousand Oregon-bound emigrants per month were passing through Council Bluffs, Iowa, located within sight just across the Mississippi River from Omaha, Nebraska. What had begun as a mere trickle of wagon trains carrying emigrant men, women and children, to Oregon and California turned into a flood. More and more ordinary Americans, from all of the older regions of the Union, had decided to abandon their residences in hopes they would be able to begin new lives in the Far West.

Another excerpt from the letter to Hadley described for the people of south-eastern Wisconsin the travel conditions of the wagon train to which the Taylors had entrusted their lives. Taylor estimated there were "about twenty effective men," which included three "Methodist preachers." The train consisted of thir-teen wagons and "about 200 head of cattle." The group was serious about re-specting the Sabbath and did not travel on the seventh day of each week. Taylor thought that most trusted equally "in God" with "their own arms." Some "horse trains" left before them. It was a consensus of opinion that to trust in just finding enough grass for such trains was "barely safe."

The Watertown, Wisconsin newspaper had committed itself to printing re-ports from the Oregon Trail by Mr. Taylor in order to help its readers who might be preparing to embark on this great exodus to the west. The final paragraphs of this letter included advice about the type cattle (young, strong and not too heavy) emigrants should include in their party. Cattle were important since they could pull a wagon and also provide fresh milk and butter. Wagons should be strong but light. Taylor stated that "sloughs" or "slews" were "perfectly horrible," in other words very hard on the wagons. When Taylor penned this letter the train had already passed over three hundred-ninety-seven miles "from the Mississippi." In that distance he estimated there had been "2000 miserable slews." Since the road was so rough he ruled out any wagon or carriage made with a heavy top. To safely get over the sloughs wagonloads had to be less than nine hundred pounds, and less than eight hundred pounds in wet weather. Since it had been a rainy spring so far, a wagon with a thousand-pound load would sink.[83] Without saying why, Taylor remarked that he did not believe that emigrants should start out by way of Cedar Rapids or Iowa City. He finished this letter stating that "some fast companies" had begun earlier but that his train, by moving more slowly but more steadily, already had past them on the trail.

In his next letter Mr. Taylor introduced some qualities he considered necessary for travelers. Chief among these was patience. His train was halted, waiting for their turn to ford the Platte River. The letter was filled with the sense of almost palpable anxiety they all felt at being forced to wait, knowing full well that the more time passed before they crossed the Rocky Mountains, the more chance a heavy winter snowfall could fill the mountain passes. Pawnee Indians stole a few more of their oxen every night. The following letter by Mr. Taylor appeared in the *Watertown Chronicle*, July 13, 1853.

Pawnee Country, June 4, 1853

> Friend Hadley—We are now 90 miles up the Platte on the Loup Fork, in company with about 250 wagons, blocked up here, near what was called a ferry before it was flooded, waiting for the water to subside. We are in the heart of the territory of the Pawnees, the most skillful thieves that can be; and some are paying dearly for their misfortune. In this neighborhood they have stolen about 50 head of oxen, and every morning we hear of from two to six oxen being run off. About 200 Pawnees came here three days ago and are lying here with us, but with what intention we know not. We are not afraid of our lives—but we find them very annoying. During the day we keep our cattle constantly in view, and at night chain them up and keep a double guard. All do the same—but it is impossible to keep their hands off property when they attempt to get it. They will almost steal a horse from under his rider.

The letter concluded with the following addition made on June 7. At last they got permission to cross the Platte River and thus to continue their journey. The

---

83 "Letters of S.H. Taylor to the *Watertown* (Wisconsin) *Chronicle*," Oregon Bound 1853," *The Quarterly of the Oregon Historical Quarterly*, March, 1921-December, 1921, Frederick Young, Editor, 122 and 124, SODA (Southern Oregon Digital Archives), accessed Jan, and Feb., 2007 and again Jan. 6-12, 2008.

long wait had been a kind of reality check for all. Taylor had begun to appreciate the odds against them, perhaps for the first time:

> June 7—We have a prospect of crossing the Loup today. There are about 100 wagons here now—but few coming in. We see many cattle trains of 100 to 500 head—probably about 1500 head now here. Many wagons have gone up to the fords, one of which is 35 and the other 70 miles above.—Fords on this stream are essentially dangerous. Its waters are a very mass of quicksand, rushing along with the velocity of a mountain stream. In fording our cattle they sink right down into the sand, and the farther they sink the faster they sink, while the current is so swift that even ferriage is attended with some hazard.[84]

In early June Taylor's company reached Wood Creek, Nebraska. Mr. Taylor described seeing Chimney Rock and Scott's Bluff in the article published in the *Watertown Chronicle*, September 14, 1853. Buffalo bones lay almost everywhere they looked. He noted also the buffalo herds were retreating. On June 21 Taylor wrote of seeing three graves of people who died from consuming too much spring water. The cattle were seized with "westward fever" and seemed to want to go as far as twenty-six miles a day. Meanwhile it had gotten very hot; the temperature reached "112 in the shade." Nearly all of their cattle had cracked hooves or hooves that were worn through.[85] He said that because the cattle were lame the whole train had had to slow down considerably and that otherwise they would already have reached Fort Laramie. He recommended that emigrants try alcohol instead of oil as the best practical treatment for treating cattle whose hooves were sore or cracked.

Possibly because she was the wife of Stanley, whose letters were published by the small southern Wisconsin town's newspaper, Clarissa Taylor's letter to the editor's wife, her friend Mrs. Hadley, appeared on August 10, 1853. Mrs. Taylor left us an unforgettable report on prairie conditions as they appeared to a woman. At last the wagon train had reached the relative safety of Ft. Laramie. When the Taylor's family left Watertown, their infant daughter had been sick. Clarissa also noted the local flora, including what she described as "beautiful wildflowers," as well as the graves of a few emigrants who weren't able to fulfill their dreams of going west.

Watertown Chronicle, August 10, 1853

Fort Laramie, July 6, 1853

Dear Mrs. Hadley—

> You will recollect that we left home with a very sick babe, She began to mend from the first day of starting, and continued to do until she,

---

84 *Ibid.*, 121.

85 *Ibid.*, 121-122.

'with the rest of us,' is now in enjoyment of good health. We have had a fine traveling season, although some mud to wade through, and although there is a great deal of sameness in the face of the country we have traversed, yet I find it very interesting, and am not yet willing to return... The graves of departed travelers are another interesting feature in this country. We have seen but four of '53'—three of their tenants were killed by lightning; another was a babe of fifteen days...

While at Fort Laramie, the train witnessed at close range a violent and terrifying lightning storm not unlike one that had killed the three previous emigrants mentioned above. She stated that everyone was "shook" by a sudden storm. Fortunately the lightning struck the ground behind the train. The death of the newborn baby was an unrecorded tragedy. She was somewhat disappointed by the plain appearance of Fort Laramie, which she described was just "a few log houses enclosed by a wooden picket fence."

Continuing, there was good news from a "return train of Californians" who said the Taylor train already had passed through the hardest part of the route. So far they were all in good health except for the sore feet of the cattle. Most of the wagons were working. They were headed into the Black Hills. So far, at least, "Indians are very scarce."

Saturday after we had encamped, more than forty wagons passed on our road and a goodly number was at the same time in sight on the opposite side of the river. A great many cattle and sheep are crossing the plains this season. Our company have lost one horse by accident, and one wagon—sold two cattle on account of lameness; the rest are in pretty good heart to continue our journey.

Hellen [Helen?] has dried a great many flowers, expecting to send them to her mates in W. and is very much disappointed that a letter will not hold them. I have scribbled thus far on the ground with a rather troublesome babe hanging to my lap—Please excuse and remember me to all inquirers.

Yours very sincerely,

CLARISSA E. TAYLOR[86]

Later, the emotional strain and feelings of loneliness took a toll on some members of the wagon train. In another letter Mr. Taylor described the profitable livestock trade that had sprung up at Ft. Laramie. But they had little time. Doubtless, although nothing is noted here, they were well aware of what had happened in 1846 to the unfortunate Donner Party. The Taylor wagon train reached South Pass in mid July. Mr. Taylor expressed his own anxiety over their slow pace as they had progressed "just" 150 miles from Fort Laramie. Perhaps Taylor was fretting as to why they hadn't been warned by others about footsore cattle. Mr. Hadley published Taylor's letter of July 17 on November 2.

---

86 *Ibid.,* 130-133.

Mr. Taylor said there were twenty-five traders doing business just twenty miles from the fort. Together the traders had "over one thousand head of cattle" and aimed to make a three to five hundred percent profit. He also described how to treat oxen's feet with a homemade mixture of alcohol and camphor. He also repeated some advice he gave earlier about using lighter, well-built wagons.

> July 24—We are now in the mountains about four days from the South Pass—in the midst of poor feed but enjoying a little more rain than for a month past.[87]

At this point Taylor interrupted the letter to note there had been a death of a member of their party because of "mountain fever" on July 4th. He continued

> ...I have never known, anywhere, a time of such universal good health, as has prevailed this season from the Missouri to this point, on both sides of the Platte. The distance is 740 miles, the time eight weeks, and there have been 30 deaths among 30,000 emigrants. We have heard of but about three cases of sickness, and have known of no deaths except as we have seen by the way of perhaps six or eight graves of this year....

> No emigrant should come on this road without plenty of dried sour apples and cows giving milk.—Their value is incalculable...

He remarked on the great value of both antelope and buffalo steak. In fact his opinion was that buffalo meat was better than any steak to be had in Watertown or St. Louis, Missouri. He also called for including as much flour as possible for making bread on the trail. He stressed the importance of a yoke that would fit the oxen well and a big enough tent ("10 feet wide by 6 ½ feet high"). Almost as an afterthought, Taylor added:

> If a man brings along the right pole and tackle he can catch catfish in the Platte (as far as fifty miles up from Ft. Laramie), the Elkhorn, Loupe, and Missouri Rivers.[88]

On the final day of July the train arrived at the Dry Sandy Creek, a branch of the Green River.

> Dry Sandy Creek [a branch of the Green River between Fort Laramie and Independence Rock], July 31

> We are 16 miles by the summit of South Pass, actually descending toward the level of the common earth—though descending very slowly indeed, and through a region of little feed and less water. We are 7640 feet above the level of the sea, our guide books say, and almost to the line of perpetual snow. The Wind River range of mountain abutting on our right, loom almost over our trail with their sides white with snow almost to our level.... We have passed over, perhaps, the highest point of unbroken surface on the continent—yet we should hardly be conscious of being in a high altitude, so gradual has been our ascent.

---

87 *Ibid.,* 136-137.

88 *Ibid.,* 140.

> But the remains of last winter's snow, here and there lingering on the northern hillsides and the abundance of mosses on their summits, the cold chilling air, and the difficulty of weak lungs to breathe when a little wearied, indicate our situation....[89]

While some parties traveled on Sundays, Taylor stated that their party always rested on Sunday. He explained that stopping on Sunday helped them to lose "far less [a] percentage of cattle than any other company" going over the Oregon Trail. He warned about not allowing any cattle to drink if there were alkali salts on the surface. Furthermore,

> Where 200,000 cattle have passed this season, there are, for 400 miles, from one to four carcasses to the mile—and probably one-half of this 200,000 are fed on the lime grounds and furnish nine-tenths of the dead. Grass can be everywhere found on the high land. It is in spots—dry but nutritious—thin and scanty but very hearty....[90]

The party had now reached the Bear Mountains but it was also already August. At this point in his letter Mr. Taylor discussed the future route that he thought his company should take. His letter on August 7 expressed the hope they could avoid getting lost crossing the Humboldt Sink by taking the so-called "Brophy cut-off" directly over the Sierras to reach the Rogue River valley, their chosen destination. He reiterated that the Pawnees were the "only tribe to be feared." Almost in the same breath he praised "the Sioux, Ottoes, Tapoos, and Crows" as "nobler Indians." He said that all four tribes were waging war on the Pawnees. He added that when he went in search of a stolen oxen in the Black Hills he was befriended by "those Indians," meaning one of the four tribes listed above, and "I found them ever ready to give me the best place in the lodge with the best buffalo robe and best buffalo meat." He also mentioned how "the diggers—miserable robbers—are now "nearly annihilated" "by the agency of the small pox."[91]

Extinction of many small tribes in the west due to smallpox was a tragic reality and common by 1853. The letter continued with more advice about which items emigrants would need, like extra pocketknives and good ox-bows, when they started on their journeys on the Oregon Trail.

He explained about some of the additional expenses that would be paid including the cost of ferry tolls, which he conservatively estimated would cost from twenty five to thirty dollars. Taylor's company had "swum" their stock across the Missouri and Mississippi Rivers, thus saving the cost of any ferry. Taylor estimated that one should count on losing about one fifth or twenty per cent of their cattle. Regarding other domesticated animals he wrote

> ...If any one wishes to take hens, they can manage a half dozen or so with little trouble. There are some in our company, and they ride well,

89 *Ibid.*, 141-142.

90 *Ibid.*, 143.

91 *Ibid.*, 144-145.

being let out at evening, and have laid nearly all the way. There is no trouble to taking a dog, unless a bad traveler, by seeing to it that he has water supplied to him on the 'dry stretches.'...

He warned against taking along a pregnant cow that would give birth on the trail. Furthermore:

A *can* [Italics in original] holding 6 to 20 qts., keeps our sour milk and cream, and makes our butter by the motion of our wagon. Everything should be carried in tin cans and bags.[92]

The final two letters (December 17, 1853 and January 14, 1854) pertained specifically to the region of southern Oregon and northern California. Many early California settlers, including some that eventually settled on the north Mendocino coast, originally settled in Oregon before traveling south to California. The southern central town of Jacksonville, Oregon in the Rogue River valley was only a few miles north of the present California-Oregon state line.

Taylor's party had some problems beginning at the Green River in southwest Wyoming, still a long way from southern Oregon. He spoke glowingly of how volunteer "rangers" helped to save them. His letter of December 17, 1853 published on March 29, 1854, reported their arriving in the Rogue River Valley on October 26. His party included twenty-three wagons, eighty-seven people, over three hundred head of cattle and "1700 sheep." Also twenty horses and mules completed the party. Many in their party had had to go hungry at times, and he was sorry they had joined "a great multitude" at the Green River since they delayed arrival time by three weeks. He was extremely grateful to the rescue party that met them in the Sierras as they brought flour for bread which sustained them. The rangers who saved them consisted of about fifty volunteers who brought along three mules carrying one thousand dollars worth of flour. If people could not pay for their bread, they were given the bread for free. Those who could pay did so at a very low rate. They were aided also by detachments of armed men who posted themselves at night and rapidly pursued any Indians who dared to raid the wagon train. This letter was written in Jacksonville, Oregon.[93]

---

92 *Ibid.,* 146-147.

93 *Ibid.,* "Pickles, and I presume, pork, can be kept in cans while air tight.—The flesh of poultry, "cooked down," is found an excellent article of food. The dried eggs were a failure. Tin ware should be substituted for earthen, and sheet for cast iron. Russia is the only sheet iron, that, in a stove, will last through. An excellent substitute when a stove when no baking is to be done, is a sheet of iron like a stove top, to be put over a fire hole in the ground, a common means of cooking, and one which the traveler soon learns to make and use. It is just as good as a stove for every purpose but baking. Every one needs flannel under clothing here. In regard to supplies of clothing for the future, every one is convinced that anything not needed for the road, costs a great deal than it comes to. Take nothing for use after getting through—excepting money, of course, tho' I assure you, you will have much less of that than you expected, when you get there. No water should be used for drinking or for cooking, nor allowed for cattle, unless in a running stream or containing insects; otherwise it is probably alkaline." He finished up

Rescue parties from Oregon and northern California combed the Rocky Mountains and especially the areas just east of the crest, from the Sweetwater River to the Green River and the Bear River in Wyoming and northern Utah. They rescued numerous wagon trains from suffering or death from thirst, starvation, privation, or Indian attacks during the 1850s and 1860s. In some cases Mormon responders rescued emigrant parties.

In the next part of the letter Taylor reported that the settlers found that Oregon prices for most items including foodstuffs were much higher in Oregon than in Wisconsin. Surviving the first three months was a difficult task for many. The plowing season and the wet weather extended from late November through the end of February, even early March. He might have added that it often rained up through April. He noted that most settlers did not bother to create haystacks since cattle could range free throughout the year, something that was not possible in chilly Wisconsin. The settlers stored supplies of potatoes in log houses. Geese and turkeys were absent.[94] He described in terse, frontier shorthand a shared sense of optimism and hope that was characteristic of many. Taylor wrote that he thought there would be "much trouble" coming from the Indians, "that community," in southern Oregon and northern California. During their trek to Oregon he noticed there had been more trouble from the Salt Lake City tribes than from any near Bear River.

Oregon settlers obtained lumber from cedar and oak trees. Taylor made a rough estimate at from "three to four thousand" in the whole Rogue River Valley, while the village of Jacksonville at "three to four hundred." At first he noticed that a woman ran the local "drunkery," or combination bowling alley and saloon, later he noticed there were "ten or twelve" families in Jacksonville. He described seeing "merchants in their stores" and "mechanics in their shops." Most of the buildings, except for one called "Robinson House" were rough affairs of shakes slapped together with cotton windows (not yet any glass). While the merchants and mechanics were thriving as yet there was "no cooper, gunsmith, carriage maker or shoemaker." There was just one saw mill open but three more were in the building stage in the Rogue Valley. It was the last month of 1853 and a "grist mill" was planned yet not in operation.[95] The basic plan for a permanent community had been set although it wasn't yet complete.

Taylor concluded that prices for necessities like beef, bacon, salt, candles, potatoes, coffee, sugar, butter and milk to be "enormous." Reiterating how problematical it was for new residents to survive the first few months, he said, "Some of our folks say they never before found 'existence so much a problem.'" One of his

---

this letter saying that the next time he wrote, "if he lived," it would be from Rock City, Oregon.

94 *Ibid.,* 149.

95 *Ibid.,* 150-151.

neighbors had to part with a valuable wagon for just "$100 to $160." Furthermore he wrote, "I presume four-fifths of those who have been here but three months, experience great trouble in getting enough to eat....[96]

Stanley Taylor noted there were not many trout or salmon, but deer and wild fruit could be found in large quantities. It must have been surprising to people back in Wisconsin enduring long, hard winters to read that grapes were fresh, even in mid December, in southern Oregon.

In the following passage, Taylor omitted reporting about many peaceful tribes of Oregon and California Indians while focusing only on a so-called "Indian war." The conflict had begun the preceding summer of 1853. In a sudden about face from his description of the kindly treatment he'd received when he was looking for his stolen oxen in the Black Hills near the start of their journey along the Oregon Trail, he described how uncivilized, "degraded and cruel" the Rogue River Indians were.

> The valley is about 75 miles long and perhaps 8 wide, beside the valleys of the creeks. The lower part of the valley, half of it, or thereabouts, is reserved for the present for the Indians. They attempted last summer [summer, 1853] to drive out the whites, and after a war of three months, during which about 40 whites and 100 Indians were killed, peace was concluded by the surrender of the best half of the valley to the whites. These Indians are a wild fierce tribe, of kin to the Diggers on the Humboldt, and about the lakes this side of there, and the Snakes of Snake river.—They are degraded and cruel beyond measure. It is said they murder for pastime. They will any of them shoot a man to get his hat....[97]

Still, compared to some settlers, Mr. Taylor's opinion with regard to fighting between whites and Indians was measured. Reflecting a view held by many modern scholars and other contemporary observers, he thought the "Mormon military" provoked war with the Utah tribe. Taylor advised future wagon trains to take the southern route "through the Humboldt" as opposed to going anywhere near Salt Lake City.

Once again, in case some readers of the *Chronicle* had not been paying attention, Mr. Taylor stated that newcomers in southern Oregon or northern California would find it hard to survive for the first few months but that once one was established in a recognized trade, life got somewhat easier. He also noted the "dehumanizing processes" that everyone had to go through as they worked their way across the Great Plains.

> And you can tell them that if people are not made over, or rather half unmade, by the dehumanizing processes through which they go from Kanesville here, they would never submit to living in such houses, with such an absence of the conveniences and comforts of eastern life,

---

96 *Ibid.,* 151.

97 *Ibid.,* 152.

and such a destitution of intellectual and moral opportunities, if they had not already learned on the plains to submit to anything. You can tell them that too; and tell them they can never, in living here, get paid for coming over the plains. I am not homesick; I am not prejudiced; I can only tell you the facts....

Mr. Taylor felt he had to fulfill his own personal pledge that he had made to some of the residents of Watertown to describe his "Oregon bound" experience. After making the trip, however, he did not recommend it for most of his readers. In fact, he discouraged people from trying it. He wrote:

Of those who have come without their friends, I have heard not one express an intention to bring them here. The general expression of such is, 'I am glad my family are [sic] not here.'...[98]

Mr. Taylor reported that many wanted to leave the West and eventually return to the Midwest or the East.

We are all told that by another year or so we shall prefer it to the East. I know not how that may be; but I know that a large portion of those who have been here eighteen months, the time of the settlement, intend to leave.

While there were a few discoveries made every day in the mines, Mr. Taylor maintained that mining was a very risky business. The dangers from cave-ins were great and, for most, the rewards were few and far between. He mentioned that to "see the elephant" might be tolerable for a young man but one usually could spend two years of their life doing almost anything else.

Thus ended Mr. Taylor's second-to-last letter, in 1853, which he addressed to his dear friends in Wisconsin. What Mr. Taylor had stated about the mining industry was a commonly heard view on the ground in Oregon and California mining regions, and, in fact, nearly everywhere throughout the west. Great success came to only a precious few (such as James "Old Virginny" Finney in Nevada or Henry "Old Pancake" Comstock) among hordes of people from many nations, including parts of the U.S., who came west seeking to strike it rich in the gold mines, "to see the elephant."

In his last published letter, Mr. Taylor described a conflict between natives and an armed settler party that had taken place on January 13, 1854, at Cottonwood, Oregon. Mr. Taylor reported what he had heard from others about what had happened. We can deduce some of the sources of conflict. There is nothing about the Indians, how they felt as they were being pressured by white people, or why they attacked in the first place. If a settler newspaper reported a "difficulty with the Indians," this really meant there had been a conflict, or perhaps even a massacre. Sometimes it was one in which many Indians were massacred and a number of whites were either injured or killed.

---

98 *Ibid.*, 153.

Citing a familiar theme in the story of the westward movement, Taylor wrote to the *Watertown Chronicle* on January 17, 1854 that a thirty man force of white volunteers engaged a group of Indians about forty-three miles "on the road south to California." He thought that the Indians had been stealing horses. At first the whites had been "dispersed with the loss of their rations and ammunition-having four men killed and four seriously wounded." The battle had lasted one entire day. He stated the "Indians are of the Shastee [Shasta?] and Rogue river Tribes." He thought that a portion of them lived within "nine miles from here." The engagement was fought near a community of Cottonwood. He also reported that volunteer parties were being formed in Yreka and Cottonwood with the aim of raising a force of two hundred "regulars."[99]

There was a pronounced change in tone in this letter from all others. The conflict near a remote mountain cave "in the Chastee [Shasta?] valley" had ended with eight white casualties — four dead and four wounded — out of a force of "about 30 whites." Since he wasn't present at the battle, he couldn't report on the number of Indians killed and wounded, but it may have been as many or even more than the whites lost. Late in 1858, and once more again late in 1859, bloody battles took place along the Trinity, Klamath and Humboldt Rivers and near Round Valley. These so-called "Indian wars," or massacres of indigenous people, were on a much larger scale, with the result that late in 1858, after the struggle had ended, approximately one thousand Indians from the Humboldt Bay area were transported far to the south to the Mendocino Indian Reservation at Fort Bragg. Thomas J. Henley was California's second Superintendent of Indian Affairs. In one of his last significant messages to the Office of Indian Affairs in Washington, he reported that this transfer took place in January, 1859. It involved bringing them from the Humboldt Bay region by schooner to Fort Bragg so they would remain on the Mendocino Indian Reservation.

The press and Gov. John B. Weller's administration termed this conflict "Gen. Kibbe's War." It was named after California's white militia's commander-in-chief, Gen. William C. Kibbe and was a campaign simultaneously fought by militia forces in northern California along the Klamath and Trinity Rivers and near Round Valley in northeastern Mendocino County. Whether or not these particular Indians had taken part in the resistance, the so-called "Indian disturbances," was immaterial to most whites. The purpose stated for moving such a considerable number of Native Americans so far from their homeland was so they would not know how to return. Of course this forced removal was inhumane and somewhat ludicrous. California Indians could always find their way to or from anywhere they wanted in northwestern California since they had been born and raised here.[100] Many who were thus moved simply walked back to their tribal areas

99 *Ibid.,* 159.

100 *Ibid.,* 159-160.

where they tried to resume their lives following the same patterns of fishing and hunting they had always followed.

Having sold off and left their homes in Watertown, Wisconsin, in the early months of 1853, Taylor's group led by Methodist preachers began their trek with buoyant although naïve enthusiasm. Their high hopes were tempered by the hardships of the trail but lifted again when they received aid from some of the Plains tribes. After they reached the Rogue River Valley, the harsh realities of the frontier caused their attitudes toward the native peoples to deteriorate. Their many hardships brought forth stronger feelings of anger and loss. On the other hand, the Indians defended themselves and their way of life in the only ways they knew how. Mr. Taylor and his group seemed clueless as to the profound alterations they and the other settlers like them wrought upon southern Oregon and northern California.

CHAPTER 9. FOUNDING OF THE MENDOCINO RESERVATION AND FORT BRAGG, LT. HORATIO T. GIBSON, U.S. ARMY

> What neglect, starvation, and disease have not done, has been achieved by the co-operation of the white settlers in the great work of extermination.
>
> — Special Agent J. Ross Browne, "The Indians of California," from Browne's *Observations In Office, Harper's New Monthly Magazine*, 1864.

Partly responding to a May, 1855 petition through Mr. Robert White, an *ex officio* Indian agent, signed by some fifty-one nervous whites who lived on the north Mendocino coast, California's Superintendent of Indian Affairs Thomas J. Henley decided to open an entirely new Indian reservation about seven miles north of Big River's outlet and at the future mill site of the Mendocino Lumber Company. This reservation was named the Mendocino Indian Reservation. Some local whites, including most local Indian elders, questioned the need for a reservation. The petition to Supt. Henley said that some of the local Indians were stealing food from their homes when they were gone. It included several settlers who lost personal items like clothes and food or, in the case of Sam Watt, his whole crop of seed potatoes. Capt. Rundall's house was burglarized; a Mr. Caspari lost all of his possessions, and the houses of one Mr. Mitchell and one of Capt. Thompson's houses allegedly was also burglarized. Those who signed the petition threatened to start a "war of extermination" unless the state took some action. However the signers did not fear an imminent Indian attack. The same lumber mill, one started at Big River or Mendocino by partners, Jerome B. Ford and E.C. Williams, employed twenty-six out of the fifty-one signers. A considerable number of present-day Ft. Bragg residents maintain that the signers had been coerced with a threat of being fired if they didn't sign the petition. Regardless of why some community leaders, like the Hegenmeyers, J. P. Simpson, and Jerome B. Ford, for example, signed the petition, there was a conflict of interest among them together with other whites and local Indians who might have become mill hands or lumber jacks. If Indians remained on tribal lands, some of which had thousands of acres of standing timber on them, they could negotiate from a strong position. However, if they were resettled on reservations, they would lose all of their property rights. The three community leaders, who led the fight to induce others to sign onto the petition, as mill owner/managers stood to gain a great deal if a reservation was established. Soldiers were brought in to keep order. The settlers wanted the soldiers to keep Indians on the reservation and away from their homes and businesses. In 1854 Supt. Henley had initiated the Nome Lackee Reservation, which was located a little more than ten miles southwest of Red Bluff in neighboring Tehama County. Already Congress had appropriated one hundred and eighty thousand dollars so that Supt. Henley could establish three new reservations. Therefore settlers couldn't have timed their petition any better.

The four members of the exploration party to lay out the site of the reservation were James Tobin, Robert White, John P. Simpson, and Samuel Watt (or Watts), the last three of whom were residents of Mendocino County. On May 12, 1853, President Franklin Pierce approved the Mendocino Reservation as had been requested by California State Senator H.P. Heintzelman. As the southern boundary the team selected the Noyo River since it was one of only a few streams that could provide a safe anchorage for all vessels that drew up to ten feet of water in any weather. The Mendocino Reservation, like almost all of the other reservations that were created in the state, consisted of approximately twenty-five thousand acres. It extended just over a mile north of what was then called "Hale Creek" (or Hair River, now Ten Mile River). From mussel beds that ran along the whole length of the coastline in the west, the reservation extended across sand hill and grass lands, patches of clover, and three hundred acres of Bald Hill, to the western edge of the Coast Mountains. It also included many acres of dense pine, redwood, yew, and oak trees. Beginning in 1856 with a total of a few more than three hundred seventy-five Indians, the Mendocino Reservation operated for ten years, until about 1866. During this period the Native population varied and rose at one point to as many as thirty-five hundred.

There had been other proposals besides establishing expensive reservations for handling what white California settlers called "Indian affairs." Until March, 1853, when Joel Palmer became Superintendent of Indian Affairs for Washington and Oregon and began there to institute the reservation policy, the federal government's official Indian policy was *laissez faire*: all natives were allowed to roam freely. As long as they coexisted in peace with others, they were considered free to come and go wherever they pleased.

To illustrate how broad some of Supt. Henley's thinking was, in the spring of 1855 Supt. Henley thought seriously about creating a reservation for California's Indians east of the Sierras. It was a possible although probably geographically impractical project that, at one point at least, had appealed to many California legislators, including Gov. John B. Weller, 1858–1860. As is sometimes the case today, this idea was ignored while events continued seemingly to favor development in another direction.

The Mendocino Reservation's first Agent-in-Charge was Henry (or H. L.) Ford. Ford was known to almost all of his white California contemporaries as one of Captain Frémont's key lieutenants during the Bear Flag Revolt and the Mexican War in California.[101] When he arrived Subagent H.L. Ford was enthusiastic about the reservation's site since it offered isolation from large settlements of whites and a plentiful supply of fish, deer and elk, as well as good farmland. With the help of some local Indians the recently appointed subagent constructed a new headquarters building one half mile north of the Noyo, eight dwellings and a smokehouse. According to Supt. Henley's directions everyone should be out of bed by five, eat breakfast at six, and be at work in the fields by seven every day. Two other sub-Indian stations or farms that also date from 1856 were the so-called "Cully-bool" (later Cullybull) Station just below the Noyo under John P. Simpson and the Bald Hill farm under M. C. Dougherty. Robert (Bob) White was the first overseer and head gardener at Mendocino Reservation.

In some ways 1857 was a more successful year than the first at the reservation. If progress in reservation-building was measured by an increase in numbers of Indian residents ("wards"), then by the end of the year 1857 the Mendocino Reservation seemed to be on the way to success. Yet there were profound problems that no one would ever solve. The first and foremost was how to keep the Indians on the reservation. Many of them, especially the males, continuously tried to leave. Another was the problem of schools for the young Indians. There was not one cent allocated either by Congress or by the California Legislature to build a single Indian school at any of its California reservations. Subagent Ford recommended that Congress hire a schoolteacher to serve the Indians at the reservation.

According to the records and despite some negatives, the initial two years of farming on the reservation seem to have been a success. Wheat, potatoes, barley, peas, and oats were planted on over three hundred fifty acres of land. Moreover mixed crews of white and native fishermen brought in thirty thousand pounds of cod as well as ten thousand pounds of small fish. A great deal of the cod was dried and salted. In 1857 there were twenty-five houses built for Indians as well as twelve larger buildings. According to Edward Vischer, who visited the reserva-

---

101 A few Native Americans also were transferred to the Hupa (or Hoopa) Reservation. An example of such a tribe was the Chilula in 1850, a tribe that Ethnologist Alfred E. Kroeber described.

tion as a member of J. Ross Browne's fifteen man hunting party in the fall of 1857, there were by this time offices, a large storehouse, employee cottages, Subagent Ford's residence and mess halls.[102] Dr. Thaddeus M. Ames took on the position of the doctor in charge of a large hospital on the reservation.

The reservation also operated a twenty-ton schooner between Mendocino City and the reservation ferrying supplies. According to an annual report for 1858 by Supt. Henley, a storm occurred that nearly sunk the ship. The schooner's captain was drunk in Mendocino City and unable to pilot his ship to safety. Resourceful Indians took the ship out to sea and sailed it around until it was safe to return to Mendocino. There is no record that they received anything except possibly a few kind words for their actions.

A more serious crisis occurred during the spring and summer of 1857 when food supplies ran short, so short, in fact, that at least three natives died. Due to the food shortage, Dr. Ames had to close the hospital, despite the fact that some of the Indians were not well; he felt that it was more humane to allow the Indian patients to go back to trying to live off the land than to starve within the walls of the reservation hospital. Those who survived had to revert to eating acorns, berries and clover. During the spring of 1857, supplies of rice and grain at the Mendocino Reservation ran so short that a still unknown number of natives died of starvation, although in a deposition given during an OIA investigation in the fall of 1858 Subagent Ford stated that he never actually knew about any Indians who starved to death. Other white employees at the reservation confirmed their deaths. The sadness that Subagent Ford felt might possibly have played some

---

102 H.L. Ford's actual name was Noah Eastman Ford. Noah E. Ford was born Aug. 24, 1822 in North Conway, Vermont. On one side his family was Welsh, Dutch on the other, without going into all the details. One of his grandfathers had been a Revolutionary War soldier. Noah Ford was in the second year of training to become an Army officer when news that his brother, the real Henry L. Ford, was sick and dying in Vermont. As the brothers were close, Noah had applied for a leave of absence to be at his brother's deathbed. When the Army denied his request and Henry died, Noah decided to withdraw from the military college, change his name from Noah to Henry Lambert or H.L., and immigrate to California in 1842. Once in California he worked at various occupations, ranch hand, boatman, trapper, and soldier. Getting word that the U.S. settlers were going to declare independence, he joined the Bear Flag Revolt. He was present on the morning of June 14, 1846, at Sonoma when the Bear Flag replaced the Mexican flag. He enlisted with Fremont's Battalion, serving throughout the Mexican War.

During the Bear Flag Revolt, June 14-July 4, 1846, Lieut. H.L. Ford led one of the three detachments. He drove Capt. Jose Castro, commander of the Mexican forces, out of northern California. During the short, significant existence of the Bear Flag Republic during late June and early July 1846, Lt. Ford's men routed a force of the Mexican Army at Olompali, a small valley located on Hwy. 101 about two miles north of the present-day city limits of Novato. None of the Bears were killed, but several members of the Mexican force were wounded. One Mexican soldier, or two, depending of different accounts, was killed. See also Edward Vischer's (Vischer lived from 1809-1879.), "Reminiscences of Mendocino," *Hutchings California Magazine*, III. (October, 1858), 145-160, as quoted by Fred B. Rogers, *Ibid.*, 165.

role in his accidental death almost two years after an investigation concluded in September 1858.

A former overseer at Nome Lackee Reservation, Simmon P. Storms, was both the founder of Nome Cult Farm (or Round Valley) Indian Reservation was also its Agent-in-Charge. A former Grass Valley rancher, Storms spoke most of the Indian dialects and also had been present during some of the earlier treaty negotiations. Simmon P. Storms and H.L. Ford at Mendocino Reservation were designated "Subagents" by the Office of Indian Affairs (OIA). The Mendocino Reservation operated until well after the conclusion of the Civil War, about 1868, when the Indian residents were marched to Round Valley.

Meanwhile, the interplay of powerful forces, the self-serving U.S. mantra of Manifest Destiny, gold fever, and the growth of the lumber industry, was bringing about changes on Mendocino County's north coast during this critically important first year of 1857. As Subagent Ford had led both white and native employees in establishing a successful Indian reservation, Supt. Henley consulted with the Army's staff officers to establish a new post at Fort Bragg. A detachment of the US Army from the San Francisco Presidio founded a camp about a mile and half north of the Noyo River. Despite the fact that, technically speaking, the Army's troopers were intruders upon Mendocino Reservation land, work started on structures for the army post.[103]

The first problem to be overcome was a drastic shortage of building materials. An Office of Indian Affairs employee, Captain Cook, assisted by supplying materials to the soldiers. The reservation Indians helped out also, both by moving supplies and equipment and by building structures.[104] By September, Lt. Gibson reported to Army headquarters that three buildings were complete and occupied,

---

103 Although it is now the so-called Guest House, Ft. Bragg's hospital stood on a knoll near the northwest corner. Although probably not known by the soldiers at Ft. Bragg, the entire military post had been carved out of land that once was part of the reservation. The large brick Guest House that now is a museum on Main Street run by the Mendocino Historical Society, was occupied by the guest house (which later became The Guest House Museum) of the Union Lumber Company. Completed much later, in 1892, this Victorian home suggests a way of life of many years ago; pleasant gardens, ornate woodwork of the nineties, stained glass windows overlooking the entrance hall and a spacious redwood interior. A State of California Historical Marker commemorates the location. Subagent Ford died in early July 1860 at Nome Cult Farm (Round Valley). He and Supt. McDuffie were there to drive some livestock from there to the Mendocino Reservation. Most historians believe he accidentally was shot through the neck when his pistol, which he was carrying in a saddle bag, misfired. Ironically, perhaps years before, his mother-in-law, Mrs. Wilson, warned him that she feared he would lose his life due to his careless handling of his pistol. See Fred B. Rogers' "Bear Flag Lieutenant," *California Historical Society Quarterly*, XXX, June, 1951, 168.

104 The Company M, 3rd Artillery troopers who built Ft. Bragg were led by Lt. Horatio Gates Gibson. Lt. Gibson, a young lieutenant, had been so impressed by his superior officer Captain Braxton Bragg, when both were serving in the Mexican War, that he chose to name the new camp after his former commander, Fort Bragg. Captain Bragg

even though they were not completely finished. He hoped that the officers' quarters would be completed by October, 1857. Remaining to be built were a stable, a guardhouse and storehouses.

In November 1857, Lt. Gibson and Company M hurriedly left Ft. Bragg on orders to support other Army units fighting Indians in eastern Washington. Lt. Gibson's unit returned to Fort Bragg during the summer of 1858. Throughout the remainder of 1858 work continued toward expanding the base. The officer's quarters were just north of the parade ground. To the west of the officer's dwelling was the commissary, quartermaster storehouse, and a stable. A hospital was built on the northwest corner of the fort. The parade ground included the guardhouse and stables that Lt. Gibson's 1857 report had mentioned.

Some Ft. Bragg soldiers had sexual relationships with Indian women. In most cases these liaisons, whether or not they became actual marriages and whether or not children were the result, usually were not recognized by either the Army or by the civil authorities. The negative side of these relationships was the transmission, back and forth, of venereal diseases. Another result were the births of infants such as the second Henry L. Ford, Jr., who was born at the Mendocino Reservation in 1860, grew up, was trained to practice law in Eureka, and made many positive contributions to the state's development.

Under Agent Henry L. Ford's tutelage the Mendocino Reservation grew in size from about three hundred Native American residents to about three thousand four hundred. In Agent Ford's August, 1857 report to Supt. Henley, he noted that three hundred fifty acres of reservation land had been planted in wheat, oats, barley, peas, potatoes, and turnips. Forty thousand pounds of fish had been caught, of which about half had already been dried for use in the coming winter. Two major roads had been built to Little Valley (some called it "lil valley.") and to the town of Mendocino. More than five hundred acres of land was fenced. Frame houses were also built. In addition reservation employees directed Native American workers in finishing a large log building, a hospital, together with twenty-five houses specifically for Native American use. The reservation physician, Dr. Thaddeus M. Ames, had vaccinated eight hundred forty-two Indians. As in Storms' report from Nome Cult, at Mendocino Reservation one of Agent Ford's early reports advocated segregating Native Americans from all other California residents, especially the white settlers, because of the spread of venereal diseases. Since 1852, when the federal government began building its California reservation system and the Tejon Reservation had begun operations a few miles north of Bakersfield. in California, the idea of separating Native Americans from Euro-Americans had been a primary purpose of the reservation system.

---

made a heroic charge that may have won the entire Battle of Buena Vista for the American side.

Today if one reads only the official reports by reservation employees, such as reports by H. L. Ford and other reservation agents and subagents, it appears that progress was being made. A handful of employees, especially those few who could use their own internal influence as supervisors to extract a form of slave labor from Indians of both sexes or sexual favors from female Indians, were completely content. Unfortunately, below the surface, the real situation was not so serene nor anywhere near as positive as it appeared to Agent Ford. Mr. G. (George) Canning Smith was Head Clerk of the Mendocino Reservation at this time. For a number of years before this, Superintendent Henley and Head Clerk Smith had been on generally friendly terms with each other. At some unknown point Superintendent Henley spoke to Smith about the possibility of Smith becoming a customs inspector or collector at Little Valley on the extreme northern edge of Mendocino Reservation. At the time the job of collector of customs, a middle level job in the U.S. Treasury Department, was a highly sought after position since it was a federal job therefore secure and almost immune from political changes that frequently brought about wholesale and capricious changes in personnel. Some positions, such the California Superintendent of Indian Affairs went to political appointees. For example, the first Superintendent, Ned Beale, had been replaced in 1853 by Thomas J. Henley. As long as one was conscientious and stayed ahead of the work load, this position provided almost complete job security as well as a somewhat higher rate of pay.

In Head Clerk Smith's particular case, if chosen, he stood a decent chance to earn at least twice his normal clerkship pay. Moreover he also would be entitled to much more in unofficial benefits or perks, such as greatly enhanced prestige and a better way of life. Another positive factor to being a customs collector was the chance to move up to some higher state or federal political office. Previously G. Canning Smith had been elected to a brief term as a judge. It was not beyond the realm of possibility that he might dream of serving in a higher position in government than being the head clerk at the reservation.

Nevertheless because he was an ethical public servant, Head Clerk Smith wrote a scathing report that charged Supt. Henley with gross mismanagement, even deliberate fraud of the federal government in his disbursement of the Mendocino Reservation funds. These were serious charges. It would take the OIA a considerable amount of time and trouble to investigate and verify them before any punitive action could be taken, such as a demotion or dismissal. There was never any possibility of criminal charges against the superintendent.

There were three serious charges against Superintendent Henley. In the spring of 1857, he had sold a herd of cattle and oxen driven by a Round Valley group of cowboys that included members of his family, from Nome Cult Farm across the Eel River through Sherwood Valley southeast to the Mendocino Reservation on the Pacific Ocean. Head Clerk G. Canning Smith noticed that the federal government paid Supt. Henley top dollar, as if the whole herd had been composed of only full-bred American cattle. In reality, and in Mr. Smith's eyes, the cattle had included some half breed cattle that were worth much less. Supt. Henley, who had come to California from Missouri, was a ranching business partner to William A. Wilsey. Once in California, the Wilsey family and the Henley family had retained ties, especially in Round Valley.

A second source of dispute was the founding of a saw mill on the south bank of Noyo River, just across the southern border of Mendocino Reservation, on land outside of the reservation's limits. The saw mill was owned and operated by a white settler named Alexander MacPherson (the name has also been Anglicized to 'McPherson' in a few records). The problem here was twofold. Native American workers at the mill were being paid less than whites who also worked at the saw mill. Reservation members also cut and helped transport timber from the reservation to the mill site. Lumber thus produced was sold with the proceeds going solely to MacPherson's company. There was a rumor going around Mendocino Reservation that MacPherson and Supt. Henley were business partners and were splitting the profits.

A third charge of serious fraud against Supt. Henley involved his choice of the source of where to buy a supply of potatoes for the same reservation. In the late spring each year at the Mendocino Reservation supplies of dried fish, rice, and other staples were usually depleted. In 1857 this happened earlier than had been usual. As a result potatoes were to be supplied for a few months for the Native Americans to eat until the reservation's food crops could be grown and harvested. But Supt. Henley and Subagent Ford refused to follow the common sense practice of buying the needed potatoes from the many local Mendocino County farmers, buying them instead from San Francisco merchant companies that charged more for potatoes than any of the local farmers would have charged. The result was higher cost to the government. Ship transportation from San Francisco one hundred fifty miles north to the Mendocino Reservation was both riskier and costlier. Two OIA vouchers, the first on April 1, 1857 in the amount of $2,180.91 and a second one, on May 9, 1857 for $2,535.75, had been approved and signed by Henry L. Ford. The two potato vouchers constituted conclusive, hard evidence that there had been significant instances of mismanagement by Agent Ford and Supt. Henley.[105]

In addition to charging the federal government more than it should have paid for this important staple, Supt. Henley at the very least showed favoritism toward his reservation storekeeper, R.K Dodge at the expense of the federal agency once again. According to the depositions of local settlers and reservation employ-

---

105 The Army chartered a schooner to move equipment up the coast from "The City" (San Francisco) to Mendocino City and then north of that to a site about a mile and a half north of the Noyo River.

ees gathered and recorded by Special Agent Browne, Special Agent Bailey and Superintendent Henley from August through September 1858, Henley and Dodge overcharged the government a second time at the local level. Thus, if the charges were true, the OIA was being defrauded on a regular and systematic basis, in the main by its own California superintendent. There is no evidence about why Supt. Henley was present during the process of collecting the depositions, although as we shall see, he cross-examined some of those who recorded their depositions, including Head Clerk Smith.

By the spring of 1857, even the few potatoes that the reservation had left over from the preceding summer were gone. As we have seen, due to the lack of food Dr. Thaddeus Ames, physician in charge of the hospital, said that he hoped the Indian patients could survive for a few months on their own in the wild. In fact, at least ten Native Americans died as a result of starvation in the late spring of 1857. A year later Agent Ford testified that he had not been informed that any Indians had died. In his deposition in 1858 he denied knowing about their deaths.

In spite of the charges made by Head Clerk Smith against Subagent Ford, some historians might find valid reasons to defend the work that Captain Ford did while in charge of the Mendocino Reservation. Two years after the food crisis during 1859, the reservation produced more than seven thousand bushels of grain, three thousand of potatoes, and many tons of vegetables. If success can be measured in terms of foodstuffs produced, the Mendocino Reservation's burgeoning harvests until the early 1860s were resounding successes. Again, one must give credit to the white farmer-overseers and the backbreaking labor that was performed under what were difficult if not nearly impossible soil and climate conditions.

Depositions taken during the Indian Office of Indian Affairs' investigation are not the only source of information about the Indians and the reservations. Agent J. Ross Browne published his own views about the California Native Americans in a three-part series of articles in *New Harper's Monthly Magazine* published in 1861. Special Agent Browne wrote in bold and sarcastic terms with reference to his own investigation of Superintendent Henley's California Office of Indian Affairs.

Special Agent Browne summarized,

> In short, the original purpose of language was so perverted in the official correspondence that it had no more to do the expression of facts that many of the employees had to do with the Indians. The reports and regulations of the Department [the OIA] actually bordered on the poetical. It was enough to bring tears into the eyes of any feeling man to read the affecting dissertations that were transmitted to Congress on the woes of the red men, and the labors of the public functionaries to meliorate that unhappy condition. Faith, hope, and charity abounded in them. 'See what we are doing for these poor children of the forest!' was the burden of the song, in a strain worthy of the most pathetic flights of Mr. Pecksniff [a character in Dickens' *Martin Chuzzlewit* with

whom most readers were familiar]; 'see how faithful we are to our trusts, and how judiciously we expend the appropriations! Yet they die off in spite of us—wither away as the leaves of the trees in autumn!

At this point in his 1861 article Special Agent Browne presented a harshly critical assessment to the general public in *Harper's*, thus putting his own future as a public servant in jeopardy. His writings were drawn from his own extensive public service experience in the Far West, from the Minnesota Territory, Arizona, Washington, Oregon, and eventually California, where he attempted to clean up the bureaucratic mess that Supt. Henley and others had made of the OIA's reservation system for California Indians. "Decency in official conduct must be respected and the public eye regarded!" Agent Browne was talking about his years as special agent for the Office of Indian Affairs, 1857 and 1858, when he attempted to serve the OIA as an impartial observer. In that position he was frustrated by what he saw as serious corruption and waste in the administration of the reservation. He noted, "There was something so exquisitely comic in the idea of taking official instructions literally, and carrying them into effect, that he could not resist it. The humor of the thing kept him in a constant chuckle of internal satisfaction; but it was the most serious jest he ever perpetrated, for it cost him, besides the trouble of carrying it out, the loss of a very comfortable per diem." The article concluded, "The results of the policy pursued were precisely such as might have been expected. A very large amount of money was annually expended in feeding white men and starving Indians."[106] Unfortunately for the Indians, none of this brought about any positive changes in life on the reservation. At this point Special Agent Browne lost his federal posts at the Treasury and the Indian Affairs Department.

The Mendocino California Indian tribes, as they were increasingly being outnumbered and out-gunned, had no chance of defeating their white foes in a battle on any north Mendocino coast field. The presence of Fort Bragg added insult to injury. Even when the base closed and all the troops withdrew in 1868, the old Indian lands had begun to lose much of their natural ability to sustain native people. The individual Indians faced an unsolvable, cruel dilemma: get in step with the ever more dominant white society or simply face extinction with whatever grace and dignity possible. Progress of the logging industry and gradual improvement in transportation by sea and by land brought temporary incomes for a few Indians and for many predominantly white workers and rare fortunes for a tiny minority of lumber barons while slowly but surely destroying the great redwood forests.

---

106 Vouchers #17 and #18, April 1, 1857 and May 9, 1859, "Letters Received by the OIA in 1858," *Ibid.* 0417-0418. Probably these vouchers were noted by the Office of Indian Affairs in its investigation of Superintendent Henley.

Tales of fortunes made in the lumber boom along the north Mendocino coast as well as in the Humboldt Bay region and areas along the seacoasts of Oregon and Washington in the second half of the nineteenth century reinforce the impression that free enterprise along with the steady improvements in communications and transportation, especially with the advent of railroads during the last two decades of that century, worked well and was a great success. Nevertheless certain groups, especially the natives, Chinese, other Asian people, and African-Americans, were excluded from this scenario of success and plenty. In particular, the Native American population as a whole suffered, albeit possibly unintentionally, in many cases, from discrimination or exploitation. Since they were both readily identifiable and culturally different from the emerging powerful, predominantly white ruling elite, and because their preferred lifestyle of hunters, fishermen, and acorn and fruit gatherers no longer was sustainable, Indians lost out in far greater numbers in the fight for survival.

CHAPTER 10. THE INVESTIGATION OF THOMAS J. HENLEY
CALIFORNIA SUPERINTENDENT OF INDIAN AFFAIRS

"Am acquainted with G. Canning Smith. Have heard him say in the office that he
had the dead-wood on Col. Henley. That Col. Henley had promised to get him
an office and had not done it."

—Wm. H. Ray, Aug. 17, 1858

During the late summer of 1858, in response to charges against California's
Superintendent of Indian Affairs Thomas J. Henley, two Office of Indian Affairs
(OIA) special agents, J. Ross Browne and Goddard Bailey, rode over hundred
miles of rugged terrain north from San Francisco to the Nome Cult Indian Farm
in Round Valley. California's Superintendent of Indian Affairs, Thomas J. Henley accompanied them. It was the start of a traveling investigation that moved
from Round Valley through Redwood Valley to the Mendocino Reservation, and
ended in San Francisco. Approximately forty depositions were taken on many
aspects of reservation life in the fourth year of the Mendocino Reservation's existence. Superintendent Henley exercised his right to cross-examine some of the
participants, especially Head Clerk G. Canning Smith. Once the depositions had
been recorded from the most relevant Mendocino County residents, especially
at Nome Cult Farm and the Mendocino Reservation at Ft. Bragg, they were sent
to the Office of Indian Affairs in Washington where the Commissioner of Indian
Affairs made his decision to relieve Supt. Henley and replace him during the summer of 1859.

The first testimony came from Agent Simmon P. Storms, the founder and first
Subagent-in-Charge of Nome Cult Indian Farm. Besides not being reimbursed

for a loan as promised by Supt. Henley for a ranch that Storms purchased from a settler named Brizentine for Judge Hastings, Subagent or Overseer Storms said that "J. R. (Ross) Browne had made charges in reference to the Mendocino Reservation." Dr. Ames had "furnished Mr. Browne with the information upon which some of the charges were based." This deposition as well as most of the others recorded can be found in the Appendix on p. 197. The breakdown in the system, coming as it did when many white settlers were questioning the worth of the whole reservation system in general, could not be ignored for long by the Office of Indian Affairs.

The second individual whose deposition was recorded on August 11, 1858 was the acting physician at Round Valley, Dr. J. W. Burgess. John Burgess had also been in charge of the Commissary, including the mess hall at Round Valley. Burgess was Subagent Storms' second in command, Dr. Burgess was a faithful employee, loyal to Subagent Storms and devoted to doing his duty. First he related that a Dr. Ames ran a hospital on the reservation. When food supplies ran short Ames had to discharge patients who were still ill. He then said that he, Burgess, was not paid but was issued "vouchers" (nothing more than a promise to pay) that he made out with the amount owed in blank. He stated in his deposition that using vouchers as a means of payment to all the employees and for payment of necessary items such as foodstuffs in hard times, was unusual and a reason for protest by the reservation employees. Dr. Burgess's deposition backed what Dr. Ames, the doctor in charge at Mendocino Reservation, had alleged: there had been shortages in the food supplies.

Following Dr. Burgess was Charles H. Bourne who reaffirmed Head Clerk G. Canning Smith's scathing report to the Indian Affairs Department that had prompted the investigation of Superintendent Henley. Bourne, an early Round Valley settler who didn't work at the reservation was a respected "Indian fighter" (a term other settlers reserved for anyone who'd been involved in conflicts with Indians) who had saved the lives of settlers while, at the same time speaking out for just treatment of the Indians. Mr. Bourne, who was originally from Pennsylvania, was one of the first whites to settle in Round Valley having arrived in 1856. Mr. Bourne's testimony carried weight since he was not a greenhorn settler and didn't work for the OIA.

Mr. Bourne stated that the cattle sent from Round Valley to the Mendocino Reservation were not full-blooded American cattle but instead were Spanish cattle, an inferior breed. Government stock mixed freely with the livestock of private ranchers at Round Valley. Branding was the only way to keep track of the ownership. Since barbed wire didn't exist until much later, there was often a problem even when everyone was being honest. Early Californians were concerned with and protective of the quality of their beef.

Following Bourne, Alonzo Kinsley, a drover (vaquero or cowboy) who actually took part in the cattle drive from Round Valley to Mendocino Reservation in 1857 gave testimony. Kinsley's deposition supported Smith regarding the cattle. He was a regular Nome Cult Farm employee who had participated but got no additional payment for his services. His estimate of the worth of the cattle was higher than was Jesse Henley's or Charles Bourne's was.

Next, Jesse Henley, one of the superintendent's nephews who had settled in Round Valley, testified in his deposition that at least one of the cattle had been injured during the long shipment from Kentucky to northern Mendocino County. Cheaper so-called "Spanish cattle" had been in California before the whites brought in the more expensive "Durham breed." The very diversity in the stock meant that there was often a difficulty in assigning the correct value to the cattle when they were bought and sold. On the open range, such as at Round Valley and at many other locations in northern California in the latter 1850s, the buyer had to beware that he wasn't paying too much for the breed of cattle that was purchased. Jesse Henley's deposition is number 5 in Appendix IV.

Jesse Henley's deposition was the last one recorded along with the others at Round Valley. The date was August 11. The three-man investigating party made its way southwest across a thick redwood forest of the coastal range toward the Fort Bragg/Mendocino Reservation region to record the last half of the depositions. Beginning with that of Mendocino Reservation's doctor, Dr. Thaddeus M. Ames, the depositions by the settlers and reservation employees continued.

The investigating team moved from Nome Cult Farm directly southwest towards the south Mendocino coast, taking two depositions along the way. Robert White and John P. Simpson, had co-founded the town of Cahto, between Covelo and Ft. Bragg near Laytonville. For a period of fourteen months, John P. Simpson had been the overseer at the Cullybull Indian Station, an outpost of the Mendocino Reservation. In the first part of his deposition Mr. Simpson discussed how W.C. Davis, a man of good reputation, sold his claim "in the fall of 1856" to the reservation as well as his potato crop, to create the Cullybull Station. As he discussed how the MacPherson saw mill had been built, Mr. Simpson suggested that about thirty white men had had a hand in constructing it. In conclusion, Simpson reported that Mr. White told him about one day in front of the headquarters, one "Matteo, Chief of the Kineamares" confronted Supt. Henley telling him that unless his people received some food soon since they were starving, that "they'd be forced to leave the reservation."

John Simpson's deposition certainly didn't help Supt. Henley's cause as he confirmed that he'd heard that "two or three" Indians died during the food shortage. But he also said he wasn't one who believed everything the Indians told him since they often complained to him of being hungry even after he had just fed them. Sometimes he thought it was alright for the Indians to leave the reservation if they would return. Mr. Simpson maintained that many Indians left the reservation during the food shortage who would never return. This was a pattern noticed by others including J. Ross Browne.

The next Euro-American settler to testify was Simpson's longtime partner, Robert White. The two men had met in New Orleans and had immigrated to California late in 1848. Mr. White had held the position of overseer on the Mendocino Reservation. They had been among the first Mendocino County pioneers and had joined state Senator Heinzelman's party that decided on where the Mendocino Reservation would be established late in 1856 and early 1857. The first question by Special Agent Goddard Bailey put Mr. White on the spot asking whether or not he thought MacPherson's saw mill should have been allowed.

It wasn't too surprising that Mr. White either couldn't or wouldn't answer some questions posed by Special Agent Bailey about the business relationship between Supt. Henley and Alexander MacPherson. While he stated that MacPherson had paid some of the Indians,, when he ran out of cash he hadn't paid some of the others. Mr. White said that some Indians had not been paid for the work that he knew they had done at the MacPherson saw mill.

As someone who had dealings both with Supt. Henley and Alexander MacPherson, Mr. White was in a good position to know about how stores were loaned back and forth from the reservation's storehouses or commissary. When it came to the question of R. K. Dodge's tent store that he'd been permitted to set up on the reservation, Mr. White supplied the investigators with a few details.

Not much can be concluded from what Mr. White said about the quality of the cattle. The last few points made by Mr. White involved the quality of seed used at the reservation. When it came to either defending or attacking Head Clerk Canning Smith's character, Mr. White also was neutral or generally evasive. Apparently during Smith's watch as judge, three men may have been arrested for selling liquor to the Indians, a relatively common offense.

Rumors about the investigation must have circulated for weeks before it came to Mendocino. The depositions that followed showed further weaknesses that by the fall of 1858 had begun to eat away at the integrity of the California reservation system. Public support for financing the reservations, always shaky, had been rapidly evaporating both at federal and state levels as various rumors about Supt. Henley's corrupt practices swirled about eventually reaching the press. The federal government's investigators recorded a surprising total of eight depositions on the same day, August 16, 1858. Some participants may have written out their depositions in advance as it seems doubtful that in actuality all testified in one day. Still, in their effort to solicit candid, unrehearsed testimonies, the investigators probably tried to prevent the participants from comparing notes before testifying. The commissioner of Indian Affairs as well as members of Congress did not wish to over-react and fire any hard-working, innocent employees. Or, perhaps it may have been just easier to take the testimonies any way they could.

When Alexander W. MacPherson and his partners in his firm decided to build and operate a saw mill on the reservation's property, a few Indians applied to work at the mill. Once they had started to work, others noticed and asked to work also. In spite of the fact that they received half what whites received for similar work, or in some cases nothing at all, most Indians knew better than to complain.

The first deposition taken at Mendocino was from Agent H. (Henry) L. Ford. He must have learned what some of the charges were against his boss, Superintendent Henley, even though Ford's testimony showed he wasn't privy to a complete list of the complaints about Supt. Henley's performance. As someone caught up in a groundswell of popular unrest at the same time someone who had a lot to lose and nothing to gain from the investigation, Agent Ford took his time in making a lengthy deposition.

He specified the limits of the reservation and explained how, at Supt. Henley's request, Agent Ford had purchased a small land claim (Mr. Davis' potato field) to add to the reservation. In so doing he may have helped avert trouble as some of the Indians were complaining that Davis "set his dogs on them" when they had to pass by his property. He confirmed what Mr. Simpson had testified about how much Davis was paid for his land and the potato crop but denied that any kick-back went to Henley.

Agent Ford denied that he had heard of a payment of two hundred fifty dollars "or any other sum for effecting the sale of the said (Davis') claim." Having stated that now he thought the southern limit of the reservation to be Hair Creek, he continued to discuss how he had not opposed MacPherson's saw mill since MacPherson had gotten permission to build it. Apparently permission had to be granted by Superintendent Henley.

Ford didn't state how or when he met the Alexander MacPherson, who, as noted above, had been employed by Jardine, Matheson and Company in the Far East, perhaps in the opium trade. MacPherson may have introduced himself to the agent when he arrived on the north Mendocino coast. It is probable that Ford learned of MacPherson's connections to this large trading company and thus guessed that MacPherson's credit would be better than that of any of the other prospective mill owner/managers. In addition, Ford favored the project since he thought "the erection of the saw mill on the Noyo" could lead to increased "facilities for obtaining supplies" for the reservation. Helping to build the saw mill meant "employment afforded at good wages to those Indians for whom we had no use on the farm." Here Ford admitted that not all of the Indians had enough work at the reservation. Natives with too much time on their hands were dangerous, or at least it seemed so to many mid-nineteenth century whites.

If trade increased, everyone on the Mendocino coast would benefit from it. The point about good wages also was significant since Ford knew many of the Native Americans, especially the males, couldn't stand to work in the fields doing the repetitive work required to produce good crops. Many of them balked at fieldwork and as often as possible left the reservation in order to hunt or fish. There may have been a stigma associated with farm work as they could have seen it as woman's work. On the surface, getting the new saw mill began to appear to Agent Ford like an obvious "win-win" situation. There were nine Native American wood cutters who downed reservation trees that either went into the building of the Noyo saw mill or were milled. At first most of the lumber went back to the reservation. Some Indians also went to work at the saw mill for "fifty cents a day." His deposition apparently referred to two earlier settlers (Wolf and Gen. Estill) who had tried but failed to get his support for the proposed saw mill. While filling in some details about the first year of his work as Subagent at the Mendocino Reservation, none of the information he gave related to the investigation.

Agent Ford allowed MacPherson to borrow supplies and tools from the reservation till at times. It is not known whether they were returned. Agent Ford explained that the wheat crop "was short" in other places as well as on the reservation. He reported rumors that MacPherson was paying Supt. Henley something for agreeing to allow the erection of the saw mill. According to MacPherson as he told Agent Ford, Supt. Henley did not get anything back for agreeing to the deal. Agent Ford said that according to MacPherson boards that started out as logs from the reservation would be sold back to the reservation at the rate of eight dollars per thousand board feet, in other words, at cost of the labor of both the whites and the Indians.

As was understood by anyone who worked with or had any contact with Indians in the Far West at this time, liquor and Indians did not mix. It was one of the main reasons for reservations being established in the first place, since segregating the Indians from whites and others, it always had been thought, would eliminate or lessen the Indians' exposure to the evils of alcohol. Things did not work out as well as officials back East hoped they would.

Agent Ford tried to be clear about the quality of the beef that had been sent over to the Mendocino Reservation from Round Valley in the autumn of 1857. His testimony supported Supt. Henley in most regards. About the next matter however Agent Ford made a shocking statement: he said he had not been told that any of the Indians had died from starvation. This did not jibe with either of the preceding testimonies about Agent Ford's ordering Dr. Ames to close the hospital because it was feared that patients might die from the lack of food.

Agent Ford's statement that the reservation Indians had not suffered as much as Indians "back in the Valleys," while certainly true, made no difference as far as his own responsibility was concerned. It was also an obvious mistake to have permitted the reservation supply of food to get so low. He had loaned some of it to MacPherson and, regardless of whether the food rations were returned, his judgment was questionable. Agent Ford ended his testimony with a hopeful, if hollow and pretty obviously specious, prediction about being able to feed "double the number of Indians" if the current crop came in as well as expected.

While Agent Ford may have been less than honest about the lack of food, he had done what he had to do and what he thought was right in the circumstances to help MacPherson build the new saw mill —even though it rested on reservation property. While this saw mill would later be bought out and operated independently by MacPherson and his partner, Wetherbee, at this time the mill actually belonged to Jardine, Matheson & Company, the important British Far Eastern trading company. Agent Ford never really came up with a satisfactory answer as to why the Indians had starved to death while they had been in his charge. From two to as many as ten lives had been lost. Some who decided to leave the reservation also doubtlessly perished.

Dr. Thaddeus Ames MD, Mendocino Reservation's physician, was next to testify. As mentioned above in the Burgess deposition, Dr. Ames had been one of the first to detect a red flag and to report to Subagent Storms and possibly to the Office of Indian Affairs that there was something seriously wrong at the Mendocino Reservation. In the meantime Dr. Ames expressed frustration that some of his patients had left the hospital, probably before they were well enough, to work at Mr. MacPherson's new saw mill.

Dr. Ames stated that he discharged "four or five" of his patients since the reservation was out of rice, which was the food most needed at the time for his patients suffering from gonorrhea. There can be no doubt whatsoever as to Dr. Ames' good intentions. He was so honored by them that an unknown Indian carver created a beautifully inscribed powder horn, made from an elk horn, with his name, the date, and Mendocino Reservation written on it.

Dr. Ames remarked that personally he favored the saw mill. He also clearly stated that the problem of white men having sexual intercourse with the Indian women and "giving them disease" was not a new one nor was it attributable to the new saw mill. It was tersely termed by reservation officials like Subagents Storms, Ford, or Dr. Ames, as "the venereal."

Dr. Ames played a vital role at Mendocino Reservation and its society. His decisions determined whether the reservation hospital would survive or not. At one point, just a year or so earlier, this hospital served over three hundred Indian patients. Now it had been downsized to only about thirty patients "in the hospital and rancherias." Up to this point, VD hadn't been too large a problem among the reservation Native Americans. But now it was becoming a larger problem, especially for the so-called "wild Indians for the past eight or nine months."

Dr. Ames thought the Indians had contracted VD primarily from having contact at the reservation with so-called "Christian Indians." He failed to clarify who or what he meant by this term. He omitted mentioning the presence of the soldiers at Fort Bragg and their sexual intercourse with the Indians. He confirmed the fact that there had been a food shortage.

The next participant, Mr. Lyman F. Hinckley, was the reservation's chief carpenter. Mr. Hinckley was in a position to have a very good view of the timber cutting and harvesting operation. He was a close observer of what actually was going on simultaneously at the mill and on the reservation.

Lyman Hinckley played a dual role, first as supervisor to the Indian woodcutter crews on the reservation, and secondly as the head carpenter for the reservation. While he started work in 1855 earning one hundred dollars a month, in January 1858 the government reduced his pay to seventy-five dollars per month. Sometime in the early part of 1858 he almost quit working at the reservation. However he "was induced to stay upon the understanding that I was to be placed in charge of Indians getting out timber for Mr. McPherson and to receive from him $25 a month." This arrangement continued until April 1. In the fall he started working for MacPherson while continuing to be paid by and to "draw my rations from government." He estimated the number of Indians "from ten to thirty, but usually there was an average of about twelve." There were "fifty" more who were "good choppers" on the reservation, doing a competent job as far as he could tell. Mr. Hinckley was in favor of the mill and obviously had experience working with both the Indians and the whites who were employed by MacPherson. Mr. Hinckley surprisingly admitted that MacPherson had borrowed "about a thousand dollars" from Mr. Hegenmeyer and from Hinckley. Mr. Hinckley stood in the middle between Agent Ford and the owner/manager of the saw mill, Mr. MacPherson. He had to be careful about not offending Agent Ford; if the Indians were needed for reservation work, that was to have the first priority.

During this short period from about 1853 to 1860, Alexander MacPherson looked for a way to branch off from his position of being just another employee of a large British trading firm to starting up his co-owned independent lumber company. It was obvious to MacPherson that he might become wealthy while developing an industry that would one day employ thousands.

Lyman F. Hinckley's deposition provided concrete information as to how many Native Americans went to work for MacPherson, from ten to thirty, but usually the average was twelve, at the site of the new saw mill. He stated that there were also enough Native Americans to work the fields at the reservation as well during this time. Mr. Hinckley employed "eight or nine white men, who were paid by Mr. MacPherson" at the same time he supervised the work of the Native American wood choppers. The number of Indians who chopped wood for the mill varied but Hinckley reported that an average of twelve were employed from October 16th to February 7th, about three and a half months of the year.

He concluded that in his opinion the mill work had been good for the Native Americans, a conclusion that others had reached. Subagent Ford had been careful to cover himself with the standing order that no Indian could work at MacPherson's if he was needed for work on the reservation. Mr. Hinckley also contradicted Dr. Ames in saying none of the Indians complained "of suffering from hunger." Mr. Hinckley stated, as did several others, that he did not know whether any liquor was sold to the reservation Native Americans. Thus Mr. Hinckley had the same response as had Subagent Ford about the food shortage.

Continuing with the depositions, William ("Bill") Ray, was head fisherman of the Mendocino Reservation. As reported by Mr. Ray, at least one third to one half of the protein intake of both the white reservation employees and the Indians was derived from the consumption of fish or seafood. This vitally important food source consisted of a variety of fresh water and salt water fish, salmon, cod, halibut, seals and sea lions, scallops, mussels, crabmeat, or other kinds of shellfish. There were two reservation boats: "a yawl" and "a skiff." Mr. Ray added that the saw mill had used his boats. One particular boat was left damaged. Possibly Mr. Ray hoped to be reimbursed for the cost of repair of this boat by the federal government. It is doubtful that this was realized. Both Mr. Ray and Mr. Hinckley remarked that boats were shared between the saw mill and fishing. The head fisherman also explained how a boom across the Noyo River had been erected to move heavy logs from within the reservation across the Noyo River to a landing site near Mr. MacPherson's saw mill on the north bank.

Several points were made by Mr. Ray which add significantly to our understanding of Euro-American-Native American relations. Because he employed individual Native Americans on his boats, Mr. Ray came to know them as well and perhaps better than any other white reservation employee at that time. Mr. Ray believed that the presence of the new saw mill and especially the "boom and logs" actually increased the amount of some of the catch, especially freshwater fish. Mr. Ray added that he thought the amount of salmon caught was less than before the MacPherson mill was constructed on the Noyo River. There were no records kept to either confirm or to disprove his beliefs.

Mr. Ray's supported Chief Matteo's concern about food shortages at the reservation thus contradicting Subagent Ford, Supt. Henley, and others whose testimonies argued that there had been no critical food shortage on the reservation. Chief Matteo was one of the Sonoma Mission Indians who had been forced to go to the Mendocino Reservation after it opened in 1856. It was true that the Indians who tried to go it alone in the inland valleys and forests, as Special Agent J. Ross Browne reported to his superiors in the Office of Indian Affairs on numerous occasions, suffered more than Indians at the reservation from hunger and privation. These so-called "wild Indians," a term used by settlers to describe indigenous natives who were not on reservations, were dying in great numbers from 1845 until around 1900.

A number of the white men who testified made the point that most of the time they thought the Indians were well supplied with food on the Mendocino Reservation. The overseer at Ten Mile Station, Joel Lewis, even went so far as to describe the reservation as an "Indian Paradise." Mr. Ray's deposition, like those of Dr. Ames and others, refuted this view. Some reservation Native Americans had, in fact, starved to death during the spring of 1858. Chief Matteo feared that the food situation was so grave that he confronted Superintendent Henley to ask him for his permission to leave the Mendocino Reservation and return to Bodega. The Native American chief understood the reality of the reservation's food shortage situation better than the any of the whites did. Yet they also lived in fear that if they complained too often or to the wrong person they might be killed. The lack of food in the spring of 1858 was unusual for the reservation, yet Subagent Ford claimed that he didn't know that the Indians were starving. The chief said that if the Subagent Ford doubted that he was telling him the truth he should come to his camp, the Indian rancheria, and see for himself. Subagent Ford could have done more to find out what was really happening but he didn't.

On the next day after testifying Mr. Ray had remembered something important, He went back to the investigators asking them to take a supplemental deposition. He testified that he was "acquainted with G. Canning Smith" and he "heard him say in the office that he had the dead-wood on Col. Henley; that Col. Henley had promised to get him an office and had not done it." While this was hearsay, Ray went on to say that "shortly after this conversation, Smith left the reservation and went down to the City."

Supt. Henley tried to save his skin by promising a promotion to Head Clerk Smith. Henley hoped he could convince Smith to drop his complaint about the overcharging for poor quality cattle and other misdeeds of Supt. Henley that Smith had made to the Commissioner of Indian Affairs in Washington in the spring of 1858.

The next deposition came from Superintendent Henley's Round Valley business partner, William A. Wilsey. As noted earlier, the two men had worked together as ranchers in Missouri before they had immigrated to California. W.A. Wilsey's deposition was short, yet it contained some significant points. Mr. Wilsey basically denied that he and Supt. Henley had any current business relationship, or that they had a kind of so-called "gentleman's agreement" to share profits from cattle-raising or to make money through Supt. Henley's purchasing decisions as the head of California's Office of Indian Affairs. When directly questioned about it near the end of his deposition by Special Agent Browne if he "owned cattle in partnership" now with Supt. Henley, Mr. Wilsey didn't say no. He declined to answer the question. Under the circumstances with the most powerful individual of the Indian Affairs Office in California being investigated for fraud it must have been obvious that Wilsey purposely was hiding damaging material from the investigators.

It was August 16, 1858. By this time, the late summer of 1858, it was abundantly clear to Bailey and Browne, the two special investigators, that Mr. Wilsey and Supt. Henley shared a close business relationship. The questions he was asked weren't technically difficult to answer and were really fairly straightforward. Despite this, Mr. Wilsey refused to answer and his evasiveness was suspicious. Four times in his brief deposition he declined to answer or give any details of his business dealings with Supt. Henley. He denied that he and Supt. Henley were business partners while refusing to state whether or not he took care of Supt. Henley's San Mateo herd "on shares." To the question about "five hundred head of cattle now in Nome Cult Valley," once more, Wilsey "declined to answer."

Following Mr. Wilsey was former Head Clerk G. (George) Canning Smith, the whistle blower. In what was one of the most dramatic testimonies in this extensive investigation, he was questioned by Browne about the alleged promise, amounting to a bribe by Supt. Henley to Smith for a promotion. Of Henley it was said that he would "use his influence" to get a lucrative job for Smith. When questioned by Browne, Smith declared that he "did not accept" the offer. Furthermore Smith said that he was told that he could resign his current post in anticipation of the promotion and Supt. Henley would "provide for me in the meantime."

Head Clerk Smith was the first, and the only reservation employee with the courage to directly challenge Superintendent Henley by sending his report critical of Supt. Henley to the Office of Indian Affairs in Washington in the spring of 1858. Supt. Henley attempted to force Mr. Smith to retract his charges with the promise that Smith would receive the position of Collector of Customs at Big River. The head clerk's decision to bring this to the attention of the OIA marked a turning point in early California's reservation system history for it sent a message throughout the nation that the Office of Indian Affairs would step in to enforce a fairer standard of honor and behavior for its officials. Interestingly enough apparently someone had stolen the list of charges from Head Clerk Smith's office. That person probably supplied the charges to Supt. Henley soon thereafter. Regardless of who it was, Smith stated that he "never informed Col. Henley of my intention to make these charges." Smith said that "Capt. H. L. Ford prepared to sue on the part of Col. Henley that I should retract the charges." And that if the head clerk did so, "Col. Henley would use his influence to obtain the post of Inspector of Customs at the Big River. I did not accept the proposition."

What followed was a verbal duel, under oath, between Superintendent Henley and Head Clerk Smith. Smith steadfastly refused to give up his right to speak in his own defense. His testimony to a great extent hinged on whether or not

Agent Ford had been truthful when he talked to him about the promotion. If Superintendent Henley thought he could badger Mr. Smith into changing his mind about the charges once the pressure was on, he was sadly mistaken. Smith stuck to his guns and would not back down.

Head Clerk Smith stated that Agent Ford had told him it was Supt. Henley's wish that he go to San Francisco to apply for the promotion. Special Agent Browne asked "[Did] Col. Henley a day or two after you arrived in San Francisco in April, go with you into the office of the Collector of Customs [Col. B. F. Washington] and recommend you for the appointment of Inspector at Big River?" The head clerk answered yes. This was the end of the questions regarding the customs appointment. The questioning then turned to the time before Mr. Smith was employed at the Mendocino Reservation. In 1854 Smith had been elected judge in western Mendocino County. He refused to answer a series of questions about his work as judge or Justice of the Peace by Supt. Henley

After the investigation Supt. Henley might have been able to retain his position, but the facts bore out most of Mendocino Reservation's Head Clerk G. Canning Smith's charges. No quick fix could remedy the serious problems that had developed at many of the Northern California Indian reservations. The so-called "Mendocino Indian War (1858–1860)," between Indians and the Eel River Rangers, had begun on the outskirts of Nome Cult Farm (Round Valley Indian Reservation) and on the banks of the three branches of the Eel River. Simultaneously, a broader conflict, "General Kibbe's War" (also sometimes called "Red Cap's" Conflict), broke out across the entire northern portion of the state, from the Sacramento Valley near Red Bluff in the south to Humboldt County in the northwest including Native American tribes as far east as Susanville. California's Indian warriors made a futile effort to defend their freedom and prevent their many tribes and tribelets from being "relocated" onto the reservations.[107]

Unfortunately conditions did not improve at the Mendocino Reservation. So much federal money had been expended in vain that at last, late in 1866 the Office of Indian Affairs started the process of closing this early northern coastal Mendocino reservation. The federal government forced most remaining Native Americans to march over fifty miles northeastward to Round Valley high in the Coastal Range (the Mayacama Mountains) near to the Tehama/Mendocino County Line. It was about a fifty-mile trek through dense redwood forests, lush valleys that had been the homelands of some of the Indians, and, finally, dry, rough terrain to Round Valley. After the relocation of all of its Native American residents, Mendocino Reservation's structures were sold off to nearby Euro-American set-

---

107 J. Ross Browne, "The Indians of California," *New Harper's Monthly Magazine*, 1861, 28, as quoted in J. Ross Browne's, *Crusoe's Island: A Ramble In The Footsteps Of Alexander Selkirk with Sketches of Adventure in California and Washoe*, New York, Harper's Brothers Publishers, Franklin Square, 1871, republished by The University Of Michigan, University Library, 300-301.

tlers. The money so raised was to be used to help buy supplies and equipment at Round Valley. Actually little money was made from the sale of the deteriorating structures.

The last depositions took place in San Francisco. Horace Maloon, a San Francisco resident and San Francisco Mint employee, an acquaintance of G. Canning Smith. corroborated Smith's testimony providing specific details. He contended that Spec. Agent Browne backed the scheme for the promotion of Smith.

For a time in 1858 Special Agent J. Ross Browne had to handle himself with discretion. Since his own position might be cut or any change in the political situation might lead to his being replaced. Canning Smith was pressuring Special Agent Browne to try to enlist his support to obtain the Collector of Customs (or Inspector) post. Smith knew that this post would have paid him about double what he had been paid as Mendocino Reservation's Head Clerk. For several reasons Special Agent Browne put Smith off rather than be forced to make any promises that he couldn't keep or that might weaken Browne's own position as a secret Special Agent of the Office of Indian Affairs.

Henley had made serious mistakes in judgment such as letting the food supplies get so short at the Mendocino Reservation that the Native American wards died of starvation. He had also used his position to build a saw mill that helped enrich one particular settler (Mr. MacPherson) at the same time it returned almost nothing to the reservation or to the government. He had pawned off a second rate herd of livestock brought over from Nome Cult Farm (or Round Valley Reservation) and gotten back full price from the federal government. Several employees (Davis, J. Henley, Kinsley, and, to some extent, even Subagent Ford) had now formally testified that the cattle were not worth full price.

The investigation moved onto San Francisco with James Tobin as the next witness. At this time Tobin wore many hats: Indian agent, prominent San Francisco merchant, guide to an army detachment of approximately twenty Army soldiers to Fort Bragg, and a frequent hunting companion to J. Ross Browne. In one of Browne's humorous writings about their yearly hunting foray, he nicknamed Tobin "Uncle Toby." Another famous member of the Rangers was Texas Ranger and Mexican War hero Col. Jack Hays. Browne immortalized them all in a revealing booklet, *The Coastal Rangers.*

Mr. Tobin reported that Mr. Smith had told him that he was angry with Supt. Henley since the superintendent had cheated him out of the Treasury Department post. As a result, he promised Mr. Tobin that he "would do his utmost to be revenged. Tobin noted that he "prefer[ed] not to use his exact language as it is not fit for ears polite."

Special Agent Bailey questioned Tobin as to why sub vouchers were not filed along with those used by Mr. Dodge. The voucher system allowed the federal government to check to be sure that its funds were being spent honestly. Sometimes these receipts constituted the only way for the Office of Indian Affairs to check up on the distribution of its funds.[108] Mr. Tobin was rightfully proud of the fact that he and Mr. Dodge had co-operated in San Francisco in running a successful business that "bought and sold to all the world." Mr. Tobin had made it a point to single out G. Canning Smith for criticism.

The summer of 1858 was nearly over. Nights were getting longer and cooler and even the daytime temperatures were dropping. The two special federal agents, J. Ross Browne and Goddard Bailey, must have been relieved that their trip to northern California and their recording of formal testimonies was almost over. The alder, buckeye, and willow leaves were turning and beginning to fall. Special Agent Browne and Special Agent Bailey realized that it was time for a change.

In the last deposition San Francisco resident John H, Wise testified about the relationship of Special Investigator J. Ross Browne and Supt. Henley. The two men had locked horns before. Wise reported that Browne had remarked, "Either I or Henley must go overboard." Again Mr. Wise confirmed that Head Clerk G. Canning Smith had made "very strong" charges against Superintendent Henley. Following this deposition were two vouchers signed by Subagent Ford for the purchase in San Francisco of potatoes. These records along with all of the original dated depositions resided under the heading "Letter Received by the Office of Indian Affairs" at the National Archives in Washington.

These seemingly innocuous vouchers shed further light upon the superintendent's misdeeds. Like the future prices of pork bellies in Chicago, cotton in New Orleans, or gold in San Francisco, the largest traders or bankers controlled the price of potatoes in San Francisco. Potato growers from the Santa Cruz to Mendocino often had to leave their potatoes to rot in their fields for the price might drop below a certain minimum.

Two vouchers were for potatoes purchased in the spring of 1857. They demonstrated once more that Superintendent Henley had mismanaged the business of his federal department. First there was a receipt to Eugene Kelly and Co. for $257.50 for clothing on July 17, 1858. The next two receipts proved that Supt. Henley, through Subagent Ford, had been buying potatoes in San Francisco instead of locally from Mendocino County. On April 1, 1857 Ford had bought 2,697 lbs. of potatoes at 3 cents a pound. On May 9, 1857 he also had bought 4,525 lbs. of potatoes and paid $2,535.75.[109] In these two transactions the federal government's money was paid to R.K. Dodge, the same man who later became the sole

---

108 Details about these events may be found either in Estle Beard and Lynwood Carranco's 1981 work, *Genocide and Vendetta: The Round Valley Indian Wars of Northern California* (Norman, University of Oklahoma Press) or in my more recent *Killing for Land in Northern California Indian Blood at Round Valley 1856-1863* (New York, Algora Publishing, 2005), reprinted 2006.

109 Potato voucher #17 and potato voucher #18, April 1, 1857 and May 9, 1858, *ibid.* 0416-0418.

storekeeper at the Mendocino Reservation. Mr. Dodge enriched himself at the expense of the federal government.

The Office of Indian Affairs rarely replaced any of its white employees once they were in office, whether it was its agents, sub-agents, superintendents, or other employees even if they were suspected of double-dealing or other forms of fraud. Despite the fact that it wasn't easy to find qualified replacements, by the beginning of 1859 the California public had become outraged through newspaper articles about Supt. Henley's misdeeds and malfeasance in office. In the late spring of 1859 Supt. Henley was informed of the impending change. His replacement, James V. McDuffie was told that he was being promoted. During May of 1859 Superintendent Henley was relieved of his duties. While conditions did not improve sufficiently under Supt. McDuffie's term of office for the next two years, the Mendocino Reservation enjoyed a somewhat more productive year in terms of its crop production in 1859.

In the meantime lumber mills were being built throughout northern California coastal areas so rapidly that by the mid 1850s it might be compared with the Gold Rush itself. Reservation trees were cut down by reservation Native Americans at almost no cost to anyone except to the underpaid Indians. The resulting lumber products, shingles, boards or other wood products were transported by means of government-owned boats to Fort Bragg where they were loaded on board oceangoing ships that carried them to such ports as Sydney, Hawaii, Portland, Seattle, Los Angeles, San Francisco, or Canton or Hong Kong, China.

Virgin old-growth redwoods produced the massive beams that, to this day, act as the primary supports for many fine San Francisco and southern California Victorian homes and other structures. Some of this wood came from redwood trees that had survived for centuries on land that became part of the Mendocino Indian Reservation.

*

Within a few years after the investigation of Superintendent Henley, Goddard Bailey held the position of clerk at the Office of Indian Affairs Headquarters in Washington DC. During the summer of 1860, Bailey was involved in a scheme that involved his stealing some bonds from the department's Washington safe. The plan was to take the bonds to a bank and obtain a loan for the value of the bonds. Bailey was then to hand over the money to William Russell of Russell, Waddell & Majors.[110] This firm was one of the largest freight hauling companies in the nation. Russell, Waddell & Majors fulfilled contracts with a great many of the US Army's far-flung forts throughout the west in pre-Civil War years. However, due to some delays in payment by the Army, Russell, Waddell & Majors had

---

110 Russell, Majors & Waddell was the freight company that founded and ran the first pony express company. The story of the pony express and this remarkable company has been told in a recent book authored by Christopher Corbett, *Orphans Preferred The Twisted Truth and Lasting Legend of the PONY EXPRESS*, New York, Broadway Books, 2003.

fallen deeply into debt in 1860 and needed money to maintain its operations and pay its thousands of teamsters.

This scheme might never have become a national scandal if the bonds had retained the same value, or, at least, if they had not increased in value. All of the stolen bonds had to be returned to the Office of Indian Affairs' Washington safe before the end of calendar year 1860, or the plan would be exposed with Bailey (and possibly also Russell) going to prison. The problem was that rather than decrease in value, as Bailey and Russell had hoped, the bonds had increased in value before the end of the 1860—which meant that the company would have had to come up with more money at the end of the year to secure the bonds from the bank that made the loan to clerk Goddard Bailey in September 1860. At the end of the year knowing the game was up, Bailey reported his crime to the Commissioner of Indian Affairs. The Commissioner had no choice but to fire Bailey and reveal the facts about the theft to the press and to Congress.

As a result of the discrepancy and fraud, as soon as it became public, Congress began a full highly publicized investigation. Already severely weakened by its failure to obtain many weapons from government arsenals across the South before these arsenals were one by one taken over by southern states, the Buchanan Administration, in January 1861, in a lame duck mode of operation, now had a second ominous and ugly scandal on its hands. Goddard Bailey eventually was tried and went to prison. President James Buchanan is recalled by most historians as the weakest president in the history of the United States.

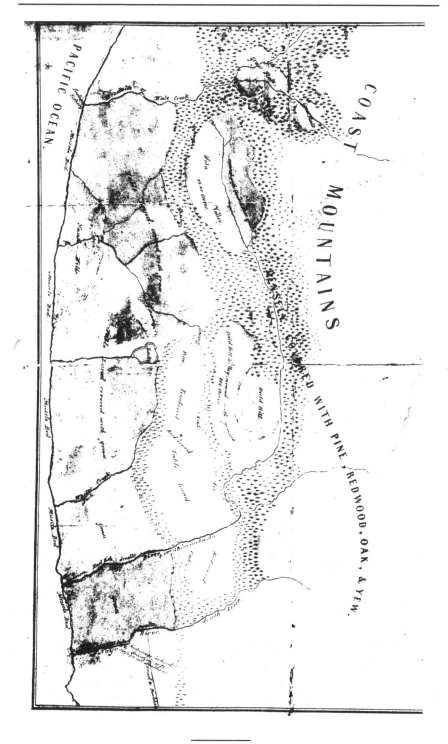

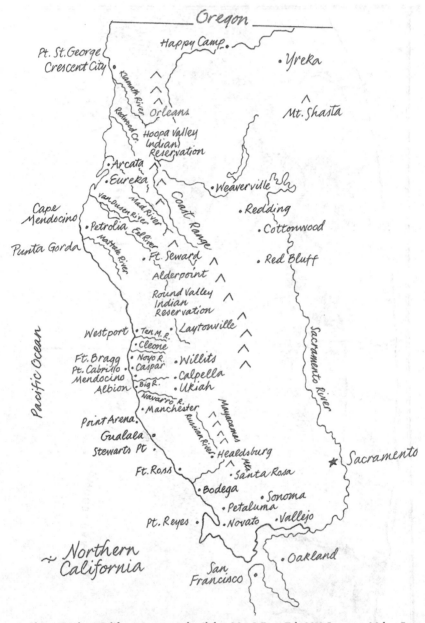

Above: Northern California in greater detail than Map 1. Date, Feb. 2010, Jeannette Mahan Baum-gardner and Ms. Barbara Harris.

Previous Page: The original map of Mendocino Reservation, "National Archives, Washongton, D.C.", date ca. 1854. Northern border at Hale Creek. Note the term, "Indian Fisheries," near Hale Creek's outlet. The northern border was set at the Noyo River. This early map's limits correspond roughly with Fort Bragg's City Limits, especially on the Noyo. Courtesy of Noyo Hill House, Ft. Bragg, CA.

Oxen team transporting heavy logs down a ravine. Date, unknown, possibly late 1880s. Courtesy of Guest House Museum, Ft. Bragg, CA,.

Above: Anchored schooner in Mendocino Bay at the outlet of Big River. A lumber loading apron chute extends from the bluff on the right. Source: Kelley House Museum, Mendocino, CA.

Below: "The wooden schooner, "J.C. Ford," loading lumber under chute in Mendocino Harbor. The J.C. Ford was build in San Francisco in 1882. It was a three-masted single deck schooner with a wooden hull, 123 ft. x 31 feet x 10.3 ft. and could carry 243.61 gross tons, ca. 1885. Courtesy of Kelley House Museum, Mendocino, CA.

Above:: An unknown group of Chinese workers paused to propose a toast beside the Caspar Lumber Company. Many Chinese worked as cooks in northern California mills. Source: Kelley House Museum, Mendocino, CA.

Left: The hill, upper left, is "Medicine Point" located in the northwestern portion of Round Valley. L to R: Sam Young, Edith Van Allen Murphy, Lucy Rogers-Young when Lucy was 90. 1941, Covelo, CA. Courtesy of Beard, Robert J. Lee Photo Collection, Held-Poage Historical Research Library, Ukiah, CA.

Left: Fur trader, date and source unknown. Courtesy of Bancroft Library, University of California at Berkeley, Berkeley, CA.

Below: "Moving Day, Camp Number 2, Albion Lumber Company. Date, unknown. Courtesy of Noyo Hill House, Ft. Bragg, CA.

Left: Etta Stevens Pullen. Date, unknown, ca. early 1870s. Etta Stevens, age 16, emigrated from central Maine to Little River, Calif. in 1864. She left her home in Maine with father, Isaiah along with two other sisters, and her stepmother, Rebecca. Source: Kelley House Museum, Mendocino, CA,

Below: Postcard depicting the wharf at Albion in 1897. Lumber from the mill was hauled on railcars to the end of the wharf where a crane loaded it onto schooners. First published by Nicholas Wilson, Jon Newgard Collection in the Kelley House Museum, Mendocino, CA.

CHAPTER 11. MENDOCINO COAST SETTLEMENT TAKES HOLD

> Tom Hoe, head cook at the Albion cookhouse, and who has been cooking at various places on the coast for the last twenty years, had his heart gladdened last Sunday morning when his wife gave birth to a little 'China girl.'
>
> —*Mendocino Beacon*, February 22, 1913

On June 6, 1849 Alexander Wentworth MacPherson, a young Scotsman with extensive experience working for a large trading company, jauntily leapt from the deck of a ship from China onto San Francisco's Embarcadero. He was destined to found the forerunner (MacPherson and Wetherbee) of the mighty Union Lumber Company of Fort Bragg. The young businessman had been born in Inverness, Scotland in 1822. Hired in 1842 by Jardine, Matheson & Co. as a management trainee, MacPherson had worked in the Far East from 1843 through 1848. Throughout the 1830s Matheson and Company, a large Scottish trading firm, then the world's largest company, had profited from operations in Asia. Jardine, Matheson, and Company, also developed the China trade which brought opium grown in India by ship into Chinese ports like Canton and Hong Kong. One of its foremost American rivals was Augustine Heard's Yankee firm, which also owned a fleet of sailing ships, based in Boston, Mass.

It was Alexander MacPherson who built the first saw mill north of the Noyo River. While neither the US Army's Fort Bragg nor the Mendocino Indian Reservation survived, MacPherson's saw mill and the giant company he founded with government help certainly did. By the early 1890s it was the dominant company on the north coast, if not in northern California.

As whole crews of seamen were jumping ship at San Francisco to travel up to the High Sierra gold mines, MacPherson arrived in California with orders to buy or lease San Francisco real estate. The company sought lots and warehouse space to use for the storage and distribution of imported goods to be sold in San Francisco. A year or two after his arrival in San Francisco, MacPherson wooed and married a Peruvian-born woman, Petrita Gonzales. She was ten years younger than he. With her bilingual skill, extremely practical in a region greatly influenced by Hispanic culture, and with pale blue eyes, charming manners and light brown hair, Petrita was an excellent match for this handsome, polished and ambitious young Scotsman.

Using money extended to him by his company and also by another early northern California settler, William Richardson (Richardson's Bay), in 1852 MacPherson leased his first tract of Mendocino coastal timber land near the Albion River south of Jerome Ford's mill on Big River. In 1854 he installed the north Mendocino coast's first steam-powered mill with a sash saw on the Albion River. It had a modest output capacity of four thousand board feet per day. This was a technological advance over older saw mills already operating in northern California.

Two years later in 1856 the addition of a large circular saw more than tripled the daily capacity of MacPherson's mill to fourteen thousand board feet per day. Not too proud to accept a helping hand for a short time when MacPherson first moved to the north Mendocino coast MacPherson had shared quarters temporarily with Lt. Horatio Gibson at Lt. Gibson's officer's residence on Ft. Bragg.

As noted above, during a critical, three-year period, 1857 to 1860, Mr. MacPherson was building his first his saw mill and establishing his lumber company. Subagent H.L. Ford followed Superintendent Henley's instructions to provide MacPherson with Indian labor. Lt. Gibson's soldiers also assisted him in the process. MacPherson's connections and company influence put him on the inside track when it came to recognition by the California Legislature. In 1859 the Legislature passed a bill that recognized MacPherson as the only one authorized to build a wharf at the mouth of the Noyo River to the Pacific Ocean. This important piece of California legislation allowed him to charge ship owners for use of the Noyo River wharf. It was an additional source of income for MacPherson to use in acquiring more timber properties. Although many privately owned fishing and pleasure boats use the harbor located just below the present Highway 1 overpass, MacPherson's wharf no longer exists. Today, perhaps about at the same site near the original saw mill and wharf, the U.S. Coast Guard maintains a small station with two cutters and a smaller rescue speedboat.

In 1864, Alexander MacPherson, with his new partner Henry Wetherbee, bought out the share in the saw mill originally owned by Jardine, Matheson and Company. Henry's job was to establish and run a San Francisco sales office while MacPherson continued to manage the Noyo River saw mill. Together they had founded what soon grew to be the largest lumber mill company on the north Mendocino coast. By the end of the 1860s MacPherson and Wetherbee had three mills in operation, two at the Noyo and one on the Albion. Each year brought in more experienced lumberjacks, many of whom were Irish, Canadian, English, or Scandinavian immigrants, to cut the redwood trees and transport logs to the mills at the Albion, Little River, Big River (The Mendocino Lumber Company), the Noyo and other independent mills like the Casper Lumber Company. There were also more Americans who resettled on the north coast. During the years after 1864 four more lumber mills sprang up on the Albion River flat with the last one opening in 1902. There were more than eighteen different mills scattered along numerous streams and rivers along the north Mendocino coast. Some of their names were Albion, Alpine Hill, Caspar, Cleone, Ft. Bragg, Glen Blair, Greenwood at Elk, Handy Creek, Little River, Mendocino, Navarro, Noyo, Rockport, Salmon River, Usal, Wager Creek, Wending/Navarro, and Westport.

Chinese emigrants also played a key role in the development of the lumber industry on the North Coast. In 1867, William Kelley sold a 33' by 80' lot on Albion Street for one hundred seventy dollars in gold to "Ah Sy" or "Mr. Sy." According to Ms. Bear's article, when the name Eli Wa Sing's name was written on the 1868 Mendocino City street map, this name was a "representative of a larger cooperative group." Three years later, in 1871, Ah Sy deeded the property over to another Chinese-American, Chong Sung.

Another well-known North Coast pioneer Chinese-American was Charles Li Foo. According to his obituary in the *Mendocino Beacon* (April 9, 1898) Mr. Foo arrived on board a ship headed by Capt. Brown from China in 1865. Foo's first job was working as a lumberjack. As a member of crew there was an accident. A large tree pinned Foo to the ground with the tree mangling one of his legs. He was found trying to amputate the leg with a pocket knife. Somehow despite excruciating pain Foo returned to work. By 1871 Foo trained and became a barber. In 1871 his name was listed as a hairdresser in the Pacific Coast Business Directory. According to the *Mendocino West Coast Star* (July 3, 1874), Charles Li Foo's wife, of Cuffey's Cove, had been arrested by authorities for "lunacy" and had been hospitalized in an "asylum." The next newspaper mention of him came on May 4, 1878 in the *Mendocino Beacon*'s advertisement:

> Charles Li Foo, Cuffey's Cove,
>
> California. Barber Shop and Bath
>
> House, Hot and Cold Baths at All
>
> Hours. Also Dealer in Fruits, Nuts
>
> and Confectionery. My motto:
>
> Please Customers.

Names of north Mendocino coast communities sometimes changed. Mr. Foo's barbershop was in a shop on Main Street in Greenwood (now Elk). Like many of the other structures in the Albion-Little River area, this building was owned by the L.E. White Lumber Company. The shop was located at the north edge of a gulch that is called Li Foo Gulch. Also at Cuffey's Cove, Choy Yan Fook (aka James Kenny) worked for so many years at a lumber loading chute for James Kenny's Lumber that he earned the American name out of respect.

After a saw mill began operating at Gualala ("Wa-ha-la") in 1862, Ah Bing was the engineer for the Gualala Logging Railroad Company. He was an excellent mechanic who kept the rolling stock in top shape. In 1990 local historian Ms. Dorothy Bear described him as "a husky fellow who spoke excellent English and dressed in American clothes." His last local run was on Engine No. 4 in 1926. He later moved to San Francisco and eventually journeyed back to China. Charlie Dock emigrated to Gualala in 1868 where he ran the general store for more than thirty years. He lived in the area for sixty years until he died in 1928.

There was a lumber mill that operated at the outlet of the Garcia River just north of Point Arena from 1869 to 1894. Notes written by Nannie Escola, and quoted in Ms. Bear's article (D. Bear and David Houghton, *The Chinese of the North Mendocino Coast*) stated,

> Mr. Russell Stevens made the roller chute at the Garcia. A China-man contracted to furnish Chinamen to float lumber down the flume and to keep the lumber from jamming in the flume. There was a China camp up river, but after the mill burned and the flume used for [railroad] ties the Chinamen were let go.

Almost every saw mill on the North Mendocino Coast employed Chinese cooks who served tens of thousands of meals to mill workers. As was the case in staffing crews who manned the schooners, the variety as well, as the quality of the food, served at a mill were important to the workers who, year in and year out, provided the muscle to accomplish the work needed to continue to grow the lumber industry. The Albion Lumber Company on the Albion River and Alexander MacPherson's Noyo Lumber Mill were no exceptions. Despite four fires that destroyed the Albion Lumber Company, for each of its eighty years of operation (from the early 1850s to the mid–1920s) its cookhouse beside the river provided thousands of meals to its workers.

Mendocino's daily newspaper occasionally mentioned members of its Chinese-American community. On February 27, 1913, the *Mendocino Beacon* reported:

> Tom Hoe, head cook at the Albion cookhouse, and who has been cooking at various places on the coast for the last twenty years, had his heart gladdened last Sunday morning when his wife gave birth to a little 'China girl.' Congratulations from Chinese all over the coast were received and Tom is a proud man.

Lee Sing John, the founder of the Hee family, cooked at the Caspar Mill cookhouse. William H. Kelley and Richard Rundle had founded the Caspar Lumber Company on Caspar Creek in 1861. It became the longest lasting independent lumber mill on the North Mendocino Coast. The Caspar Lumber Co. also employed another fellow named Wah Bow as its head cook at Camp No. 1 cookhouse.

Beginning in the 1880s many Chinese began working for Calvin Stewart's newly established Ft. Bragg Lumber Company. They were steady workers who acquired excellent work records. Many of them were welcomed to live in Ft. Bragg's Chinatown, an area of central Ft. Bragg that centered on Redwood Street in the first two blocks east of Main. As the Gay Nineties progressed, the Chinese community grew in numbers and in influence. Taught by Ms. Laura Nelson, a Ft. Bragg private school serving the Chinese community opened in 1890.[111]

Redwood and fir logs went from remote groves to the lumber mills with the help of the first Chinese immigrants on the north coast. As more Douglas fir and redwood logs were cut further away from the mills on the seacoast transporting them to the mills became increasingly difficult. As the largest stands nearer the mills were cut down, the loggers had to move further and further inland through rugged terrain. Oxen teams equipped with chains dragged the logs over rough trails to the mills. The lumberjacks learned that the oxen would not tire so quickly if the crews constructed skids over which logs could be rolled. As time went on water tossed on the skids would accelerate the process of moving logs. Buckets containing water were tossed onto the skids by "water-slingers" who usually but not always were Chinese workers. Work like this was back-breaking labor for the crews who had to lift and carry heavy wooden buckets filled to brims with water. As previously noted Mendocino Reservation Indians helped to cut the trees and transport them across the reservation property on logging crews. Oxen, horse, or mules were employed in moving the logs along a so-called "sled." In many cases steep ravines with heavily forested banks impeded the work. Before arrival of the railroad after 1900 lumber crews employed large teams of many pairs of oxen.

Native Americans weren't the only ethnic group that suffered from discrimination and, at times, from overt persecution. Two Chinese-Americans, Lee (Ling)

---

111 See "The First Steam-powered Sawmill," Dorothy Bear, copyeditor, *Mendocino Historical Review*, IV, No. 2, Mendocino Historical Research, Inc., Mendocino, CA, 1974.

Sing John and Eli Tia Ky (or Key), were featured in Dorothy Bear's locally published account (1990). Lee Sing John might have been one of the survivors of the *Frolic* shipwreck in the summer of 1850. He achieved almost legendary status in the area. He worked as one of the cooks in the lumber mill at Caspar. The other man, Eli Tia Ky, worked as the cook at Dan Milliken's mill later on in the years just before 1890.

Perhaps the first commercially successful, stand-alone Chinese-American family business on the North Mendocino Coast belonged to the Look family. Eli Look was listed in census records (He was listed in the Big River District.) in the year 1870. The name recorded was "Ah Key," which was a due to the census officer's mistake. "Ah" in Chinese meant "Mr." or "Mrs." The actual name of the person thus recorded was that of the early Mendocino store owner, Eli Tia Key, with the Eli being the family name. The Look family of Mendocino City started with Eli Tia Key, his wife, Su Wang, and their four children. An 1874 ad in the *West Coast Star*, appeared in the following way:

Eli Tia Key, DEALER IN,

Cigars, Tobacco, Rice, Tea,

Boots,

Shoes,

Clothing,

Matting,

Etc, Etc.

MAIN STREET, MENDOCINO.

The Look family maintained the store until Tie Kie sold out to a man named Lee Tin Yow.

The same notice in the *Mendocino Beacon* (January 10, 1881) that indicated the change in store management also stated that soon Mr. Eli would be moving to San Francisco. Despite the notice his two sons, Look Tin Eli and Look Pong-shan (Lee Eli), capably ran the Mendocino store during the early 1890s. The same two men later held important positions in the Russo-Chinese Bank of San Francisco. The elder son, Tin Eli, was the bank's "confidential advisor," the one responsible for handling nearly all of the bank's business with Chinese at home and in China.

Continuing to work together, in 1906 the brothers co-founded the first Chinese bank in the United States, the Canton Bank of San Francisco. Tin Eli was employed in San Francisco by the Sing Chong Company, a lucrative importer of Chinese and Japanese goods. In 1915 Mr. Eli founded the successful Chinese Mail Steamship Company.

By 1875 the population of Chinatown in San Francisco was approaching fifty thousand. While some tongs or brotherhoods of Chinese men were merely fraternal groups, others had an outright criminal nature. It is not surprising that the Chinese in San Francisco as well as in other west coast cities and towns formed fraternal orders or brotherhoods since the Chinese in general were greatly discriminated against. Chinatown in SF became a center for tongs, nineteenth century gangs, which forced many Chinese people to pay tribute or face being killed. Mr. Eli's success in banking made him such a likely possible target on a tong's hit list that he fled for his life to China where he lived out his life.

As we have seen from John Work's and George Gibbs' journals, and Jerome Ford's memoir of the earliest settlements on the north Mendocino coast, Indians played an active role in each step forward. During the 1850s one of the strongest men physically who lived in Northern California was dubbed "Squeaky Charlie." Squeaky Charlie's actual Indian name was *Hi-sho-na-ma* or "man with many scars."[112]Standing well over six feet *Hi-sho-na-ma* weighed in at three hundred pounds. In his prime he was all muscle and never passed up the chance to fight. Frequently he challenged and defeated all comers in feats of strength or fistfights. He may or may not have been a chief, but unfortunately, no one ever recorded what tribe Charlie was from. If he was like most Indians from this area, he was probably from a Mendocino or Sonoma County Pomo tribelet.

The Army responded to reports of settler attacks on Round Valley Reservation by dispatching a company to Round Valley to establish Fort Wright late in 1862. *Hi-sho-na-ma*, who could cover the Indian trails faster than most white men could ride on horseback, became the regular mail courier from Round Valley to the coast. Throughout the 1860s he regularly fought and beat all other male Indians of whatever tribe. There were numerous tales told and retold about his feats of enormous strength and endurance. He regularly traveled the fifty rugged miles from Nome Cult Farm to Mendocino Reservation in less than one day. By 1870 "squeaky Charlie" settled down to life in a Ukiah rancheria. Eventually *Hi-sho-na-ma* died in a fight with George Boxer, another Indian.

A regular shipment of supplies came to Fort Bragg from Sherwood Valley over rugged terrain. Another Indian, who earned the nickname "Muley Jack," often carried the supplies in return for food or for a new shirt. It usually took two strong men to roll one replacement wagon wheel over the coastal hills from Sherwood Valley. On one occasion Muley Jack carried a heavy wagon wheel by himself on his head. For some reason the Ft. Bragg soldiers requested that he wait a while until some other wheels arrived before they paid him with a shirt. Jack

---

112 Dorothy Bear and David Houghton, "The Chinese of the Mendocino Coast," #91, Winter/ Spring, 1990, Mendocino Historical Research, Inc. Box 922, Mendocino, CA, copy on file at Noyo Hill House, Ft. Bragg, CA. Bear and Houghton described the power and terror of San Francisco Chinatown tongs. One tong maintained a 'murderer's death list' on a wall at Dupont and Clay Streets.

---

grew impatient with this. When the others didn't appear, Jack carried the wheel, which he had lifted up again onto his head, halfway back to Sherwood Valley. Finally a group of soldiers on horseback caught up with Jack who asked for the shirt he had been promised. According to the local writer Ms Dorothy Stillmon (*The Long Trail*, 1967) despite being impressed by this feat of strength, the soldiers never paid Muley Jack what they owed him.

Despite the change of leadership in the office of Superintendent of Indian Affairs for California from Thomas J. Henley to James Y. McDuffie in May 1859, there were few real changes at the Mendocino Reservation. Indian women bore the brunt of the abuses from soldiers, the settlers and the reservation employees. One agent (possibly Frank Warren) sold off cattle as the herd increased and used the resulting income to buy more private land for his own ranch instead of turning the funds over to the government. Subagent Simmon P. Storms at Nome Cult Indian Farm in Round Valley as well as other agents at other California reservations also followed this practice.

Indian women had to carry one hundred pound bags of grain from the reservation over fifty miles on rugged trail, across streams and rivers down to Ft. Ross. One of the rancher's employees rode along behind a group of terrified women carrying a black snake whip that was used to goad them along when any lagged behind the others. Just as he had hired Mendocino Reservation Indians as both lumber cutters and teamsters during 1858, A.W. MacPherson, also hired Native American women to carry heavy bales of hay or grain up the Noyo River to the logging camp. Subagent Ford received fifty cents a head for the labor of these Indian women. The Indian women had no choice but to comply without complaint since they faced harsh punishments if they objected in any way.

The continuing financial drain of the Mendocino Reservation finally led to its closure. The actual order to close the Mendocino Reservation came during the spring of 1868. The federal government began selling off all the Mendocino Reservation land as fast as it possibly could to settlers at the paltry rate of $1.25 per acre. The amount of money thus raised was not recorded. Was the small amount of money thus raised used to pay back some of the wealthy Americans who had bought government bonds to pay for the munitions, armaments and Army pay that eventually brought the Confederate States of America to its knees? The answer to the question remains shrouded and almost certainly will never be known.

The Army marched a desolate group of three hundred Indians across Mendocino County to Round Valley Reservation in 1869. There they faced intense competition for food and shelter.[113] Among hundreds of nighttime campfires, some managed to eke out an existence by going back to the wild. Only one thing was clear: Native Californians never saw one cent for the land they had labored for over ten years to clear, build, farm and improve.

---

113 Peggy Stillmon, *The Long Trail*, published by the Mendocino Historical Society, 1967, 34.

One of the white beneficiaries of the dissolution of the reservation on August 1, 1872 was Duncan Mackerricher who, until then had been an employee of the Caspar Lumber Company for about a year. Mackerricher bought six hundred seventeen acres of what was formerly reservation land at the purchase price of one dollar twenty-five cents an acre. About one year later he bought three hundred more acres of ranch land from E.J. Whipple for three hundred seventy-five dollars. The Mackerrichers named their ranch Laguna and later changed its name to Cleone, the Greek word meaning gracious and beautiful. The words might be used to describe all of the North Mendocino Coast.

Meanwhile Alexander McPherson continued running the Noyo River mill and profitably managing the company properties. As one of the City of Fort Bragg's foremost founders and pioneer lumbermen, Alexander MacPherson built a large home on the Noyo River's northern bank. For many years he and Petrita entertained summer visitors and welcomed newcomers to the town in his spacious, well-built house. It was located at the site of the present-day Harbor Lite Motel overlooking the Noyo River, just a few hundred feet northeast of the Highway 1 bridge and of the site of the mill in Ft. Bragg. MacPherson Street is one of the main north-south streets in downtown Ft. Bragg; it is the second street west of Main Street. A.W. MacPherson and his family lived in San Francisco until the couple's children grew up. Summers were always spent at the Noyo River. In 1872, the MacPhersons moved to the north Mendocino coast permanently. It was Alexander's job to manage the Mendocino timber properties. Tragedy struck in 1875 when Petrita died. She was buried in San Francisco. Late in the 1870s, a hostile group of Albion area businessmen led by L.E. White began legal proceedings against MacPherson in order to divest him of his Albion holdings. From the middle of the 1870s legal fees to protect the company began eroding profits.

Early in 1879 one day Alexander apparently had a problem mounting his horse as he was leaving the mill. While he made it home on his horse since it well knew the way, MacPherson suffered a stroke at his house. For more than a year he was unable to speak. He fought off death but finally expired on February 19, 1880. His will specified his burial at a favored site on the bank of the Noyo. Unfortunately, after his burial, the exact site was lost, so that when the family wanted his body exhumed to be placed near that of his wife in San Francisco, the site could not be found.[114]

While Alexander MacPherson was gone, his company, especially the large saw mill on the banks of the Noyo River, continued. It was expanded and added onto in 1885. By the late 1880s many mills were merged together to form the Union Lumber Company, incorporated in 1889. For the next one hundred thir-

---

114 See "General Grant's order, GENERAL ORDERS No. 74- HEADQUARTERS OF THE ARMY, ADJUTANT GENERAL'S OFFICE," Washington, August 24, 1868. Public—100, Donor #43, Ben Booth, Mendocino Coast Historical Society, F-120006-1-99, Box 15, File 3, at Noyo Hill House, Ft. Bragg, CA.

teen years, Ft. Bragg and the redwood lumber industry were almost synonymous. The Wisconsin-born businessman, Charles Russell Johnson, who went by "CR" throughout his fruitful career, headed the company in the first half of the twentieth century. The eventual closing down date for the saw mill and operations of the company, which, at the time, had become a part of the giant Georgia Pacific Corporation, was November 7, 2002. As soon as the mill stopped operations questions remained about what to do with Ft. Bragg's beaches, other land holdings, and one very large building that had been part of the Union Lumber Company.

The postscript to the history of the McPherson saw mill has not yet been written. As recently as the end of 2009 a settlement between the City of Ft. Bragg and Georgia Pacific Corporation was announced that will allow the city to build a walking trail along through the properties owned by the lumber company that will be open, eventually for public use.

CHAPTER 12. "DOGHOLE" SCHOONERS LINK THE MENDOCINO COAST TO THE WORLD, FORT BRAGG BECOMES A CITY

> "Because men were endowed with tenacity, they sailed, but they never won their battle with the restless waves. The sea became a route to discovery, settlement and development of Northern California."
>
> —Ms. Nannie Escola.
>
> "You no scratch, you stay on — you scratch, you get off!"
>
> —Seaman John Valentine

There are many colorful stories about the schooners and small ships that sailed in and out of the Mendocino County coast, the eighty-four mile stretch of the Pacific Coast from Gualala in the south near the Sonoma-Mendocino County to Needle Rock above Ft. Bragg in the north. One of the largest obstacles to settlement and development of this coast was the lack of deep water ports. Schooners had to come in and out of areas no larger than a hole a dog might fit itself into, to turn around and lay down. Thus these small one- to four-masted ships came to be called "doghole schooners."

During the period from about 1860–1908 tiny shipyards within this region produced many "doghole schooners," which were the only form of transportation for the rapidly growing lumber industry. These ships also carried groceries, passengers, hardware, and almost every piece of large furniture needed by residents of the villages, farms and towns in the area. Most shipbuilders simply began their businesses first by telling a lumber tycoon, "Saw me the lumber and I'll build you the ships you'll need to carry your products to market."[115]

Captain Thomas Henry Peterson worked in shipyards in San Francisco and the Puget Sound before getting a call from the Little River Lumber Company to build the first schooner in Little River. He built a total of twelve two-masted schooners at his Little River shipyard. All were less than two hundred tons with lengths varying "from 68 to 115 feet"[116] but broad of beam to carry large loads of lumber over short distances.

Peterson also constructed and launched ships in Russian Gulch, Whiteboro, Albion, Mendocino River, Noyo, and Cuffey's Cove. The list of other shipbuilders included John Ross, H.C. Wright, and the Walworth & Reimer (W & R) Company at Point Arena, Fletcher & Bryant as well as Crawford at Navarro River, and Thomas' brother John Peterson and another man with the surname Peterson at Albion. About forty-five sailing ships originated somewhere along the north Mendocino coast almost all of which eventually ended up as shipwrecks along this same coast.

Many kinds of merchant vessels (for example, brigs, barkentines, and schooners) plied the waters and the harbors of the burgeoning hamlets, villages and towns on the north Mendocino coast. Any vessel not propelled by oars is defined as a ship. There were more than eight kinds of sailing ships that played a role in the settlements and the saw mills. The largest type of ship was a so-called "square-rigged ship." It had "square-rigged sails" on all three masts (not shown). The second type was a bark. It had three masts but square sails on just the first two with schooner rig on the last. Next was the brig, with square sails on two masts. A topsail schooner had two masts, schooner-rigged except for fore topmast. Schooners might have from two to as many as seven masts, with regular schooner rig on each mast. Without a doubt the most common type of sailing ship was the schooner. Usually built with two tall masts, the schooner was a highly maneuverable small vessel that carried lumber as well as many other kinds of wood products and other freight.

In her notebook, now at the Kelley House Museum in Mendocino, Ms. Nannie Escola, a dedicated schoolteacher and local historian recorded each schooner's place and date of origin along with the record of many shipwrecks. Escola patiently gathered data from many sources. She noted that on board the schooners a kind of democracy existed; everyone from the captain to the youngest,

---

115 "Fort Bragg's Founding Father, The Forgotten Man of the Mendocino Coast " *The Independent*, Nov. 26, 1980, on file at Kelley House Museum, Mendocino, CA. Referring to the closing of the Union Lumber Company, Denise Stenberg, presently the Director of the Guest House Museum, Ft. Bragg recalls, that is about when it all stopped and then the wrangling about what to do with it began." E-mail to author, October 28, 2009.

116 "Saw Me the Lumber and I'll Build You the Ships," Barney Hekkala, *Journal of the San Francisco Maritime Museum*, no date, on file at Kelley House Museum, Mendocino, CA.

most recently hired crewman had a very difficult and, at times, perilous job to perform. She summarized the place that the ship captains and their crews held in the hearts and minds of most residents of the region.

> [In] past generations, men who sailed the canvas winged wooden craft [did so] out over these bars. [It was] a time when men pitted their courage and knowledge against an always threatening sea. Because men were endowed with tenacity, they sailed, but they never won their battle with the restless waves. The sea became a route to discovery, settlement and development of Northern Calif. For years the people of the area depended on sail ships—later steam—for commerce and prosperity. Everyone knew the skippers and men in the crews.[117]

Ships and schooners that served California's growing coastal populations from Humboldt Bay to San Diego Bay generally were constructed from either Douglas fir or redwood. Before the mid-nineteenth century almost all ships on the West Coast had originated either in Europe or were built at East Coast shipyards. Small locally managed shipyards, such as the one owned by Thomas and William Peterson at Little River, usually constructed schooners. Others originated at larger shipyards in San Francisco, in Washington State at shipyards near Seattle, or at Portland, Oregon.

During the middle of the nineteenth century, lightning strikes were especially fearsome events for seamen and passengers. Nannie Escola wrote,

> Thunder and lightning storms [were] dreaded by seamen at sea, for it is not an unknown thing for vessels to be struck at sea. The lightning striking the top masts, running down the mast and sometimes striking the vessel tearing a hole and if this is below the waterline the vessel is in danger of sinking.

Sometimes even small animals played a role in north Mendocino coastal affairs. During one of the last years of the nineteenth century a Chilean vessel shipwrecked near the outlet of the Navarro River south of the Albion River's mouth. As the ship floundered in the process of sinking, one of the crewmen, John Valentine, scooped up the ship's cat and held it under one of his arms. The water was high and John needed to walk carefully or lose he would his balance in the high water. Placing the cat on top of his head for safety, John said, "You no scratch, you stay on—you scratch, you get off!"

Valentine, who was later known to the people of Ft. Bragg as "Kanaka John," was a local fixture until his death in about 1930.[118] In the next two entries, Ms. Escola described two incidents that damaged yet apparently did not sink the affected ships:

---

117 *Ibid.*

118 From a dedication to a large notebook of news clippings collected, compiled and preserved by Ms. Nannie Escola. Kelley House Museum, Mendocino, CA., June 4, 2008.

Sch. J. C. Ford was struck by lightning at sea.

Lightning storm, Jan. 30, 1858

Sch. Kaluna, 30 hrs from Mendocino with 125,000 ft of lumber- On the 22inst while lying at anchor at which shivered the main top mast which shivered the main top mast and severely injured the main mast.

Recording facts, gleaned mostly from newspaper articles in such sources as the *Fort Bragg Beacon* or *Advocate*, Ms. Escola followed the history of each ship's date of origin, building site, and builder, when and where it was shipwrecked, and who served as captain. The schooners were small ships that were at the mercy of treacherous tides and winds. The north Mendocino coast contains some of the most rugged stretches of coastlines on earth. Among the many common shipwreck sites Fish Rock was the place where the greatest number of ships sunk.

A typical two-masted schooner built by Thomas Peterson at Little River in 1875 was the *Electra*. The *Electra* sailed in and out of Mendocino and Fort Bragg as well as San Francisco, even San Diego, for over twenty years. At just ninety-two tons she was generally highly maneuverable, when there was a wind. On August 12, 1890 the small ship had to be towed into Ft. Bragg by the steamer *Cleone* since it was becalmed outside the port.[119] The *Electra* served the north Mendocino coast until it was shipwrecked in 1894.

The following six schooners were typical of many ships that played an essential role on the Mendocino County's coast by linking its communities to the rest of the world. They were crucial carriers of redwood lumber to ports throughout the world. Note also that many small saw mills, such as The Caspar Lumber Co., usually loaded most of their finished lumber on just one or, in some cases, a few schooners.

Sch Abraham Lincoln – Abe –

Built for H. Richards.

Wrk. Stewart's Point, 1880 – Fisherman's Bay

Took the first load from Uncle Abe's chute — therefore name for chute.

Abby or *Abbey* 200 T 3 masted

Operated by Caspar Lumber Co.

Named for Abbie E. Krebs.

Harry Larson was Captain on her for many years.

Built at Fairhaven, California for J.G. Jackson. 98.5 by 29.5 by 8.3

119 See "Just Around the Corner," Claude A. King, *Ft. Bragg Advocate*, News Feature Page, Nov. 24, 1955. See also Appendix V for more facts about the ships and the schooners that served the north Mendocino coast before 1900.

Schooner Arispe,

  Wrk. at Fish Rock May 26, 1854.

  More vessels wrecked at Fish Rock than any other port on coast.

Schooner Archie and Fontie 95 T

  Built for H. Richardson, Stewart Point and named for his two sons, Archie and Fontaine

  Wrecked at Fort Ross, March 31, 1902.

Sch. Ajax

  Wrecked at Point Arena, May 20, 1868.

Schooner *Barbara* – 2 masted

  Built by Thomas Peterson- Little River — 1877.

  Gross Tonnage 113.02 Net T 107.38

     Length 89 feet

     Beam 28.3 ft.

     Depth of hold — 7.1 ft.

  Named for Barbara Stickney — a 16 year old girl at Little River.

  Wrecked at Shelter Cove — Dec. 2, 1889. *The Beacon*, Dec. 14, 1889, reported,

> The *Schooner Barbara*, Capt. Peterson, parted her lines at Shelter Cove on Dec. 2 and went ashore. Several holes were knocked in her bottom and stern port and rudder are gone. The crew were saved. Dec. 21, 1889. An attempt will be made by the wrecking steamer *Whitelaw* to haul off the Schooner *Barbara*, which went ashore at Shelter Cove on Dec. 2. The schooner is badly damaged but it is thought by Capt. Whitelaw that she can be hauled off and towed to the city for repairs.[120]

As noted above, the *Schooner Barbara* had a gross tonnage of 113.02. Gross tonnage was one of five different kinds of tonnage used to describe sailing ships. More specifically, "gross tonnage applied to vessels not cargoes. It is determined by dividing by 100 the contents, in cubic feet, of the vessel's closed-in spaces. It was used for dry dock charges." On the other hand, the *Barbara*'s "Net T" or "net tonnage" was "her gross tonnage minus deduction of space occupied by accommodations for crew, by machinery, for navigation, engine room and fuel and was used for port charges and canal tolls."[121]

---

120 See the *Ft. Bragg Advocate*, August 13, 1890, from Nannie Escola's Notebook, Kelley House Museum, Mendocino, CA.

121 See a section of Ms. Escola's notebook titled, 'Sailing ships—schooners,' 2, 13, Schooner *Barbara*

Railroads were late in coming to the North Coast. The western edge of the redwood forests in north Ft. Bragg was over two miles east of the coast. Transporting a constant, steady supply of suitable logs for the mills was an issue for the mill owners. One crude little railway grew into an enterprise called the Fort Bragg Railroad and Lumber Company. As a local newspaper, *The Mendocino Beacon*, noted on July 25, 1885,

> This is a large enterprise altogether involving the expenditure of a good deal of money of which the company seems to have plenty at command. The railroad will probably cost a hundred thousand dollars to reach timber enough for the first supply. It will be extended as it shall become necessary to penetrate deeper into the forest.

> Whether it is the contemplation to erect a town at Fort Bragg we are not informed but this we judge to be the natural result. We know of no more inviting spots for a town. It was an educated eye which selected it, thirty years ago for a military post, and it has been the admiration of all passers by ever since. It is a charming plateau extending from the Noyo to Duff River (Pudding Creek, original parentheses) affording ample room for a city of hundred thousand inhabitants.[122]

Unlike the development of the town of Mendocino (or Mendocino City, as most at first called it), which was founded and grew up slowly as an American town, Ft. Bragg had no official name until it was incorporated in 1889 by a group led by Calvin Cooper Stewart. Born in Linn County, Iowa, April 4, 1847, Calvin Cooper Stewart came to the West Coast across the plains with his parents in 1853. After spending short periods of time in Washington and Half Moon Bay, in 1857 the family moved to Stewart's Point, which was named after them. Stewart actually came of age in Vallejo and established a shipping point at Bridgeport, twelve miles north of Point Arena, in 1872. In 1875 two of the Field brothers founded a small saw mill on the North Fork of the Ten Mile River. In 1877 Calvin settled down and marryied Frances Cooper. He and his brother-in-law, James Hunter, rebuilt the Newport Mill. When all was going smoothly, this mill was capable of producing about five thousand board feet daily. It had a double circular saw, a single edger, and a planer. However the outlet to the ocean was too narrow and small to accommodate larger schooners. Mr. Stewart had to start to look for a better site to establish a larger mill.

Shortly after this, in 1882, a Wisconsin-born lumberman named Charles Russell (CR) Johnson bought a part interest in the Stewart firm. It was renamed, Stewart, Hunter and Johnson. "CR" borrowed funds from his father in Michigan and friends in Wisconsin. The company bought a large tract of land from

---

16-17. Kelley House Museum, Mendocino, CA.

122 *Ibid.*

McPherson and Wetherbee. The purchase included the entire site of the Union Lumber Company as well as most of the land included in present-day Fort Bragg. By June of 1884 the company employed thirty-five men and had built a mile long railroad. Logs went to the mill over rails laid on an inclined plane. Horses pulled the empty cars back up to the tops of the hills. Before this cattle or oxen had been used to pull sleds containing the logs to the end of the rail line. A device run by steam called a "steam dummy" took the place of the animals.

The old boundaries of the military post were from the south side of Laurel Street, east from the railroad depot to just beyond Franklin, south along the alleyway to one hundred feet south of Redwood Avenue, west to just beyond the mill's office, then north again to Laurel. The Guest House (Guest House Museum today) was built at the west end of the fort's original boundaries only a couple of blocks from the ocean. A citizens' meeting was held on June 26, 1889. By the vote of 118 in favor to 39 opposed, the motion to incorporate the town passed. Five Trustees, John Randolph, O.F. Westover, Calvin Stewart, Frank Bucholtz, and C.R. Johnson, were elected. At this meeting Mr. Stewart was delegated to draw up the first plans for the city.

During the 1870s A.W. McPherson had bought much of the reservation/military camp's original property up. After McPherson's death, the newly formed company, owned primarily by Stewart and his new partner, C.R. Johnson, took over this property along with more that it purchased later and rebuilt the mill after it burned in 1888. In 1892 Fort Bragg Lumber Co. merged with the Noyo River Mill becoming the Union Lumber Company. After the turn of the century the Union Lumber Company became for a time the third largest lumber company in America.

It was sometimes difficult for observers to follow the rapidity of change taking place everywhere on the West Coast. For example, the Union's future general in charge of all armies in the Civil War, Ulysses S. Grant, made three required visits to San Francisco each year from 1852 to 1854. In his memoirs, the future Gen. Grant recorded how that city went from a raw gold-crazed home of saloons, dance halls, whorehouses, and faro gambling dens to a city he described as 'staid and orderly' upon his final return in 1854. In addition to noting how miners and tenderfoots would end up falling (and then often subsequently drowning to death) through holes in the crudely built, wooden sidewalks along the waterfront, Lt. Grant described how land speculation driven by greed made some rich while most lost everything becoming increasingly bitter and frustrated.

> Besides the gambling in cards there was gambling on a larger scale in city lots. There were sold 'On Change,' much as stocks are now sold on Wall Street. Cash, at time of purchase, was always paid by the broker; but the purchaser had only to put up his margin. He was charged at the rate of two or three per cent a month on the difference, besides commissions. The sand hills, some of them almost inaccessible

to foot-passengers, were surveyed off and sold into fifty *vara* lots—a *vara* being a Spanish yard. These were sold at first at very low prices, but were sold and resold for higher prices until they went up to many thousands of dollars. The brokers did a fine business, and so did many small purchasers as were sharp enough to quit purchasing before the final crash came. As the city grew, the sand hills back of the town furnished material for filling up the bay under the houses and streets, and still further out. The temporary houses, first built over the water in the harbor, soon gave way to more solid structures. The main business part of the city now is on solid ground, made where vessels of the largest class lay at anchor in the early days. I was in San Francisco again in 1854. Gambling houses had disappeared from public view. The city had become staid and orderly.[123]

Growth followed a similar pattern along the north Mendocino coast. In addition to laying out the new city of Fort Bragg's limits, Calvin Stewart was the first president of the Fort Bragg Bank. By 1892 he became restless and again struck out on his own in the tanbark business. Tanbark was in great demand to tan leather. Selling out his share of the Ft. Bragg Lumber Company, Stewart and his brother-in-law James Hunter teamed up with Thomas Pollard and Edward Dodge, who co-owned the Eel River Lumber Company in Humboldt, County, to buy the wharf at Bear Harbor. They also purchased twelve thousand acres of timberland. This large tract extended from the Pacific to the South Fork of the Eel River around Piercy. Calvin Cooper Stewart's career did not end until his passing the age of ninety in 1937 at the town of Perolia.

Part of the story of the West Coast's early cities and towns was the nefarious role played by so-called "red-light districts." Women were not permitted to vote or to be seen smoking in public, yet they were exploited as prostitutes for monetary gain. On the north Mendocino Coast common laborers and lumbermen who supplied the mills with logs usually worked twelve-hour days, six days a week from mid-March through early October. This was followed by a five to six month rainy season. Young men who brought down the big trees, during the dry season each year, day in and day out in a dangerous and always stressful occupation, might be expected to seek feminine company. As is well known, there were far more males in proportion to available females in early California, perhaps until quite late in the nineteenth century. With a shortage of women, especially desirable women of marriageable age and of a like ethnicity, young men sought out the so-called "ladies of the night" to sate understandable human needs. Many men did not wish to marry or to have children within a family due to the possible financial burden involved.

---

123 "Ten Mile Lumber Co. To Move to Ft. Bragg," July 25, 1885, *Mendocino Beacon*, courtesy of Sylvia E. Bartley, "Local History Reference, accessed at Noyo Hill House, August, 2008. The author is also indebted to Mrs. Sylvia Bartley for help with this description of the life of Calvin Stewart.

In the growing town of Ft. Bragg there were at least two places where lumbermen could spend their free time and their hard earned-wages in pursuit of sexual gratification.

The first was actually on a small island just off the coast. It was called "the island of joy." Its owner/manager was a man named Gus West. It was destroyed by a fire in 1921. The second was a block and a half of Redwood Street that was Ft. Bragg's primary "red light district." Before 1900 this area had been Chinatown. As the Chinese moved away seeking to settle in more desirable places in the West, this area became the center for prostitution.

The area extended from an alley located one half block east of Main Street to the east side of McPherson Street, or about a block and a half. A second location was the so-called "island of joy," a one-room shack on one of Noyo Harbor's bluffs. It was owned by Gus West. Ladies of the night entertained customers there nightly until a fire, which was either set or accidentally broke out, destroyed the building in 1921.

Two persons whose names were linked to the first red light district were Maggie Horn and her partner, Rock McMullen. Every visitor to Maggie's house was regaled by Maggie's favorite motto: "For every man, since life began, is tainted with the mire!"

Most of the Chinese-built structures in this part of town today have been remodeled many times over and bear little resemblance today to what they looked like just after 1900. At that time young women who entered a brothel at the tender age of fifteen (more or less) could never go back once they began practicing the "oldest profession." Once in awhile life in the brothel got rough. Rock McMullen would be called upon to pistol-whip a would-be thief or someone who got seriously out of line by physically attacking one of the girls. If a man said, "I'm going down the alley," there was no mistaking what he was about to do.

The houses where the prostitutes plied their trade were modest structures that looked like any other by day. A girl displayed her charms to lumbermen as they entered the front room, or "crib," as it was called in Ft. Bragg. If a man was interested and could pay the price, he would be admitted to the rear of the room where a bed was always ready. Since women were never allowed inside any of the twenty-nine Ft. Bragg saloons, if any of the girls wanted a drink, she had to tell someone in the neighboring crib what she wanted. Word was passed along from person to person until it passed across the end of the alley to the closest saloon. A girl might put in her order in this way, "A bottle of beer and a bag of durham (tobacco)!" The bartenders knew all the girls were who drank or smoked and kept up with their tabs. Just after 1900 whiskey sold for ten cents a glass, beer at five cents a mug.

Occasionally, a particularly alluring trollop dressed up in her brightest finery would attract a crowd of leering men at the front door. Hardly noticed might be a solitary light knock on the rear door.

"One China boy."

"Get out, yousonofabitch! I take no chinks![124]

However, on rather a slow evening with no crowd about, a "China boy" might have been welcomed.

Ft. Bragg's police force consisted of just two individuals: the City Marshal and a night watchman, who were rarely seen in the red light district. Few crimes took place there. Sometimes violence might take the form of a knifing done with finesse and practiced skill. Once, when a French girl was shot three times through the heart, onlookers were heard to say, "She couldn't speak United States." However, this woman had been one of the most sought after, when alive and working. During one or two peak times of the year, Christmas or the Fourth of July, for example, higher-priced talent, usually from San Francisco, needed to be imported to the area.

A humorous episode in Lawrence Vernon's colorful account of the Ft. Bragg red light district, *A Bottle of Beer and a Bag of Durham*, described how Maggie and Rock set up tents near the old racetrack located just north of the Noyo.

> One day, in the midst of the festivities, who should arrive with a span of blacks and rubber-tired buggy, but a well known citizen of the town, and with him, one of Maggie's blonde honeys, dressed in the most egregious and flamboyant of colors. Around the track they sped, not sparing the horses. This caused some real excitement—a regular hubbub! Whistles, shouts, and cries, 'Have another drink, Tom! Go around again, Tom!' In the midst of all the flurry, few, if any, heard the small voice, 'Mommie! Mommie! Who is the pretty lady riding around with our daddy?[125]

Lumber mills provided a steady source of income to several thousand lumbermen. Most men in the lumber industry worked twelve-hour days in the redwood forests, cookhouses, and saw mills. Northern California lumber workers in general, and apparently also on the north Mendocino Coast, didn't join national labor unions like the Knights of Labor. Almost all had to toe a fine line to remain employed. One or two owners of the most successful mills, like William Carson,

---

124 *Personal Memoirs of U.S. Grant*, with a new introduction by William S. Feely, (New York, Da Capo Press, a republication of the 1952 edition, 1982), 105. Random House Webster's Dictionary defined a *vara* as a unit of length in Spanish and Portuguese speaking countries, varying from about 32 inches (81 cm) to about 43 inches (109 cm).

125 See the undated and unpublished article by Lawrence Vernon, "A Bottle Of Beer And A Bag Of Durham," 2. Noyo Hill House, Ft. Bragg, CA. One should not pass so quickly by the matter of prostitution without noting that many prostitutes either had to abort unwanted fetuses in barbaric, dangerous, and unsanitary abortions in which many very painfully lost their own lives in the process.

at Humboldt Bay granted his mill workers a ten-hour day in August 1890.[126] The powerful and sometimes benevolent Mendocino mill owners held power over all of those who they employed. Nevertheless, by 1900 the ten-hour day became the norm. If a man worked twenty-six days, it was considered a month of work. Woodsmen fell into various categories depending on the kind of work performed and were paid accordingly. According to one north coast native, Frank J. Hyman, "Head choppers received $55 a month and board, second choppers received $55 a month, sawyers $45, and 'swampers' $35 to $40." Frank's family charged $12 per person per month for board. Before gas and oil became the home heating of choice, cord wood was used. Each cord of split wood cost from $.90 up to $1.10 per cord, an incredibly low price for one today.

Before the end of the nineteenth century there was a saw mill located at the outlet of nearly every creek, stream and river along the entire eighty-mile North Mendocino Coast. The following lumber mills operated: Gualala, Navarro, Greenwood, Albion, Mendocino, Caspar, Fort Bragg, Glen Blair, Alpine, Iramulco, Cleone, Wages Creek, De Haven, Howard Creek, Juan Creek, Hardy Creek, Rockport, Hollow Tree, Jack Ass, and Usal as well as others. Out of all of these mills, only Rockport and one or two others are still operating today.

The "doghole schooners" played a vital role throughout the nineteenth century and for many years after 1915 when Ukiah and Cloverdale were connected to Fort Bragg by the first full service railroad. The local newspapers recorded the life events of the diverse everyday folks and reflected the times. A Chinese-American cook named Tom Hoe, head cook at the Albion Lumber Company's cookhouse and twenty year resident of the North Coast, had his heart gladdened when his wife gave birth to a "little China girl," and life went on foretelling California's future.

---

126 *Ibid.,* 3.

CHAPTER 13. ETTA & WILDER PULLEN, LITTLE RIVER

> Oh! How hard it is to leave our dear home, friends and loved ones for Cal. and strangers.
>
> —Etta Stevens, age 15, June 20, 1864.

With this thought Etta Stevens opened her diary. It told a story that was typical, in some ways, of many emigrants to California in the mid nineteenth century. At first glance Etta's and Wilder Pullen's saga of locating, settling, and working their family ranch at Big Gulch in Little River from the late 1860s thru 1890, might seem ordinary. Thousands of other settlers made similar journeys about the same time to the far West.

What makes the Pullen story compelling is that Etta recorded everyday events clearly without embellishment or literary flares. Without her poignant record the passage of time would have blurred the truth as surely as the Pacific fog obscures the outlines of the Mendocino Coast. While many of the following quotations come directly from Etta's diary, what follows combines letters and the diary of Gene Sampson, her sister Rachel's diary, Eugene Sampson's letters to Rachel, as well as Etta's story with a few notes by Etta's husband, Wilder Pullen.

Early pioneers to this rugged and inaccessible part of northern California, Charles Pullen and his son, Wilder, had a special gift: a remarkable, unique talent they were able to employ freely without being hemmed in by government regulations as might be the case today. Both father and son were master craftsmen, above average carpenters and millwrights. The father, Charles Pullen, built at least seven saw mills. Wilder was an on-site engineer, a natural born architect whose innate mathematical and carpenter skills were so well developed that many of his works served as models for works of later builders. Wilder's work on roads, dams, fences, and in making furniture can still be observed in a few locations today. Like the central valley's pioneer agriculturalist, John Bidwell, Wilder Pullen was also an intelligent farmer. His farm produced peaches, apples, pears, potatoes, corn and cherries as well as Jersey and Red Poll cattle.

Marriage as an institution has changed to a great degree from the mid-nineteenth century to the twenty-first. In the past marriages were often formed for political and economic reasons and a man and woman often came together from families that had been acquainted for a long period of time. By the start of the second half of the nineteenth century, or the so-called Victorian Era, many married couples had roots that were separate but intertwined. In the case of Etta Stevens and Wilder Pullen, for example, Wilder and Etta probably played together while still young children living in rural Maine. The same was true for Eugene (Gene) Grant Sampson and Etta's older sister, Rachel Stevens, who made their vows on the last day of 1868, a few years before Wilder and Etta married.[127]

As children born in the 1840s all of the above, in addition to Stephen, who was the only Stevens male heir, and Lydia attended the same Quaker Sunday School in Maine. The children may have shared in the wonder of learning Old Testament Biblical stories, like Jonah and the whale or Noah's ark, for example. The three families lived in the same eastern section of rural Maine, a farming region where the family roots went back for a number of generations.

Like many American citizens in all parts of the nation, this small group of Maine farmers experienced a rise in sectional political tensions between the North and the South after 1850. Events such as Bleeding Kansas and the Dred Scott decision contributed to the unrest that in time hastened the start of the Civil War. Early in the spring of 1861, after fighting began in earnest at Charleston, South Carolina, young men throughout New England and the Deep South enlisted to serve for the duration. Gene Sampson, who had turned twenty-one, joined the Navy. Some of his letters of 1863 and 1864 to his seventeen-year-old sweetheart Rachel (Etta Stevens' older sister) have survived the passage of over one hundred-fifty years. Rachel brought them to California in 1864.

During the summer of 1863 Gene and Rachel spent some time together at the Stevens home in central Maine. At this time they were chaperoned by an adult family member who was ever present. Near summer's end, on September 1, Gene went to Boston, Massachusetts. His ship, the *Bark Arthur Pickering,* had to be loaded with cargo. A junior merchant marine officer, Gene Sampson was expected to use not only his mind but also his back to help load the ship. Once in Boston he tried to meet his "Bro Smith," but his brother had just gotten "his appointment to the Navy." Smith already had left for Washington to prepare for an examination "at the Commercial College." Since Gene had been so short of time, he didn't get

---

127 Daniel A. Cornford, *Workers and Dissent in the Redwood Empire,* Philadelphia, Temple University Press, 1987.

a chance to see Rachel's brother Stephen. What Gene noted next possibly interested his future wife, Rachel, a little more.

> O Rachel was I expecting too much when I thought I would see you alone Sabbath Eve and have a good long talk with you. I don't know but I was, although I thought I would for I wanted to tell you how much I was thinking of you Dear Rachel whenever I was in your company this summer.[128]

After sailing to Monrovia in West Africa, Eugene's letter to Rachel on December 13, 1863, reached Hallowell, Maine by way of a British packet, dated February 11, 1864 through Liverpool,

> Dear Rachel,
>
> I hardly know why it is but the time has seemed very long since I heard [from] you, and much longer since I wrote you, only three months ago in Boston and it has been about as long to me since the mail arrived last month as all the time before. From the fact I suppose that I was expecting a letter from you as soon as I got one from home. But not so.[129]

In another letter twenty days later, Gene said he was having trouble complying with her request that he burn her letters after he read them. Their letters said essentially the same thing: just as lovers do today, they wrote of how much they missed each other. Rachel also could not bring herself to destroy his warm letters.

By the winter of 1863–4, the bloody Civil War had been underway in earnest for over two years. Battle after inconclusive battle had been fought. It wasn't at all clear from the press reports, the casualty lists that reported names of the dead, missing, and wounded, the battle reports written by war correspondents, or even from the official military summaries by the generals in charge at the fronts, that the North held a definite advantage. It was capable of refilling the ranks of its armies. On the other hand, the Confederacy was low on capable service personnel essential to continuing the war effort.

It was a frigid winter in south central Maine in 1864. Snow had fallen almost constantly during late January and early February. On February 6, 1864, a group of Farmingdale area farmers, mostly Quakers, huddled beside a snow drift in an open area known locally as 'Railroad Crossing' to see Maine's 30th Regiment, formed up in their dress uniforms, off to war. As Emily Etta Stevens, then fifteen, noted, "They all seemed in good spirits."[130] Her father Isaiah Stevens made a trip on his own to Augusta on February 25 to see the soldiers one last time. Etta listed

---

128 "Gene" instead of "Eugene" will be used in the text. Please see Appendix III for a sampling of poetry by Bret Harte. See also Appendix IV for list of the names of other members of the Pullen family who are buried in the Little River Cemetery.

129 See the file "Letters: Eugene & Rachel Verbatim," provided to author by Ms. Ronnie James, Dec., 2008.

130 *Ibid.*

the names of four of her acquaintances who had either died in combat, in prison camps, or from sicknesses during the bitterly fought Civil War. Etta already had learned most of the skills of a capable seamstress. Two months later she wrote, "I have been knitting but made a square of patchwork for the soldiers today." In the meantime her older brother Stephen was fortunate enough to be granted a leave to briefly return home from active duty.

Etta's biological mother, Mary, had died at age forty-four in 1859, when Etta was ten. Isaiah married Rebecca Coombs, who stepped in to raise and care for Isaiah's six children, Mary Alberta, Lydia, Steven, Rachel, Emily Etta, and Mary Rosilla (Rosie). Everyone in the family had to do some chores on the farm. Like most girls her age at the time Etta had to drive livestock as well as tatting, quilting, cooking, cleaning, picking fruit, and harvesting. Possibly the farm work kept Etta and two of her sisters, Rachel and Mary, from thinking about friends they had grown up with who had already left the Pine Tree State and never returned from the war.

The Civil War had started before Stephen was old enough to enlist on his own. At first Stephen's father Isaiah refused him permission to join the Union Army. On April 27, Isaiah met Stephen, who arrived home on the *Steamer Eastern Queen*. To his sister he seemed "some better" but "looks pale." Stephen was on sick leave. While he was at home he got many calls from old friends. Soon after this, he was well enough to go out and see some of his former friends. Stephen later served in the West in the Cavalry.

Isaiah's brother-in-law Silas Coombs returned in the early summer of 1864, reporting stories of giant redwoods, beautiful valleys and large tracts of virgin land, plentiful jobs and opportunity for all. The Stevens family began to make preparations to leave Maine and immigrate to California. A few days before the end of May, Isaiah sold the farm to Mr. Longley. As the young lady thought about leaving their home, Etta confessed, "Oh! How hard it is to leave our dear home, friends and loved ones for Cal. and strangers."[131] The family planned to begin the journey by steamship down the eastern seaboard, around the southern state of Florida, through the Gulf of Mexico to the Isthmus of Panama, across the Isthmus, and finally re-embarking on another ship sailing north to San Francisco. From there they would have to travel by stage and wagon across one hundred miles of rugged, dangerous mountain trails to Little River.

The Stevens family's decisions might have seemed far removed from battles on land and on sea that determined the course of their nation. Yet in the early summer of 1864, just one day before Isaiah Stevens along with his wife and daughters left their home in Maine on board the *Eastern Queen*, the Union's *Kearsarge* and the Confederate raider *Alabama* met in the English Channel, less than ten miles from Cherbourg, France. The Stevens along with their fellow passengers might have

131 *Ibid.* 2. Note: this author numbered Etta Pullen's diary since it is unnumbered.

become prisoners of the *Alabama* had it been a year earlier, when the Confederate raider earned a place in history as the scourge of Yankee commerce on the high seas, especially in the mid-Atlantic. On Sunday, June 19, 1864, a series of cannon shots from the *Kearsarge* sunk the South's most fearsome warship.

The next day, June 20, Rebecca and Isaiah Stevens, along with his three youngest daughters, Rachel, Emily (or Etta), and little Rosie, boarded the *Steamer Eastern Queen*, bound for Boston. The fourth daughter, Lydia, had chosen to remain in Maine.[132] They arrived in New York and at noon June 23 boarded the *Steamer Northern Light*. Most of the family didn't feel well but the ship made good progress. By June 28, Etta wrote the ship had past "the Bahama Island." Then they were met by a "convoy to guard us from the rebels." She noted passing lighthouses, Cuba and other islands (the Dominican Republic or Haiti?). Their trip was uneventful, except for the death of one crewman, a fireman on June 30th, "killed by some of the machinery and buried at sea in the night." A sailor's life sometimes ended abruptly, with no one to mourn him.

On July 2, they reached "Aspinvall" (Aspinwall, Panama) on the east side of the Isthmus. Fortunately they had a safe trip through the Isthmus. On July 4 the Stevens family boarded another steamer, the *Constitution*. Meanwhile, on that same Independence Day anniversary, Silas Coombs and the Pullen family reached Little River. On July 6 Etta confessed to "thinking of my dear old home tonight."[133] On July 10 they arrived at Acapulco, Mexico. Arriving in California after passing through the Golden Gate they reached San Francisco at noon on July 18. After a short carriage ride over a partially cobble-stoned road, they checked in at the Brooklyn Hotel. The family took a walk and Etta liked the city "pretty well."[134] They made transportation plans and the next day passed through the (San Francisco) North Bay towns of Petaluma, Healdsburg and Cloverdale. On July 21 they were in Anderson Valley. All of the young people got out of the wagon so it could continue moving up over hills. With sympathy for the driver, she noted, "Us young folks had to walk up most hills for two days—just two horses on wagons. Old Bill the driver knew who would walk and kept them on his load if he could." They changed horses at specified stations. Until 1890, Etta steadfastly maintained her diary. She made an entry nearly every week, making her diary an outstanding resource today. Many years later, in 1926, Etta re-discovered her old diary in a drawer. She made occasional notations in it then to clarify the original meaning.

---

132 *Ibid.*, 3. On May 21, Etta wrote "Mr. Longley and his wife came, he has bargained for the farm, Oh, I can't make it seem that we are going away."

133 See "Two 1865 Diaries: Rachel Francena Stevens (Sampson's) (1846-1911) and Eugene Grant Sampson (1840-1885) also dated 1865 Transcribed as written by (Ms.) Ronnie James, Little River, December 2007," unnumbered, p. 33, provided by Ms. James to author, December 2008. Rachel received word of Lydia's death in Maine in mid-December, 1865.

134 *Ibid.*, 4.

She noted, "The Pullen family—Silas and wife, had arrived 4th of July."[135] The weather seemed "beautiful" to young Emily Stevens. On July 25 she noted, "Father, Silas and Wilder went to Albion to get lumber to build Si's house (The Silas Coombs home is now the Little River Inn, still owned by the fifth generation of the Coombs' family)," while Etta and her childhood friend Barbara Coombs "went up in the woods and found hazelnuts." She made many similar entries over the next twenty-six years. "July 26, the Pullen baby taken sick with measles," July 28 the Pullen baby [Katy] gets worse, July 30 "the baby dreadful sick," August 4, the baby died at twelve o'clock noon. Will Pullen came, and finally, August 6, "the funeral was at 10 this a.m."

During the first year at Little River Wilder worked as a lumberjack, cutting timber. Many northern California immigrants began their lives working in lumber mills or as lumberjacks. In September Etta wrote, "Nancy, Jim, Wilde, Barb, and I went out on the prairie (which was a half-mile-swath of clay soil where thousand-year-old trees grew no taller than about ten feet high). We had a pleasant walk, but the woods not pretty like the Maine ones. All the big redwoods, they are wonderful." Also of note that first month after arriving in California, "July 28th, Father went to Big River. Delia and Rachel went down to Albion [on] horseback to see Mr. and Mrs. White. Cal went to Mr. Ford's [Jerome Ford?] at Big River to help care for their new baby."

While she was homesick at first, Etta's mood changed as she pitched in to help with the cooking and other chores. Isaiah started work as the bookkeeper and head clerk for the firm of "Stickney, Coombs, and Reeves." His wife Rebecca became the Head Cook. Her feelings were mixed for some time before and after this, yet, at Nancy's urging, she went to a dance at Albion on Oct. 22. She began to think of all the young "scholars" she knew and almost instinctively wanted to teach them. She really enjoyed going "huckleberrying" in the woods, and noted how they were adding on tables to the cookhouse at Albion. On October 31 they had the first frost of the season.

Soon sixteen-year-old Etta had no more time for brooding about what was left behind in Maine. On November 7 she wrote, "Mr. Milton and [Mr.] Bow came to Stickney's with saddle horses and a man with a team for us crowd of girls. The wagon broke down, the horses ran away, like to ran over us girls ahead on horseback. Did knock Mr. Bow off his horse and he had a badly sprained ankle." One of the Stickneys, "Aunt Barbara," also was "badly bruised and shaken up" in the incident. "But, despite the pain of the few due to this accident, everyone went on to Albion and most of them danced."

By the end of November as is common throughout northern California, the rains were heavy and nearly constant in this primitive, little outpost community

---

135 *Ibid.*, 4. On July 18, she also wrote, "We took a walk over the city toward night. The market is fine, splendid fruit, etc."

near the outlet of Little River, two and a half miles south of the town of Mendocino. On December 16 she noted, "Vessel went ashore here." On Christmas Day she wrote, "We are situated much differently than one year ago. Hard to realize the change yet." The new Californians had passed through their first few trying months in the Golden State. Many hard tests lay ahead, yet they had begun to gain confidence.

While still in Maine Isaiah Stevens, who took his family to regular Quaker meetings there, had joined the Free Masons. After their journey to California in 1864, judging from Etta's entries in her diary, the Stevens probably attended the Quaker services somewhat less regularly. Etta made many references to "Elder Ross" who also was often a guest at the Stevens or Pullen dinner table. "Elder Ross" was Rev. John Simpson Ross, who eventually built his home and founded the Baptist Church in Caspar, located to the north of Mendocino, between this town and Ft. Bragg. He performed the marriage services of Etta, Rachel, and Rosie.

Rachel taught the first elementary school class in a shanty hastily set up for the first Little River School. Before Gene arrived (in 1867), Rachel took a number of jobs as the governess or tutor for families who lived too far away from the Little River School. On September 13 Etta noted, "We have five more scholars, fourteen now. Quite a School! Oh! How I wish I could spend a day in the schools at home [back East, in Maine].

Meanwhile, as the Civil War raged on with colossal battles fought in various locations, Gene Sampson's tour had ended on the bark. The first month of 1865 found Gene stationed in New Orleans. He was assigned to the *Steamer Clinton*. The ship was repaired and refitted. In his diary Gene wrote, "Fine, clear weather. Went over to the City in the forenoon. The Calhoun's wheels finished all but painting.... Monday, 27: Wind East & Stormy. The Navy changed the name of the *Calhoun* to Gen. Sedgwick [*General Sedgewick*]." He served on board this ship sailing between Pensacola and Texas and received an honorable discharge on April 10, 1865. He was en route to New York when he learned of President Lincoln's assassination. Gene spent much of the next year assisting his widowed mother with chores on their farm near Hallowell, Maine, before signing onto a ship bound for San Francisco. He was determined, at last, to follow his sweetheart Rachel to California.

According to Etta, "In the spring of 1865 we moved from the 'Cook House' to our new home north of Little River—a claim Father had previously bought [a three-room house and loft built about 1856]." This house was the third built in Little River. It had been owned by W.H. Kent. In 1865, the year Etta turned sixteen, Little River held a so-called "Sanitary Ball," a fund-raising dance held to benefit Union soldiers, at the new Little River mill's cookhouse on the evening of April 14. (A Sanitary Ball was a dance sponsored by the U.S. Sanitary Commission

to raise money to insure soldiers could live under sanitary conditions.) By coin-
cidence, this was that same evening when President Abraham Lincoln was assas-
sinated in Washington, D.C. by actor John Wilkes Booth. Her diary later stated
that some thirty-eight schooners were loaded for the San Francisco market. On
November 14th, Etta's sister Lydia died of tuberculosis in Maine.

In November Gene returned to sea as a crewman on a sailing ship, the *Steamer
Carte*. The merchant vessel sailed to Havana, Cuba, where he bought a large supply of cigars, most of which he later sold at a profit. He returned to Boston in a
severe storm. On December 21, Gene noted,

> In a heavy N W. gale. Carried away fore topsail yard. Lost foresail
> and forestaysail, got into [illegible____] Sound at 11 PM. A bilious old
> day of it.[136]

Etta's older sister Rachel was the first teacher in the newly organized school.
Two more Stevens sisters, Nancy and Barbara, along with Vandalia Stickney,
joined Etta as students. Average attendance was nine.[137] Etta also noted, "In those
years mail was some four weeks in transit—to and from." On November 20, 1865,
Isaiah Stevens became the first Postmaster of Little River. The following year,
Etta began work at her first assignment as schoolteacher for a school located in
the Indian Creek District in Anderson Valley. She was paid forty dollars to teach
the three-month term. As was common at this time throughout many of the older
states, teachers "boarded around." This meant that during the term she lived
under the roofs of six different individual settlers. Meanwhile Rachel taught in
Boonville.[138] Etta briefly noted Gene's arrival in 1867: "We [Rachel, Gene, and
Etta?] often spend our weekends together and one time Gene Sampson of the
party, as he had by now appeared on the scene from the state of Maine coming
'around the Horn.' The attraction was of course Rachel."

A new Sunday school was set up that Wilder noted briefly in his own short
diary early in 1868. On April 15th (ten days after her eighteenth birthday) Wilder
noted, "Pulled Etta's ears nineteen times for her birthday." Etta and Wilder were
becoming somewhat more than just friends. In March Rachel, accompanied by
Mr. Stickney and Joel Gray, rode across Mendocino County to Little Lake. She
was starting to teach at another school, while young Gray had to take his teacher's examination there. The diary entries for March 1866 included mention of the
launching of the newly built schooner, the *Phil Sheridan*, at Little River. Rachel
returned from Little Lake on June 26. On the following day Etta noted, "Eating
peaches all morning. Did not go to Sunday School." In 1926, Etta remembered

---

136 *Ibid.*, July 22, 1864, 4.

137 *Op. cit.*, "Two 1865 Diaries...," 33.

138 By 1877 enrollment averaged of seventy. On Sept. 13 she wrote, "oh, how I wish I could
spend a day in the schools at home ("down east") [parentheses of Etta Pullen].",

how delicious these peaches had tasted that her sister had brought home with her from Little Lake.

During the beautiful Indian summer days of October, on the sixth Etta noted, "Lo and Gene came in the mill. He (probably Wilder) was running the circular saw to kill (time?) [parentheses added by Etta in 1926]." A week later, on Oct. 13, "A whole crowd of us went to Fort Bragg. Had a splendid time." The trip to Ft. Bragg illustrates how closely interconnected were nearly all of the small towns on the Mendocino coast. When they finally reached the "Noyo Hotel–Burn's Hotel," the manager drew himself up, stiffly informing the teenagers: "It is long past the dinner hour!" Nonetheless they were served. "Afterward we went on to Fort Bragg, then nothing but the old buildings. We roamed around from one to another of the buildings. We picked fine wild strawberries. It was where the town now stands [added in 1926]."

Wilder noted on Oct. 31, 1868, "A hard day. We had sunken logs. Father [Charles Pullen] and Sampson were in the mill here today. In the evening I went to town." On November 1, he added, "Pleasant all day. In the afternoon I went to Church. Elder Whiting preached." Later that year Mrs. Stevens (Rebecca) was ill. There had been an incident of small pox brought on by a schooner at Little River. Wilder noted on Christmas Day, "I went to the Ball and had a merry time."

In the first entry of her diary for 1869 Etta noted, "The summer of this year I taught school three months, the Navarro Ridge School at forty-five dollars per month and board." At the time she lived with the Ed Breton family more than a mile from the school. She also noted, "I went home Fridays after school and back Monday mornings, having a saddle horse and turning him to pasture during the week." There wasn't much time for a social life for the nineteen-year-old. During the next year, 1870, she returned in the summer to teach at Navarro Ridge for the longer five-month term.

On New Year's Eve 1868, Gene Sampson married Rachel (1846–1911). The couple settled down near the Richard Coombs house, although they later moved onto a 160-acre parcel on what was originally called "Sampson Lane." When it was sold, it became known as "Gordon Lane."

When he went to Little River, Gene became the town's blacksmith and did odd jobs such as helping to unload ships in the harbor. Although by 1870 Rachel had started to suffer from a foot ailment, she was Little River's first regular schoolteacher. Rachel noted the names of the ships, schooners, and barks that came and went from Little River. On March 19, Rachel noted, "Little River Mill sawed forty seven thousand eighty feet of lumber."[139] The most frequent arrivals

---

139 Regardless of their gender most schoolteachers before 1900 often boarded with students' families in many different parts of the United States, especially including the South, Midwest and West.

and departures were by two schooners, the *Little River* and the *Phil Sheridan*. On October 10, 1870, Rachel gave birth to her first child, a girl named May.

While by no means wealthy by the start of 1870, Etta was starting to make her own way in the world. Her place of residence when teaching at Navarro Ridge school changed from the Breton home to the Severance Hotel. The hotel was closer to the school. She kept the same weekly schedule as she had before. This year she had her own horse, one she named "Old Charlie." It was a sorrel-colored horse with a "white face," "a work horse, buggy horse—an all around horse." That summer she grew very fond of Old Charlie. Together with her friend, Em Le Ballister, "I rode him to Ukiah that summer from the coast to attend the Teacher's Institute."

Later in 1870 Etta felt honored when one Sunday afternoon her father trusted her to take Rachel out with "his team, a fine span of new horses" for a ride. Since giving birth, Rachel seemed to Etta to be a bit "pale and thin, but enjoyed the little ride—with 'Bill' and 'Jim' (black and bay)."

Meanwhile Wilder bought his land claim at Big Gulch from Mr. Young where he "batched it and worked in the timber, etc."

As noted earlier in 1865 over thirty-five schooners loaded with lumber left the Little River Mill for San Francisco. By this time Little River had grown into a thriving community. Charles Pullen and his son Wilder as well as others were building new mills at many other sites that eventually included Kibesillah, Ten Mile River, Little Valley, Mendocino, Albion, Whiteboro and Salmon Creek. Gradually the old growth Redwood forests that had so impressed the earliest settlers like Jerome Ford and E.C. Williams fell back further and further from the coast. By 1872 Wilder also had built a lumber chute at Big Gulch harbor, located just south of Little River.

In 1873 and 1874 two schooners were loaded with split timber at the chute Wilder had built at Big Gulch. In 1875, four vessels were loaded. This was just the beginning; in 1876 thirteen schooners or vessels loaded there. In 1877 and 1878 a total of nineteen vessels loaded. While the number of vessels loaded decreased somewhat to four in 1879, it rose again to five in 1880, before declining to one in both 1881 and 1882, the last year Etta noted that any ships were loaded. After that year Wilder turned back to his primary trade of carpentry and millwright. He built many houses, wharfs, dams, and bridges. He was frequently called upon late at night or early in the morning to go out to repair a bridge or causeway damaged by some careless stage or farm wagon driver. Serving in several capacities simultaneously was common. Wilder was a millwright, road and dam builder, farmer, carpenter, and occasionally worked for a wage in saw mills. He sometimes took trips to Ukiah to testify at civil or criminal trials.

When Etta returned to teach at Anderson Valley, Wilder served as her escort. She earned seventy-five dollars for a three-month term. From 1870 to 1873, the two had become closer. Ultimately, as noted by Wilder, there was a momentous event in early February, 1873. "Very rainy. I went up to Mr. Stevens in afternoon with team. Etta and I were married by Elder Ross. There were thirty-six present. A Big supper. I took my wife home about 11 o'clock."[140] The moon had risen and was "very bright." It must have been a romantic ride to their new home, but there was no time for a honeymoon. Etta noted on February 13, "Wilder and I took our first breakfast together." Before the wedding, Wilder had taken off four days to go to Ukiah to get their marriage license. It was a rough trip by horseback over a tortuous road.

On February 28, Mr. and Mrs. Lorenzo E. White (the couple who later owned the Albion Mill and others) along with Miss Pitcher visited the newlyweds. Etta had ridden Old Charlie to visit her father that evening. Etta was a fine home-maker, cook and dressmaker. She made many jumpers for members of her extended family as well as for friends and others. No mention of an asking price was ever made in the over one-hundred-page diary. Comments interspersed between near-constant mention of ironing and cooking make it clear that her main enjoyment was in taking walks outside to the headlands and to go "berrying."

Ships ran aground in the harbor during storms and gales. At the end of March, 1873, Wilder returned home from plowing his father's potato field, and "he and Gus went to Albion to see the vessels—eight in harbor, but two gone ashore." The spring passed uneventfully until, suddenly, on April 1, "All Fool's Day," the *Schooner Light Wing* (Capt. Henry Nelson) was shipwrecked at Little River. Four days later the Pullens celebrated Etta's twenty-fourth birthday. "Wilder commenced work for his father at Albion Mill this morning," and on April 14, "Rosie [her younger sister, Mary Rosilla] seventeen today." Early in the morning on a day soon after that, Etta's younger sister filled Wilder's pockets with apples as he left for work.

On April 22, "Was about ready to go to Little River to spend the day when a man came that seemed crazy. As soon as I could give him something to eat and get rid of him." It wasn't the only time a homeless person showed up unannounced on their doorstep. Etta changed plans and went with Rosie to Albion to see some of their friends. When she returned home with Wilder from Albion, he immediately went out to the field and talked to the old man. They later learned the deranged individual had escaped from "the Asylum," and the unfortunate man later was taken back there. On April 31, "Sam and Gus out in the boat. Got four seals and a deer that jumped over the bluff. They were here for dinner. Nothing

---

140 See "The 1870 Diary of Rachel Francena Stevens Sampson," Transcribed as written by Ronnie James July 2007 The year May Sampson was born," 7. Copy provided to author by Ms. James, Dec. 2008.

like having a husband that can cook."[141] Illness was a serious common concern. Usually there was no medical help available. For example, on May 29, 1873, she noted, "Woke up about one with a very sick faint spell, kept so bad that Wilder went for his mother about three. She came with him and stopped until breakfast and she got me up."

Schooner visits were important social events that often required Etta to set another place at the dinner table for the captain. When the *Schooner Mendocino* arrived in the Little River Harbor on June 13 with Captain Prince Gray at the helm, a group of young people boarded the ship for the short ride to Big Gulch, but then, "had to walk back." Walking was still the main mode of transportation. By June 17 the schooner was fully loaded, and, "In p.m. they hauled the *Mendocino* out to anchor at outside mooring and sailed from there." There were constant chores to do with numerous accidents that required attention. In addition, Etta kept a flock of chickens while Wilder kept sheep, goats, pigs, and later cattle. "We picked gooseberries....most every day of this month, and blackberries, then the haying went on mixed in with hauling posts." Many a meal at the Albion Mill especially after 1880 began with Wilder slaughtering a cow or bull from the Pullen family ranch. On June 26, "Reading *Chronicle* [*San Francisco Chronicle*] in eve." Despite the fact that the nation had experienced a serious financial panic, or at least a deep recession that started in 1873, the Pullens, at least, seemed well fed and housed. On July 9, "Rachel came on Old Charlie in p.m. We went up to school. Saw Rosie, Annie [Rachel's daughter?], rode home behind me on Billy." And on July 13, "A beautiful day. We took a walk around by the coast. Got some hazelnuts. Sam and Gus came up from the boat with two little seagulls for Annie. A stranger slept in the barn and ate breakfast—the fourth for the year since I was here."[142]

There were no local, state or private organizations, or so-called "safety nets" other than individual charitable acts.

In August 1873 the first telegraph was laid up to Little River and Mendocino. "They ran telegraph wire past here." On August 3 after Sam boarded the schooner for San Francisco. "I went down to the harbor – one load [?]. The ocean was as smooth as a pond. Hardly a ripple to be seen. Gus brought us two fish at noon. An old blind man called and [at?] one for something to eat."[143] The next day a new schooner appeared, Captain Peterson in command. Wilder took the captain out to gather hazelnuts. Later as the schooner was being loaded with lumber, "the captain gave us a Scotch Terrier dog—name Jack—and he was a fine faithful watch dog."

---

141 Etta Stevens Pullen diary, Feb. 12, 1873, 11. The next morning, Feb. 13 "Wilder and I took our first breakfast together."

142 See "The Etta Stevens Pullen Diary," 13, at Kelley House Museum, Mendocino, CA.

143 *Ibid.*, 14.

Whenever Wilder had to be away, her chores were doubled. She could barely keep up with the workload then, beginning early in the morning with milking Nellie the cow. Wilder, along with "more than thirty other settlers" had to go to San Francisco to the land office to contest their land claims against Alexander McPherson's first Jardine partner on the north coast, "Alexander Grant Dallas." This business took almost five weeks out of all of their lives and it ended in a bitter, heartbreaking disappointment. Fortunately, Mr. Stevens already had clear title to "one hundred thirty eight and sixty hundredths acres" or "lots 3, 4 and 5" located in Section Six and the lot numbered one of Section Seven, in Township Sixteen, North Range Seventeen West, in the district of lands subject to sale at San Francisco, California," according to Preemption Certificate No. 1328 made on January 10, 1868 in a Land Grant sealed by President Andrew Johnson.

Soon after this McPherson and Wetherbee Co. took over another large Pullen-Stevens property in an action that Etta called a "fraud." "McPherson and Weatherbee came in on the 'Albion grant.' They claimed about a thousand acres near their Albion Mill and the woods along Stillwell Gulch [Buckhorn Cove] on the north, then south and east. Their claim was that they bought these ten acres 'in good faith' hence in after years [1873] the settlers were summoned to the land office to show cause, etc. After a time, a well-drawn out time, it was decided [in favor of the Companies], so far as the settlers that they had taken up their claims since such a year—I think 1858. These lands that had been settled before that time were immune....Of course ours came under that head so we retained our home, but later through fraud lost one 40 acres of the 150 pre-empted. This done by tools of the Albion Mill Company and their larger influence at land office, or seemed so."[144]

It was a battle between the settler group who thought their claims were well established and the powerful lumber companies with their overwhelming influence in the national land office, well paid lawyers and economic clout. The settlers were bound to lose this uneven wrestling match over thousands of acres of valuable land.

This case was typical of what happened to many California immigrants who had gone west to improve their lot. Before the Civil War was over, Congress had passed a new Homestead Act. It stated that anyone could claim a plot of land if he developed it into a farm or ranch. This was exactly what Wilder and Etta Pullen as well as thousands of other families believed that they were doing. Certainly Etta's daily entries made faithfully and regularly for almost thirty years confirm that. There were no hidden agendas, no strategies for climbing a corporate or political ladder, simply hard work, day in and day out. The new settlers weren't

---

144 *Ibid.,* 16. According to Etta, "the predecessor ("squatter") had not the wherewithal, too indolent, to prove up before Wilder bought his claim and by this time the new grant claim had come in," op. cit., 16.

alone. Even California grant holders such as Jasper O'Farrell in Yolo and Sonoma Counties had to spend fortunes paying for legal fees in the attempt to protect their land claims that were supposedly assured safe and permanent by the Treaty of Hidalgo after the Mexican War.

By the start of 1874 numerous immigrant families from Portugal, Italy, and Finland were populating the coast. The Portuguese settled generally in the Mendocino area, the Finns and Italians further north near Fort Bragg. In January 1874, Etta recorded the immigration of numerous Portuguese immigrants. During the same month she obtained and started reading a book entitled "Mark Twain." Perhaps it included *Tom Sawyer* and *Huckleberry Finn*, but unfortunately she made no further notation about it. On March 21 Gus brought them the sad news that the Little River Mill had burned down the night before. At the end of March Wilder "hauled two shears for the Chute," and Etta read stories in the *West Coast Star*. On April 1, she noted, "The Portuguese gave us some fish." Despite a heavy rain that day, on April 29, "Nevertheless we all went to Little River to the launching of the schooner *Alice Kimball*. She looked nice going off the ways, stuck a bit as she reached the water, but soon floated without much trouble." They ate dinner at Mr. Stevens' house that evening. In June, 1874, Wilder became the official "road overseer" for their district. This meant that in addition to his own work as a carpenter working in many locations, Wilder also was paid a small amount to plan and supervise road and bridge construction projects. Simultaneously Wilder obtained the contract to build a new school at Salmon Creek.

Etta's sister Rachel gave birth to a boy, Eugene Stevens Sampson, on March 11, 1875. The next month Wilder completed his work at the Peterson Shipyard almost the same time that the new *Schooner Uncle Sam* was launched at a site just a little west of Rachel and Eugene's house. In May, Wilder's chute crew, Lo, Mack LaBallister and Charlie Gray, loaded the schooner *Western Home*. The vessel needed a pull from a "steam tug" out of the harbor. At the end of the month they went down to San Francisco: "Wilde took me to dentist, H.C. Davis, DDS. For 2 days I was at dentists and Wilde at Land Office, but we had callers and spent one eve with Maryetta and Tom and a ride back to Hotel [the American Exchange Hotel] on horse carts."

Like most farm families in this era, their days began before dawn and often went on until long after dark. Having dinner guests meant that Etta had to bake "apple, peach and berry pies." The weather held through most of October as Wilder worked on a new bridge at Big Gulch, and the young couple took their buggy to try out Gene's new colts, "Fly and Satan." "Wild," as she often referred to him, also had to work the cutter on the plow in order to plow his fields. Sometimes Etta would accompany her husband out in the fields just to be with him. The year 1875 closed with the entry, "Rachel and children sick with colds. Rosie there. I have been cooking. Wilder cutting brush and logs to burn (clearing land). So ends the year with another regular storm from the southeast." Her father paid her a couple of installments of "school money." It was customary for the school districts to pay the father of young female teachers at the time. The next year went along much the same. She noted that they had loaded two schooners, the *C. H Marithew* and *Concordia*. She also noted that twice that July that they had "a Digger mowing" or "haying." In other words they hired a Native American or Indian worker temporarily for a specific job.

She noted another loading for the *C. H Marithew* and the *Golden West*, another schooner. In the meantime Wilder began picking out lumber to build their new house at Big Gulch which today is known as Heritage House Resort. They attended a political meeting on October 11 in Big River to hear Dr. Cox speak. She noted he was "a fine speaker." On November 9, "He [Wilder] commenced laying the foundation." The weather was unusually good so that Wilder also framed their new house. They had a banner year for ship loading in 1876, for they loaded the highest number ever, thirteen vessels and nearly $1,400 worth of prime lumber, probably most of it redwood. She noted, "We rec'd for freight $1,390.03," but added, "I do not state expenses, but a good many in all."

The year 1877 started off with sad news. "Jack," one of their best dogs, had to be put down after he broke his leg. "Nothing but a dog, but have had him faithful and long." On February 17 she noted, "Prince, wife and baby spent p.m. here. Chinaman came for apples and chickens. Lo here." Ranchers supplied many settlers with such commodities in this era before the advent of large grocery stores. In March another new schooner, the *Barbara* (named after a Stickney girl and built at the Peterson Shipyard), was launched at the end of Peterson Lane in Little River. The captain was an old friend, Captain Higgins. On March 23, "Wilde went for his freight...that we had Sam get in the city and send for house....fruit trees, extension table and a nice patent rocker and a lounge, etc." Early in April some thirty-four former Maine residents had a party at Salmon Creek. Most of them came from Little River. On April 8, the *Schooner Abraham Lincoln* arrived at Wilder's chute; by five o'clock the following day they had her loaded and the tug *Albion* "took the schooner out."

Early in May Etta referred to "Indian John mowing," and in April "Wilde and his father plastering." Etta and Wilder "went out and built a fire in the new grate" to help dry the plaster. They also hosted a "telegraph man to dinner." May 30 was another busy day.

"I went to Little River in morning, carried Lizzie up, came home. Digger Joe and squaw [It is possible that there were two different Indians, one man named "John" who "mowed" and later another mower, "Digger Jo."] here mowing. Elder Ross called and took lunch. We went to the buriel [sic sp. burial] of Mr. Squiers in p.m. In the evening we attended the Strawberry Festival, a large crowd." At that time the mowing was done with hand-held scythes, and everyone pitched in to get the hay mowed. The hay also had to be baled and stored for use as feed during the rainy season.

During July Wilder loaded two more schooners at the chute, and in October the *Schooner Joannah* [*Joanna*] "struck the rocks going in to Little River." A storm washed the aprons off the chute in November, but Wilder got them back on shore so they could be reused. He kept up his plowing. On December 12, Etta was alone and that afternoon had an unexpected visit from "a tramp for something to eat." Naturally she was greatly relieved when Wilder returned home two days later. At Christmas, the family celebrated the marriage of Etta's youngest sister Rosie to Mark Dana Gray. They went to Father Stevens' house for the dinner and ceremony led by Elder Ross. Etta sealed the happy occasion by wishing, "May their married life be a happy one."

Toward the end of January 1878, Wilder became a bit discouraged by the loss of his chute equipment due to a series of heavy storms. On February 1, the mail was brought by Lo. Despite one or two clear days, the rainy weather continued. Rachel's husband Gene became sick, and in May the couple had to travel away from the coast for a while. There was more schooner traffic in 1878. On June 13, Wilder turned thirty. Both Wilder and Etta had reached maturity. The work didn't let up as each new month brought a new schooner to load. They barely had the time in mid July to attend a dance at Salmon Creek. On July 28, one of their favorite horses, "Lily," got loose and was nearly drowned. Wild got into his boat and rowed out to retrieve her. She had swum a half-mile out in the harbor and onto a small beach. She was tied to a log and given some hay for a bed (and perhaps for food) for that one night. The next morning "they had to swim poor Lizzie all the way back to the beach this morning, and glad was I to see her safe again and no one hurt—her legs are bruised up. She swam as fast as they could row the boat."

In November one of the schooners arrived and delivered Etta a new sewing machine she had ordered. That month another schooner "went ashore at Albion." Just before Christmas, Gene left to go for medical attention on a long sea trip to San Pedro (near San Francisco). He came home on the last day of 1878. On that same day Wilder took some chickens to town to sell and Etta concluded the year's entries noting they had loaded ten schooners from their chute.

The following February (1879) they celebrated their sixth wedding anniversary with a chicken dinner at her father's house. The spring rains had returned in earnest. Wilder planted potatoes, sowed oats, and killed a pig as Etta made "mince meat, hoghead [sic sp. hogshead] cheese and tried out lard, etc." On February 20, Wilder went to Big River with a four-horse team to pick up some freight for his father. She hoed the strawberry patch. The following month Wilder sold some potatoes at the "store." He also began repairing their front yard fence. In June Wilder returned to work building a bridge at Big River and began helping his new brother-in-law Mark Gray build a barn. She made Wilder a "jumper" as well as sewing for others. During the last week of June Wilder had to go to Cloverdale, possibly to file paperwork so he could be paid for his road work.

June passed with Wilder hurrying off each day to finish the Big River Bridge. Did he notice that his wife's condition had gradually worsened? There was no doubt that they shared some special moments of peace and love together. "July 31, I went in the woods to see Wild chop a tree to make ties." Captain Jim Higgins was their guest again in October as the *Schooner Barbara* was in for a load of lumber. They'd read about a shocking murder that had taken place on the Little Lake Road (to Willits). The outlaws were never apprehended. Early in July 1879 Etta had to see Dr. Mosher. She had begun to suffer again from various medical problems. As Wilder kept up the farm chores, she caught poison oak in her eyes on August 17. On August 30, they visited "father Pullen." On the next day Wilder took some more potatoes to town. On September 18, part of the town of Little River burned. Her notes about the fire read, "A big fire at Little River. Started in Norrigers Hotel, burned Rices house (the house next door to the hotel), and the Companies Stable, all three to the ground. Rough on Aunt Cal and Rice."

Wilder took more potatoes to town to sell. He and his crew prepared for the winter by hauling in the apron for the chute. October 6 found Etta again "commenced on the sick list," but she had regular help and visitors so that she was rarely alone. Throughout November and on December 4, Etta spoke of feeling ill, her "back aching so hard," and on December 6, "another bad spell this p.m. Oh, may I never have such sickness." In late November Wilder returned to do some more roadwork. The rains and winds were fierce in early December. It was typical for it to rain all day, as she recorded it did on December 9. She wondered if the medicine that Wilder went out of his way to fetch her did her any good at all. She was confined to bed much of the time. She was upset over not being able to be up. Christmas brought her three presents. Wilder did some more roadwork at the end of the year. There was a lot of rain, hail and even a little snow.

The *Schooner Monterey* came in on January 20, 1880. Etta's health improved and her spirits rose. Whether or not they were paid much for their work, the lumber chute operation required men to work long hours. During the following month, February, when the *Monterey* went out of the harbor because it was too rough to load her, it accidentally took a mooring out with it. Etta wrote, "Feb. 24, Tuesday, I washed. Wild and Sam were out in the Albion Tug with Mr. Brett most all day, trying to pick up the big mooring." Two days later they were surprised, for "Wild and 'Bruno' the dog, caught a live deer up by tank and let it down to barn and put him in box stall. We went to Mr. Colby's to see if it was theirs, but conclude it a wild one." The next day they "turned the deer loose. He was loath to leave the barn, but afterward deliberately walked away up over the hill on to the prairie and far away."

It turned very cold the first part of March. Another schooner, *The Emily and Shroader* [sic sp. *Schroeder*], arrived and had to be loaded with railroad ties. Diphtheria, measles, small pox, and chicken pox brought down many in the community. Wilder was busy talking to Bill Eddy about another chute that was needed. He went up to Noyo to look at the chute site. Wilder was also busy in June completing the work on another chute at Hare Creek. On Tuesday, June 13, he "went to Salmon Creek to work for Brett and White, building a mill." Work at this mill would become intense over the next few years, and Etta made numerous trips there taking her husband to the job. In the meantime she continued to work on some articles of clothing for others or cooking meals for their many guests, many of whom were relatives. In October, they, along with "Will and Mother Long," made a trip over to Round Valley and paid a visit to Dr. Melindy, who was Mrs. Long's brother.

On October 24, Etta noted, "Will and 'Mother Long' (Cornelia's mother) went to the Indian Reservation to Church and to Sabbath School with us. Both place[s] were well attended by old and young. We called on Dr. Melindy's wife— he a brother to Mrs. Long, etc." On the following day, as they started back towards the coast, "Had a nice view of the pretty valley all the way up the mountain, took lunch at the cold springs on mountain." They returned via Ukiah and arrived home on October 27.

With the advent of the telegraph, national news was suddenly much more current and available. News that took weeks to arrive before 1873 now arrived within twenty-four hours. On July 3, 1881, word arrived that President Garfield had been shot. On September 20 they learned that he had died on the nineteenth.

On November 3 Wilder got up early to go to the Salmon Creek Mill. On November 21, Mr. Wetherbee came to the house to hire Wilder to build a house for him.

Although only one schooner was loaded in 1881 and in 1882, with none recorded after that, in the meantime more mills had been built. Those already operating increased their output to the point that small chute operations like the one Wilder Pullen had built and manned near his home could no longer compete. After 1870 when new steel cables were perfected that were far stronger and more expensive, individuals could no longer afford to keep up with the big outfits as these new developments required greater capital, and the lumber business entered a new phase with only the largest, most efficient mills surviving. It was the survival of the largest, not necessarily the fittest. The largest companies bought out their smaller competitors.

Life in Little River and Mendocino fell into a pattern. Each town grew to several thousand people of many races drawn by the promise of working either in the mills or cutting lumber in the back woods. Wilder was as busy as ever working on many projects, building individual barns, blacksmith shops, houses, roads, wharfs, or mills. Building a mill involved knowledge of both the machinery and where to put each device in order to improve production. The occasional deaths of children brought periodic tragedy to the area. Wilder had to build a coffin for an Albion child on February 20, 1881. On September 25, Etta wrote, "We went to the school house to the funeral of the little Tompson [Thompson?] girl." Later that month, Wilder began working at the new Salmon Creek Mill.

During 1883, Etta's health steadily declined. In the middle of August, 1883 Etta made frequent, unusual notations in her diary about feeling sick. By August 26, "A bad spell in night so Wild stayed with me today. I am hot and feverish and get discouraged...."[145] On October 20, 1883, a small earthquake shook Little River. The following month Etta's father celebrated his seventy-third birthday with a goose dinner with "his children and grandchildren." In December she did all the usual chores. On December 11, Rachel came "to help us off." On December 12, Etta and Wilder began a trip down to the Bay Area to consult with "Madam Berman," possibly a faith healer. They took the train from Cloverdale "for San Francisco." Despite her being "tired" on December 14, she "crossed to Oakland to see Madam Berman." She made the same trip the next day. Three days later, on December 17, she saw more doctors, "twice a day for treatments."[146] On December 18 her faith in Madam Berman had run out completely. She noted that she "was glad when he [Wilder] got back (from San Francisco). I think her a quack." They finally returned home "in a drizzling rain" on the day after Christmas. "The mist let up some and we worked our way on home. Got here after dark and very, very tired after our tedious journey home, but feel thankful we are here all right." On New Year's Eve "Wilder went to Little [Little River]. Gene and May here." Making her final 1883 note Etta concluded, "A hard year in many ways."

Their lives continued pretty much the same during the first half of 1884. In August Wilder's father, Charles Pullen, passed away. In the meantime Wilder finished up work on a water tank. (In 1926, this water tank still held water.) Later that August they attended Mr. Wetherbee's funeral. During November they sold two colts, "Diamond" and "Flirt" to Mr. Thompson "(of Big River)." "We hate to let them go but suppose they have to sometime, we can't keep everything." Early in December Wilder had to haul home a "load of seed oats from the steamer in a.m." He went to work building another water tank for her father. She noted on December 22, there had been a storm and an unnamed "steamer went ashore at Salmon Creek trying to get out of Harbor." Little River had become a thriving, permanent town.

---

145 *Ibid.*, Etta Stevens Pullen Diary, Kelley House Museum, Mendocino, CA, 16.

146 *Ibid.*, 68. In 1926 Etta added, "The fever in my lip—as the common cement there never left with all the tried remedies from many doctors and otherwise never cured. These later years were some better, but never the same, always swollen and parched."

Wilder began 1885 doing his usual series of chores: shearing sheep, plowing and finishing up another water tank. Etta had a bad cold as she "ironed, worked over butter, etc." Etta made a number of references to going to a public event called "The Band of Hope," probably a camp or evangelical group meeting. During February Wilder worked at planting a new strawberry patch and planting potatoes.

Etta's father, Isaiah, donated a small portion of land on the southwest corner of his pasture to the Good Templars. This building has been restored today and is open to the public as the Little River Improvement Club and Museum. On March 11, 1885, Wilder started building the "Good Templars Hall, the land father gave at Little River." This remarkable building has a barrel ceiling. It soon became the town's community center and was used for its first library, telephone switchboard office, funerals, weddings, meetings, parties and voting. On March 12, Gene Sampson, Rachel's husband, suddenly became ill and died. Etta wrote, "I was alone with Rachel and May. Oh, what agony for them, may I not be called upon to ever go through another such scene." During April Etta spent more time visiting Rachel to console her and help her work through the worst of her grieving. There was no mention in the diary of the cause of death. During the following years Wilder and Etta spent many hours in their days helping Rachel and her three children. At this time Wilder began putting up new wallpaper in their hall. She also was busy making dresses. During May Wilder was hired to build a new cemetery fence but, "he gave this work," apparently donating his services. Later that May Wilder went to work on a wharf at Bear Harbor. Rachel and her children were frequent guests in Etta's home.

During June and July Wilder worked at "getting in the hay" for Rachel and digging potatoes. In August someone from Big River visited the ranch "trying to get Wild to build a Dam on Big River" (August 4). On August 25, "Wilder was summoned on a law case at Mendocino, it was dismissed so he got back to Rachel's where I was at noon." In the meantime Etta worked at making shirts. Wilder was "still sawing stove wood" (August 29). In September Wilder was at work setting and then watching fires to clear out gulches. He also fixed harnesses. About this time she had to have two teeth pulled. Soon after that she went to Mendocino to attend a "Teacher's Institute."

During the second half of 1885 Etta became so sick that she had to seek the help of a higher degree of medical practice than was available near their home.[147] Her fainting spells lasted longer and had become dangerously frequent. She had also developed a painful and troubling sore on her lip.

In October it was clear that something was seriously wrong with Etta. Wilder and Etta rapidly prepared to make the long trip to San Francisco. On October 6, Tuesday, she wrote,

---

147 *Ibid.,* 69.

We were to fathers, he out again to P.O. and said good bye to him there. He wants me to get health (know what it is to have an ailing wife). It is hard for me to leave home with him so poorly, but we have concluded something must be done, I can't keep on long this way, so I have listened to Wilder and we start for San Francisco. (Constantly losing flesh and strength, with sometime sinking spells in night or when lying down that I seem to be sinking down, down, down.) Came as far as Jim's tonight.[148]

By October 9, "From Cloverdale to City in a.m.—consulted (by recommendation) Dr. Green and Dr. Moore, they agreed just enough to disagree. On the following day they consulted "Mrs. Dr. Manger (a Dr. of note). She wanted time to answer. On Oct. 20, she wrote, "Real sick in morning. Went for Dr. Manger['s] opinion, called Dr. Moore again, made arrangements and agreement on terms with him for my treatment and cure." At this point Wilder returned home, leaving his wife to board at "Mr. Randletts." The Randletts were old Stevens family friends who lived in Oakland. Until the end of the month she continued to visit doctors. On October 31, she wrote, "Had to lie still by Drs. orders, another good letter from Wilder, poor boy he pities me and knows how hard it is that I cannot be with them." She continued to try to limit her activities throughout November. Wilder returned to be with her towards the end of month. In the meantime her brother Stephen and wife Helen had arrived in San Francisco from back East. Brother and sister, Stephen and Etta, along with their spouses, stayed at the Palace Hotel in San Francisco on November 30. On the same day she noted, "I look so tired they sent me home at night."

During this time Helen's mother died. She and Stephen had to cut their West Coast visit short to board a train to start the long journey back to Maine. Almost simultaneously, during the first ten days of December, Mr. Stevens passed away in Little River. On December 12, Etta wrote, "Sat. Just making ready to start for the Dr. when a letter from Rachel telling me father has passed away. How can I bear it. Mrs. Randlett went for my medicine, Mr. Flagg called to see me (father a dear friend of his). The middle of December was the hardest." On December 14 she added, "A letter from Wilder, these sad letters telling of the loved one gone to his rest, and even [ever?] in my mind my dear husband's anxiety, and sympathy, my duty to him." And finally on December 30, "Wrote Wilder in p.m. This ends a year of more sorrow than gladness. With us it has been a year of pain and sickness, sadness and mourning—what will come next?"

During the first three months of 1886, they continued to be separated. She was trying to do what the doctors ordered her to do including a number of so-called "electric baths"[149] and other treatments. She passed the time crocheting Wilder a

---

148 *Ibid.*, p. 11.

149 *Ibid.*, p. 82. Although there wasn't any documentary proof, Ms. Ronnie James, of Little River, a person who has studied the Stevens-Pullen family records thoroughly, believes

new pair of slippers as well as shopping at the "Smith Cash Store," visiting with family friends, the Randletts, Flaggs, Mrs. Kimball, Mrs. White, and obtaining a wedding dress for Allie. Added to her April 9 entry in parentheses, "(Death and marriage still linger on here, trying for health, but in vain, it seems although better in some ways, I still suffer, but I have the feeling as I had from the first. I would not have lived long, if I had not come)." Otherwise, it was unlikely that a pioneer woman such as Etta Pullen would have spent so many months in San Francisco, so far away from the ranch and her normal life in Little River. There are two entries dated the "19th."

At last she was leaving Oakland. She took with her a supply of medicine. She boarded the steamer *Yagunia* at 3 p.m. on April 19, "not sick until out past Golden Gate." On the 20th, the steamer reached its destination at about 6:30 p.m. at Little River and she noted, "Wilder and Rachel met me on the wharf, they had been there at intervals all day waiting the delayed steamer. I am a tired girl after the hard trip, but it is so good to be here once again."[150] She was still not completely well and had to be in bed part of the time until the end of April.

With the passage of time her strength gradually increased. She resumed her normal routine for the most part. In the following month they went to work settling her father's estate and legal issues. Wilder had been appointed administrator. By the middle of 1886, Etta was once again hard at work. She took time to exercise a new pair of colts. Wilder often left the house "before light." In October Wilder moved a house for the Hill family. Her 1926 parenthetical comment was "from beside the Perkins house [north of it] down across the bridge up to the sight [site] of the Old Stickney house—1864)."[151]

In mid December Etta directed a group of other women that included Mrs. Pettits, Allie, and Rosie in making two dresses for Mrs. Pettit and Rosie. On December 18 she wrote, "May helped a good deal with the work [for example May had "ironed" the day before] for I have not been of much account, Eunie came for her tonight." Apparently she was almost at term in her pregnancy.

Starting 1887, on January 3, "Still feel miserable, feet and limbs swollen." The entry for Thursday, January 6 was, "No use to give an account of this day, it will always be remembered, enough that nearly eight months of anxiety and suffering with 'nothing to show for it'—Mother Pullen with me the greater part of day and Dr. McCormick in afternoon." Without her explicit admission, it must be that

---

Etta had "some sort of gynecological complication associated with an incomplete pregnancy." This would certainly explain her need to journey to the Bay Area and her need to stay there, this time for more than six weeks.

150 *Ibid.*, 86. She had one of Dr. Horsford's Acme Vapor Baths. The term "electric bath" meant something somewhat different now or in the 1920s–30s than it did in the mid-1880s. One basic definition today refers to "an electrically-heated steam bath." This was probably closer to what Etta had during her stay in San Francisco/Oakland.

151 *Ibid.*, 87.

Etta lost an unborn child, very possibly her second. During the mid-1880s, during the Victorian Era, Etta would not have written or used the word "pregnancy" to describe her condition, yet it is difficult to interpret her words any other way. "Miscarriage" also wouldn't have been included in her diary. She was in bed during almost the entire month of January, probably with someone constantly at her side.

It was Rachel's young daughter Hazel who came to Etta's aid and apparently did the most to console the distraught woman. Etta wrote on January 27, "Hazel for company again. She was a go between and asks, 'Do you want any thing, Aunt Etta? (I never forget the little voice as she would come to my door and say those words so earnestly.)"[152] At the same time Wilder continued to plow and to keep up their normal routine.

On February 14, their fourteenth wedding anniversary, the nasty weather returned. "May and I got a rather nice dinner. We expected Rachel and the children, but too much rain and blow." Early in March Wilder sold some sheep to Mr. Jefferson. He helped drive them to their new home. She cut potatoes. In spite of her loss, she started to recover and felt well enough to take short walks. "Wild planted more potatoes and went to town." They also planted oats and carrot seeds. Wilder went to Salmon Creek to work. Later he returned with lumber to be made into yokes. He also planted corn and worked on a fence at the Cemetery for Mrs. Wetherbee, who was Mr. McPherson's partner's widow.

After a trunk full of presents arrived from Maine from her brother Stephen and Etta's sister-in-law Helen on June 12, she wrote, "All hands here to the Trunk Opening, presents to each of us from Stephen and Helen. Mark's folks and Rachel, each a present and Allie (who wasn't there)." It was a warm family potluck. Rachel brought a "roast goose." For dessert they made short work of "Rosie's cream cake, strawberries, etc. Quite a gala day."

In early July Wilder caught the flu. It was a rare event for him to be sick. He had a feverish night yet he soon recovered and was back to his normal busy workload. When the weather improved Etta ventured out to a place they called "Pea Vine" to gather blackberries. In 1926, the same place was called "Strawberry Ranch." As she did occasionally, on July 16 Etta "took supper at the Cook House along with Wilder and Mark." She washed and picked peas and berries. Wilder often rose early to get ready for work. He departed into the nearly omnipresent early morning fog. At the time Rachel's little girl Imie was sick and had to be nursed. One of the colts, "Ranger," got loose. Etta had to run out the door in order to catch and harness him. She kept up her sewing despite not feeling well. She finished a "jumper" for Wilder on Friday, July 29. The following day "Ranger" took off with the buggy. It was "smashed" but fortunately "nothing was hurt."

---

152 *Ibid.*, 91.

In August everyone pitched in to get the haying done again. There was more "berrying," and they had spuds to be dug up. On the 29th they killed a "beef." Wilder took the meat to the mill. On the following day, "Wild up very early again, dressed a veal and took it to mill." In October and November Wilder finished building a barn for the Handley's. In December she finished Allie's dress. She went to Mendocino, "did trading so I was here only in time for chores tonight" (December 24).[153] There was no mention of having loaded any ships with lumber in 1887.

Wilder's reputation as a highly competent carpenter now preceded him nearly everywhere on the north Mendocino coast. Beginning in the year 1888, Etta complained more frequently in her diary when Wilder unexpectedly had to leave her alone. She may or may not have spoken of her loneliness to him. On February 17, 1888 she wrote, "Plenty of work. [Wilder] had to see a man about fencing and cutting brush." On February 21 she confessed, "Did not feel very well. Crocheting some for Addie." February seemed about to end on a happy note with a "letter from flagg [Flagg]" but, suddenly, on the 28, " 'Beauty' a fine heefer [sic sp. heifer] failed to come up last night and hunting we fail to find her so conclude the Bluff is her end."[154] On March 12, Monday, Wilder sowed the coast field in a.m. and went to Navarro in p.m. and got himself a new "Sulky" cart. He had finished doing carpentry work at the Albion Mill and was about to resume working at the Salmon Creek Mill. On Tuesday, March 20, Etta noted, "Wilder started for Salmon Creek Mill in a.m. It makes me blue and lonesome to think of his starting another summers work there—so far from home."

Being a member of a close-knit community afforded her some comfort. On March 26, 1888, "Wilder an early start. Bell called on way to Steamer to say goodbye. I went up, called for Rachel and we went to Allies, found her with little baby boy, born yesterday [Leland]."[155] She noted on April 5, "Another birthday here." She was thirty-nine. Her health seemed to vary to a great degree for no apparent reason. On May 27 Mark and Rosie came with Captain Higgins for dinner. She had also met Capt. Higgins in the Bay Area so obviously the old captain had become a good family friend. During this summer she had a constant round of company for dinner or supper. She really couldn't pause long enough to sink into depression. She seemed happiest when Wilder had a more regular schedule or when he returned before dinnertime. On June 2, "Rested better. Did greater part of cooking, with help and a cane. Mr. and Mrs. Rebholz called, Wild came as I was washing before supper."[156]

---

153 *Ibid.*, 94.
154 *Ibid.*, 96.
155 *Ibid.*, 98.
156 *Ibid.*, 98.

They were busy until July 4, "Nice day. Wilder came last night, we took a ride to Greenwood, took dinner there, saw horse race, etc. Marks folks Jim and all Salmon Creek there, home in good season." She continued turning out shirts for her husband and dresses for other women. There was more unexpected excitement on Sept. 7, "Fri. Lots of running after stock, deal of trouble, 'Tony" [probably a horse] breaking into corn, makes me tired with other work."[157] She went out "on prairie huckleberrying" on September 12, an experience everyone enjoyed. Wilder was earning three dollars a day working at the Salmon Creek Mill. Although it was a steady income, he probably did not enjoy it after doing the more creative work as a millwright he and his father had always done.

For an unstated reason Wilder sold her stove. This meant that they had to use "Charls [her brother Charles']" stove. However they "sent for one." On October 13 Etta wrote, "Wild to Whitesboro for our new stove, a nice large one. In p.m. he set fires, I had to go out of course, had a nice burn."[158] Setting fires to reduce the amount of brush and undergrowth was mentioned occasionally in her diary. It must have been dangerous and strenuous work since there is a high danger of wildfire in the latter months of the fall in northern California. Forest fires sometimes broke out that destroyed small towns. On October 20 she took on the task of looking after Rosie's children while Rosie left on the *Steamer Rocker* from Whitesboro bound for San Francisco. She kept two girls, Dana and Addie, while Rachel took on caring for "the little boys." On Thanksgiving Day, November 30 she wrote, "Although very nice for Wilder to come last night, not so nice for him to go back so early."[159]

Etta very often had to work a whole month to finish up sewing an article of clothing such as a dress. Late in 1888 she spent most of September making a dress for her sister Rosie. At the drop of a hat, she frequently had to stop what she was doing to run down loose livestock before they were injured or lost at sea. "Lots of running after stock, deal of trouble, 'Tony' breaking into corn makes me tired with other work." She went out again "on prairie huckleberrying." Wilder was earning three dollars a day working at the Salmon Creek Mill, and the farm work continued.

The Pullens had always maintained contact with their family back East. Wilder's sister Phena had married Sam and had children. On December 24 Etta noted, "Sam down for us to write in an album he is to send to one of Phena's girls." As usual they had a pleasant Christmas Day. On the last day of 1888 she noted,

---

157 *Ibid.*, 98. Her health was still tenuous and at this point, despite her constant round of home family dinners, she spent much of her day cooking or sewing.

158 *Ibid.*, 100.

159 *Ibid.*, 100.

"Wilder up and off again while I was napping so I had to build my own fire and get after the washing. The years go and come all too quickly as we grow old."[160]

March 1889 was a wet month. After much rain earlier in the month, on March 18 she wrote, "Fine. Was out with Wild in p.m. when he hauled a load of fencing to Coast."[161]Wilder had been busy working on roads and bridges. On March 30, "Wilder finished up his bridge papers to send to Ukiah by Sam." On April 1 Wilder worked at whitewashing some of the ceilings of their house. On March 19 he was back at the Albion Mill. By the middle of the month both 'Gleaner' and 'Magic' were broken enough to be good draw horses for their rides. Wilder started working wallpapering in the kitchen. On April 20, "We had a grand excursion up Albion River in boats, then on railroad to end of road, had a fine lunch spread, our pictures taken and everything lovely for all a few showers."[162] At the end of April Wilder finished a "line fence" at the rear of their house.

The second half of 1889 found Etta sewing, baking, putting up preserves, caring for animals. Wilder was splitting wood, building a barn, maintaining fences, painting and papering the house among other jobs. They hosted family and attended funerals.

The next year began with rain and high winds. In February she was finishing Eunice's jumper. She enjoyed it when the weather suddenly improved on February 12. "Phene and her mother came, also Charlie, Rachel and children in p.m. Had a good long evening with Phene." On Sunday, February 16, "We took a walk to see Phene, Wild had to go to the mill tonight, he got delayed, found 'Fret' in the Creek but he got her out." By the end of the month it cooled and became frosty. On February 23, she noted, "The most ice yet, Ben Lane, Al Gast and Chris Nelson came in a.m. We all took a walk to Rachel in p.m." On the following day, "We had a bee splitting wood in a.m., split two loads. As Gast and Chris started home about three and Wild about five."

Occasionally on the north Mendocino Coast as well as throughout northern California, it seems as if the rainy, cold and foggy weather will never relent and that sunshine might not ever return. On March 1, Etta noted, "I got desperate waiting for good roads and struck out for Marks, found them all pretty well but Artie. I home and work done up before Wild got here."[163] On March 3, "Misty all day, Rachel and Hazel went home this morn. Eunie to stay and milk in May's place [May had gone to Big River the day before this. Eunie would turn fifteen three days later, about the age Etta had been when they emigrated from Maine to California.] He and I out hunting sheep, two over the bluff and went to sea. It is too bad." Now it was May's turn to go up to Big River to take her teaching exami-

---

160 *Ibid.,* 101.

161 *Ibid.,* 101.

162 *Ibid.,* 102.

163 *Ibid.,* 102.

nation. On March 8, "Poured most of day. Eunie went home before dark. Wilder came so late. I had got quite worried." "Wild intended to stay home a day or so but got word an order to fill so he had to go to start up. We disgusted. Rachel and children here," she wrote on March 9.[164] By the end of March the weather improved considerably. On March 18, "Wilder home for a few days, tried his new plow. Went to mill tonight." Three days later, "Good weather, Harry [The couple had hired Harry Newberry to work their ranch for a short time] gets along first rate for a beginner but I have my hands full, helped cut wood."

By 1890 there had been no notes for many years about loading ships or schooners. With the start of the new decade the lumber business shifted to larger mills that were better designed and could load ships more quickly and with less danger. In May, May went to Navarro to teach. Wilder continued working at the mill. Fortunately his earnings there were not their only source of income. They continually made decisions about which livestock to sell and which to hold onto. On Sunday, May 11, "A Mr. Hendricks here to buy Ranger, came last night late. We hate to see him go but have too many. Ben and Annie called, also Phene going home (back to Maine)."[165] Sometimes others pitched in to help Wilder with his work. May 27, "Sam down for dinner, then Annie came. We all went with Wild to haul a load of wood, from there to Rachel's for croquet, took supper and spent the eve."[166]

In July Wilder had gone back to work harvesting the hay. They took one day off, July 24, to go to Mendocino. Then she was hard at work canning different varieties of jelly and jam. As he had done in the past, working on the cemetery fence, Wilder donated part of his time for the community. July 25, "Wild working on a book case for May for Navarro School Library."[167] On the 28, "My side so lame I gave up washing, got along fine sewing, Wild hauling his wheat hay in to Corrigan." On Wed., July 30, "I got Wild to go with me berrying. We had our pails full and just down to road when Jim, Vila and Annie Lane came along, they went up on 'Pea Vine' (now– 1926– 'Frog Ranch') and most filled their pails."[168] On August 2, "Wild took May's library for her school to Navarro this morning. Brother Babcock came along and invited me to take a ride with his trotter (Black) to the mill. I went. We took dinner to Jims, called to Phenes, got home about five." On August 27, "Wild off to the mill, putting in machinery to saw—shingles. A letter

---

164 *Ibid.*, 105.

165 *Ibid.*, 105.

166 *Ibid.*, 106.

167 *Ibid.*, 106.

168 *Ibid.*, 107.

from Rachel. Rachel had taken the steamer down to the Bay Area and was about to bid on a house in Berkeley. Cow Bess hung up and broke both horns off."[169]

In early October she was back at work making mince meat pies. There was a little time to enjoy life, for on Oct. 6 she noted, "A clear cool morning for an early ride. We got down to Navarro ahead of time. I home before seven and washed."[170] Wilder had difficulties with the bosses at the mill over wages. On Saturday, October 18, "Wilder quit work on the mill, could not agree on wages."[171] His other jobs continued. On October 20, "When Eunie got along, Wild took him to school and went to town to fix up some fence. He hauled down a load of hay, sheep came up handy so he sheared some in p.m."

On October 22 Wilder was hired to build a new bridge at Navarro. They also received income from renting some of her father's land. Saturday, November 1, "Wilder has had Fathers estate rented for the past ten months and re-rented for another year from today. Chores early tonight so Eunie could go home as I went for his Uncle Wild, dark and foggy coming home."[172] On November 4, "Election day. We went to Mendocino after Wild voted in a.m. All quite busy in p.m. We put in bid for proposed new road." On November 8, some terribly sad news arrived: "We hear the shocking report of Mr. Burr getting killed at his work building Navarro Mill (Wilder working with him such a short time before), falling from frame."[173] Meanwhile their bid for the new road was accepted. In December 26, "Was out with Wilder most of a.m. staking off for width of new road." The next day, "They commenced grading for new road back of house."[174]On December 30, "Wild had to go to town to get pieces of pipe cut right after their having to take up water pipes crossing the road. Showers all day." Fortunately the weather had been fair throughout December. The final notation for 1890 read, "Wild in the woods sawing for pickets. I was up a little while but sewed most of day. Another year gone. We cannot complain of the past one, have had unusual health. May the coming year be equally as prosperous or more so." With this comment Etta Pullen's diary ended.

The diary revealed not just the details of their everyday lives. It also spoke volumes about the culture and kind of society that Yanks, as well as many other ethnic groups, established during the latter half of the nineteenth century in California and throughout the west. In 1913 Etta and Wilder sold their farm at Big Gulch (*Littleriver's Yesterdays* by Irene Mallory Macdonald, 1999). They net-

---

169 *Ibid.*, 107.

170 *Ibid.*, 107.

171 *Ibid.*, 107.

172 *Ibid.*, 107.

173 *Ibid.*, 108.

174 *Ibid.*, 108.

ted enough money to purchase Etta's early Little River home from Isaiah's other heirs. Wilder remodeled and modernized this house, which he and Isaiah had built so many years before. Etta and Wilder moved in and they continued to farm the property there. While they named it Edgewood, today it is called Glendeven Inn. Wilder died on April 25, 1925; Etta continued living in Edgewood until, surrounded by her relatives, friends and neighbors, she passed away at eighty-eight on December 10, 1937.

Just as the founders of Mendocino, including Jerome and Martha Ford, William Kelley, and others were buried in Mendocino's town cemetery, the founding family members of Little River, including Etta and Wilder Pullen, Stevens and Coombs family members are buried in the historic Little River Cemetery. Many of the pioneers' descendents still live locally. The first grave, that of the baby Katy Pullen, who died soon after arriving in Little River in 1864, can still be seen in the Pullen family plot.

Although they settled, built the West's new towns and created a new culture, folks like the Pullens, Stevens, or Coombs are usually forgotten. If it were not for the Etta Stevens Pullen diary, we would know very little about the realities of daily life for settlers on the North Mendocino Coast. The Pullens' lives were that of non-stop labor and occasional holiday celebrations, marked with sickness and death of family, friends and beloved animals, generally within a network of communal support. Corporate interests simultaneously provided employment for some individuals, including Wilder, and (at least those like the MacPherson Company, which was melded with others after 1900 into the giant Union Lumber Company) took land that had been by settled and belonged to the Stevens family and others.

Pioneer men and women divided the chores, the men usually doing heavy labor such as plowing, cutting and stacking wood, building and maintaining barn and house, and doing the greater part of the heavy livestock chores. The women centered their efforts more on cooking, sewing, cleaning, washing and ironing, rearing and teaching children, and tending the home garden as well as lighter livestock chores: milking, feeding, gathering eggs. Both pitched in when a partner had to be away or more hands were needed. Sickness, injury, disease and childbirth were frightening everyday threats. People hosted other families, kept in touch with others through personal visits, attended funerals, political events, weddings, parties, and dances.

CHAPTER 14. OUT OF THE PAST — A SURVIVOR'S STORY

"Hanging, that's dog's death. We done nothing to be hung for. Must we die, shoot 'em."

—Chief Lassik, immediately before being executed, 1862.

"Make hair raise on back of my neck. Make sick stomach. "

—Lucy Young to Edith Murphy, 1939.

While Etta Stephens was opening her diary to write about her voyage aboard steamers heading west in 1864, white militiamen in Northern California were decimating Lucy Young's family. Lucy was part Lassik and part Wailaki and was born in Alderpoint, less than fifty miles from the mouth of the Eel River.

Lucy Young was a granddaughter of Chief Lassik. For many generations the Lassik Indians inhabited the rugged region of northern California near the mouth of the South Fork of the Eel River. Their territory included the land to the east as far as the headwaters of the Madd River. The Madd River, as well as the upper Van Duzen River, was a part of their tribal land as far as Lassik Peak. Just ten years before the start of Lucy's recollections (1862), in the fall of 1852 Commissioner Redick MeKee's Expedition had passed through Lassik tribal homeland.

Lucy's father was an Alderpoint Wailaki. The word "Wailaki" means "north language." The Wailaki's heartland lay to the south of the Lassiks' including most of the North Fork of the Eel River except near its head where it overlapped Lassik land. The Wailaki were the northernmost Athabascan tribe on the Eel River. Before 1862 the Lassik and the Wailaki also controlled other parts of northwestern California. About one year later, in 1863 white militiamen shot and killed Chief

Lassik and Lucy's brother. Not long after this she also witnessed the death of a half sister and her mother. And yet remarkably she did not show any anger or hatred for the white man who took over most of the Indians' lands.

Her story begins with her memory of one of her grandfathers, who was so old that he had to be carried around in a large basket by one of his sons, an uncle to Lucy. When she was about seven or eight, in 1859 or 1860, her grandfather made a stark prediction:

> "White rabbit is going to devour our grass, our seed, our living. We won't have anything left of this world. Big Elk, the one with straight horn, will be brought here by the white man." This meant they would bring another animal, one larger than the deer. One with round feet and hair on its neck. Probably oxen or even horses.

The old man's daughter, Lucy's aunt, had pleaded with him:

> "Oh, Father, you must be crazy. Don't talk that way!"

Already by 1860 serious fighting had broken out simultaneously in various parts of northern California. "Gen. Kibbe's War" began to the south along the Sacramento River near Red Bluff and Oroville. Soon it extended northward to Shasta Mountain. It finished with battles that defeated bands of the so-called "Red Cap" and Pit River Indians along Redwood Creek, the Madd River, the Trinity and Klamath Rivers. To the south in northwestern Mendocino County near Round Valley, a militia force under Capt. Walter J. Jarboe defeated the Yuki, Nomlaki and Wailaki Indians in the so-called "Mendocino War." There were very few, if any, recorded white casualties, while hundreds of Indian braves were killed in battle or taken prisoner, disarmed and relocated to the reservations. Some warriors were murdered in cold blood.

Lucy explains why she spoke out to Edith V. K. Murphy. Mrs. Murphy was a white Philadelphian who lived for many years in Round Valley. After 1900, Mrs. Murphy taught English to the Native American people she found at the Round Valley Indian Reservation. In return, Lucy Young and others were Murphy's mentors on local topics. The Indians in Round Valley, who were descended from many different tribes, were related to the survivors of the period of bloody conflict included in Lucy Young's testimony. While the white side of this campaign has been well described, both by military participants and historians, the following rare account tells the Indians' side of this epic conflict. In 1939, when Lucy related this to Ms. Murphy, Lucy was married to Sam Young, a Round Valley farmer.

> "I hear people talk about what Indian did in the early days to the white man. Nobody ever tell of what the white man did to the Indian. That's the reason I tell it. That is a history I saw myself. My father and brother were killed in the soldiers' war before the soldiers captured us. There was a three day-long battle. Just blood, blood, blood. Nothing but killing. A young woman, one of my cousins, ran away from the

soldiers into our camp. All of us girls were running. I lost my buckskin blanket. My cousin ran back and retrieved it. I rolled it up and put it under my arm so I could run better that way.

I had another cousin who was a young man. He had a gunshot wound that creased his scalp. He was bleeding copiously. There was blood everywhere. We took him to the river, washed him off and cleaned up the wound. We bandaged his head tightly, and he didn't die like so many of the others. I asked my mother about my brother and father. I wanted to see where they had died but she refused.

'Both were killed,' was the only thing she would tell me.

I helped her escape from there and we started to run.

The battle killed almost all of our men. One little boy had his kneecap shot off. Another young man was shot through the thigh but survived. One young woman who had been kidnapped by the whites returned one day badly wounded. She was shot through the lights [?] and liver. Her front skin hung down like an apron. We bandaged her wound with a cotton dress, and she lived. Only two of our men survived the battle.

White people want our land, want to destroy us. They break and burn up our baskets. They break our pounding rocks. They destroy our ropes so we cannot use snares of hunting. We cannot get any deer-skins. They break our flint knives.

At this point, once again Lucy returned to her grandfather's last days.

The old man said, 'I'm not crazy. White rabbit has lots of everything. He's going to bring his big canoe (covered wagon) here.' My grandpa ran his hand through my hair. He called me, 'Little Shorty.'

As he gently smoothed her hair, he said,

'My child, you will live a long time! You will be in this world a long, long time.'

One day he called his grandchildren to him and said, 'Pretty soon I will be dead. I'll speak no more.' And that night he asked for a drink of water. Then he drank more water. He drank a lot that night from a small cup he always had. He died the next day.

Our people dug a broad, deep hole. They lay a large fire and lit it. The laid his body in the burning pit along with the basket and strap they had carried him around in since he couldn't walk for many months before he died. He went where people go at the last. He had very good teeth.

Lucy continued her description about how her mother, together with her two small daughters, took to the run. It was August, 1862.

"When I was ten my little sister was just seven and three feet tall. They took us all to Fort Baker which was on the Van Duzen River. A soldier there gave me a cup and a small bucket. Twice Mother ran away. When they took us to the lower country, I also ran away. Many time we ran away together, all three of us."

The last time they left Fort Baker they escaped to redwood country. Lucy's mother found a hollow tree for them to hide in. There they rested during the day, going out only at night for food or water. Lucy remembered making good use of her cup and bucket. Many times in the thick brush she nearly lost the way. She remembered to mark the trail with broken branches here and there. Once she snapped a fern down in a certain way to find her way back to the hollow tree, their temporary home.

"Way down the gulch, there were lots of hazelnuts. We eat. Traveled on. Near alders and a spring. A man suddenly raised up his head like the branches of a tree. He began running when a horn sounded. As he left they heard a branch break loudly from below.

"We saw horse tracks. Hide again. Somebody whistled. We dropped into a fern patch. A soldier had to walk by. We stayed hidden for a long time. After sundown we walked a long ways down the ridge. I heard something behind us. Dogs were barking. As she looked back she expected to see dogs. Instead a skunk family was following them down the trail.

"After walking all day we came to a little flat. There was heavy timber surrounding the clearing."

At last in what seemed to be a safe place both girls fell asleep, all that evening and through the night. Their mother dozed fitfully. She was too sick and scared to eat and would only drink a little water. She told them that if she died, to return to the soldiers and ask for help. They lived off a small supply of crackers and some beef jerky that some Fort Baker soldiers had given them.

They got up and moved on. Lucy carried some water back to her mother and sister in her bucket. They were heading over the coastal mountains to the small settlement of Cottonwood in the Sacramento Valley just south of Redding.

"Poor little sister was very tired. Can't hardly walk."

Lucy took her sister's hand as she searched for serviceberries.

"Caught sight of bear and deer tracks. Got pretty close to our own country. Li'l sister sleep but me and mother no sleep. We heard a bear coming. Mother raise up head. Moon just coming up, I listen, listen. Bear pass by.

Then Mother said, 'Children, wake up. Let's go! Sunshine big all over country.'

"We go round Lassik Peak on top of ridge. It was rocky. I looked for water. When I found some I drank some and carried some to Mother. Rest awhile. We go down creek, catch crawfish. Mother can't eat hardtack, it made her sick.

Mother cried, 'Ducklings coming down creek.' I stand in creek, caught li'l ducky in skirt. Two of 'em. Too young to run on top of water. We killum, club."

They went back to the head of the Madd River. After camping there shortly they moved onto the South Fork mountains. They stayed there for about a month eating hazelnuts and "lotsa kettn (camas) bulb." The winter rains started. They built a small bark house. Thinking the soldiers might kill them Lucy refused to return to Hoopa although her mother wanted to return.

They started a fire to smoke out some grasshoppers. Others saw the fire and realized they were still alive. Lucy went down the river looking for her uncle, Chief Lassik. When she saw him walking toward her, she cried out. He rushed to embrace her. Grabbing her hand, he walked back with her to greet her mother. It was fall again, the acorns were "getting good." Once back at camp, they broke out the oak ball and played catch. After being separated, mother and daughter enjoyed their reunion.

A young Indian man kept telling them, 'Don't be afraid. They won't kill you. Gonna' take you Fort Seward.' It was a pleasant winter partly because Chief Las-sik and some of the men had passed it with them. There was plenty of venison. The hills were full of deer. The hunting seemed easy, but suddenly and without warning things were about to get terribly worse.

A white man and his wife came. They wanted Lucy to come with them to care for their baby.

"He herd hogs, take me to South Fork mountain. He want me to stay with his woman. He planned to take the hogs to Weaverville." They had another Indian woman, who beat Lucy often. This woman didn't speak the same dialect that Lucy spoke. She stayed with them about a week but couldn't take it anymore. It had started to rain almost constantly. She lost her bucket in the river after the man beat her again thinking she'd gotten a bucketful of muddy water from a hole near their house. She ran beside a thick stand of redwoods. Later as she made her way down the trail, a grizzly bear began growling at her.

"At last I come home to Fort Seward. I see big fire in lotsa downed timber." At the same time she smelled a very bad smell.

"I go on to house. Everybody crying. Mother tell me: 'All our men killed now.' She say, 'White men there, others come from Round Valley, Humboldt County too, kill our old uncle, Chief Lassik, and all our men.'

Stood up about forty Indians in a row with ropes around their necks.

"What's this for?" asked Chief Lassik.

"To hang you, you dirty dogs," was the white officer's reply.

"Hanging, that's dog's death," Chief Lassik say. "We done nothing to be hung for. Must we die, shoot 'em."

"So they shoot. All our men. Then they built a fire with the wood and brush they had had the Indians cut for days, build big fire, burn all them bodies. But they never knew it was for their own funeral fire. This was the funny smell I smelled before. Make hair raise on back of my neck. Make sick stomach."

Again Lucy spoke to the Indian boy who was with the white hog farmer.

"Tomorrow, 'nother white man come, gonna take you off. Way down. Tomorrow white man come. Better you stay white people, better for you. All your people killed. Nothing to come back for."

"I didden say nothing, Yes nor no."

So on the next morning another white man came and took Lucy a long way away. They took both the boy and Lucy up to Blue Rock Mountain. "White man live there. Dogs begin barking. We get there, ride up to gate. White man take me off. I can't walk. Ride all day. Take li'l boy off too."

An Indian woman whom Lucy recognized came out to greet them. She was Bill Dobbins' mother. The woman took the child inside and sat down and hugged her closely. She had known Lucy's mother.

Lucy continued, "This woman live with old white man. He cooked supper. This woman don't know how to cook. He come in."

The woman asked the old man if Lucy was his daughter.

"Your papoose?" she asked.

"No."

"She put her hand on my chest.

"My Indian," she said.

"Ah-hah," white man say. "He bring out li'l baby tumbler. Give me li'l whiskey, put sugar in it, because they been out riding all day in the snow."

Then he took them all to Long Valley where he had another Indian wife. Lucy was introduced to another white man who was in Long Valley cutting wood.

"Washing face, he come in, count my finger, 'One, two, three, four days you going down, close to ocean.' I stay there, play with pups. I look back. Two small Indian boys stood there. As I look I felt afraid. I went back into the house."

That night as the man slept in a loft above her, she slept by the hearth under a blanket they gave her. The man got up early to cook breakfast.

'Get up, Breakfast ready," he told Lucy. As Lucy had her breakfast, two more Indian women came in.

"Talk quick to me."

'Poor my li'l sister,' where you from?' one asked.

"I come from the north. That bald-headed man bring me."

They said, 'He's got a wife and children. That's the way all the Indyan children came here. He brought them all.'

Lucy almost broke into tears for she missed her mother. After a while the white man returned. He and the Indian women talked for a long time. They talked as if they were about to take a big chance. By then there were five Indian women. They sat and ate a hog backbone and ribs.

The women told Lucy, 'In four days you are going to go and stay with an old couple close by.' One added, 'I got white man. I will come to see you.'

After they walked out Lucy listened carefully to be sure they were not coming back. Then, having thought about her prospects, she decided to make a run for it.

"I run in house. Match box on shelf. I put it in dress pocket. In kitchen, I find flour sacks. Take loaf of bread, take boiling meat. Take my blanket for my bed. I went out so quick that I never shut the door. Then I went to barn, open door, let all the horses out."

She'd almost forgotten that she would have to swim the Eel River. She traveled all day on the edge of the valley. She caught sight of another white man's house and a number of Indian huts. The smoke from their camp fires was a good sign. She thought she had gotten away from the white man cleanly but couldn't be sure. She also sensed that her mother and little sister hadn't given up hope of finding her alive. Then she found a footbridge to get across the Eel. She climbed up another hill and then came upon another large clearing. She could see many people and the sound of bells. The group consisted of mostly white people. They talked loudly and there was laughter. It began to get dark and she waded through water that was knee deep. It was where Bill Dobbin's mother lived. She recalled,

"Owl commence holler, coming daylight. Way this side, great big rock. Big live-oak. Hollow place. I lay blanket down. Sleep all day. Dark. I wake up."

Soon she passed by Bell Springs Mountain and was almost to Alder Point. She slept another two nights in the open. She was so tired that she had to stop and sleep for three days. She entered Fort Seward again. There were a lot of Indian widows at Fort Seward when she arrived. Along the way she knew that Indian boys watched her and a white kidnapping ring led by a man on a giant white horse nearly grabbed her.

She came upon a pot that was gently boiling with buckeye soup. Quickly she tasted it. It wasn't ready yet, too bitter. She hid herself behind a bush. She could hear a woman coming down the trail toward the buckeye soup. At first the woman didn't see Lucy. She was preoccupied with the cooking. The woman added water to the basket as she mumbled to herself about it being bitter.

Suddenly Lucy recognized that the woman was her mother, and she stepped out in plain sight. Her stirred the soup with her hand and shook some of the drops off. Then, looking around, her mother said,

"That you? My daughter!?" The distraught woman grabbed Lucy, hugged her, and held her close for a long time.

"Come back here in the morning or at midnight," she said.

"No," Lucy said. "I've got grub, got blanket, I sleep down the hill, some place."

Lucy didn't want to risk being taken again by the kidnappers. She hid out for two more nights sleeping near the creek "under big tree roots." She returned to her mother's house again the following midnight. Her mother gave her another blanket along with some food. Lucy watched the stars to tell what time it was.

Two white men caught her again. They forced her and her aunt into a large boat. They took them to a clearing where they had a house that was near Poison Rock.

Lucy stated, "I see old man pack wood. We been on look-out. He go in bark house. I look in door, big fire in middle of house. Man say, 'Li'l girl, look in door.' They get up, bring me in. Young girl lay there, sick, my half-sister. That night she die. Snowing, raining hard."

The next day the men buried the little girl's body outside the house.

She escaped again and made another long trek across the mountain range to Cottonwood. Lucy described what happened next,

"My cousin, Ellen, Wylackie Tom's woman, was there. We found her right away. Then I stay at Cottonwood all summer. After a while, my cousin living with white man.

Ellen left the white man when he suddenly wanted to kill her for some unknown reason. Lucy stayed with Ellen and Ellen's son for a while. It was a desperate time for all the Indians, especially the men.

Lucy said, "Ellen's cousin-brother [?] say to me, 'Take care of my li'l boy, cause I gonna Hayfork. Maybe white folks kill me so please care for my son! Takum way off.' "

Hayfork was named by settlers because it was where they harvested their hay and put up haystacks. A branch of the Trinity River named Hayfork runs into the South Fork of the Hyampom. Lucy, her mother, the little boy and some others proceeded south to Hayfork where they stayed for six months. While there, both Lucy and her cousin worked for a white man who cooked for them in return. Then another white man took Lucy's younger sister away. Lucy said that even if she happened to see her again she doubted if she would recognize her as her sister.

While still in Hayfork she met Sam Young, a small farmer and one of Hayfork's Indian residents. She finished her memoir by describing her courtship and marriage to Sam:

"About twenty five years ago [ca. 1914] I marry Sam. Marry him by preacher. Sam, he's good man. Hayfork Inyan. Talk li'l bit different to us people, but can understand it. We get old age pension, buy li'l place in Round Valley. Keep our horses, keep cow, keep chickens, dogs, cats, too. We live good."

* * *

Note: Lucy's account of what happened to her as a child growing up in northern California's difficult early 1860s was recorded by Edith van Allen Murphy in 1939. Just as the passage of many years may have altered some of Jesse Apple-gate's memory of the Oregon Trail, it is possible time may have changed some details of Lucy Young's account. Despite the blurring in detail due to the passage of many decades, general impressions caused by real events and real tragedies do not fade and will never change. Clearly Indians of the West were changed by the increased numbers of whites. They approached whites with more hostility and less trust, by necessity if they were going to survive.

Lucy, her sister, and her mother were forced to use their knowledge of their homeland, northwestern California, to survive in the wilderness. For example they knew they could take refuge at Fort Seward for the Army didn't make war on children or women. It is doubtful that California Army forts were completely enclosed.

Years later Mrs. Murphy placed her notes in Nannie Escola's trustworthy hands at Kelley House Museum, Mendocino, CA. The above chapter was tran-scribed by Frank Baumgardner in 2009.

EPILOGUE

Today's Indians, whose ancestors were alive when John Work's party strode along the Pacific coast up through Mendocino County in the spring of 1833 and marched north from the Russian River to the Humboldt Bay, or who witnessed Redick McKee's expedition, have valid reasons to be angry about how the white man lied and haphazardly took the lives of so many. California's reservation system, established during the 1850s, was a miserable failure in many ways. White settlement not only took lives unnecessarily but also destroyed the habitat that for thousands of years had supported the indigenous peoples' way of life. In 1852 when the Mendocino Reservation was just an idea, there were at least forty-two Indian village sites from the Russian River to the Mattole River along the North Mendocino Coast. Now nearly all of these sites are gone.

Probably no figure in American letters told California's early story better than Bret Harte. Born in Albany, New York. August 25, 1836, Francis Bret Harte lived for a while in Arcata near Eureka on Humboldt Bay. He was employed by a weekly newspaper, *Northern Californian*.

In the early morning hours of February 26, 1860, a drunken band of whites brutally murdered approximately one hundred Wiyot men, women, and children on a small island later known as Gunther's Island. The Wiyot tribe had lived and created the village of Tolowot on Duluwot Island by discarding shell fragments that had accumulated over thousands of years. The island was visible to white settlers on the shores of the Humboldt Bay from a few miles away. In order to prevent being found out, the murderers purposely used hatchets, knives, and clubs rather than their guns that would have awakened and alerted the populace of nearby Eureka. Young Bret Harte was the acting editor of the paper on that morning. His description pulled no punches: "Today we record acts of Indian aggression and white retaliation. It is a humiliating fact that the parties who may be supposed to represent white civilization have committed the greater barbarity."[175] His reward for being true to his profession was that the local toughs ran him out of town. While his news story won him respect among other writers across the state and a portion of the public, he had to relocate to San Francisco.

Given the risks inherent in the story of journeys such as those of Stanley Taylor in 1853 or, ten years later, Etta Stevens to the Far West, they were fortunate not to have been seriously wounded or worse in the process. The threat of an Indian attack on a wagon train, while it was certainly real, may have been less likely than an accidental discharge of a musket or a pistol. Bear Flag Lieutenant and Mendocino Reservation Agent H. (Henry) L. Ford, one of early California's bravest white leaders, died when he hastily reached for a pistol from a holster on the back of his horse at Nome Cult Farm in June 1860.

Research for this book required many trips to the North Mendocino Coast where I searched archives, museums and libraries. Local history museums such as the Noyo Hill House at Fort Bragg, Held-Poage Library, Ukiah, and Kelley House Museum offer what little written material somehow was preserved; there are letters, newspaper articles, diaries, notebooks, photos, family summaries, memoirs and recollections. Other records were simple handwritten notes by individuals such as Nannie Escola. Historians too often have provided exclusively the white man's history. However, one can infer from the limited and exclusive material that remains and attempt to fill in the gaps in the record, even if the result may only be a shadow of the reality of what once was.

My research revealed how often the union of one man and one woman extended beyond the nuclear family to nurture the development of entire towns such as Little River, Ft. Bragg and Mendocino. Jerome Ford's diary shows that in 1854 he traveled from San Francisco to the East Coast where he married his bride in the month of May during a rainstorm that had left the city of Hartford, Connecticut, "half under water." Martha and Jerome set sail back to Mendocino City. Together and with help from Ford's partner, E.C. Williams, they founded the first really successful saw mill company, The Mendocino Lumber Company. It is a remarkable story of courage, luck, hard work, and fortitude; not only did their marriage survive but, by 1865, the company had annual profits of over $250,000. In the meantime the Fords had five children who were brought up by the best standards of their time. Not bad for a New England boy, orphaned at an early age, left entirely to his own devices.

Almost simultaneously, as Jerome Ford was building and developing the Mendocino Lumber Company mill on the banks of Big River, both the Army fort

---

175 *Ibid.*, 109. The full transcription of Etta's diary is available at Kelley House, a full-service research facility in Mendocino, CA. The transcript of the diary is also available at the recently renovated and reopened Little River Improvement Club.

of Fort Bragg and an Indian reservation, the Mendocino Reservation, came and went. Solemn promises were made to the California Indian tribes by Congress, and locally to such tribelets as the Mitom Pomo, the Coastal Yuki and Pomo, through its 1851 Commissioner Redick McKee. Later the poorly-run Office of Indian Affairs' corrupt and inefficient California Superintendent, Thomas J. Henley, failed to fulfill Congress' mandate.

By 1870 literally hundreds of thousands of native Californians had lost their lives. The true record of this terrible time for the Indians may never be known as most of today's Indians have no wish to retell their side of such a sad and bloody story. In part due to the state's 1850 constitution that insured an inferior status for all Native Americans, Indians lived at Mendocino Reservation in a state of desuetude, a hand-to-mouth existence. Yet, despite suffering from discrimination, being many times cheated out of their rightful pay for work performed, they managed to survive. Their story needs to be told and retold, not forgotten or denigrated by the state's poorly funded elementary and secondary school systems, by its secondary schools, colleges and universities. The Mendocino Indians saved ships from being shipwrecked in storms, built structures for the Army, worked in the households of many white families, and brought in crops and great quantities of timber, fish, mussels, and seaweed from which others took the profit. They were almost daily reminded by their generally white settler neighbors of the extent of their supposed inferiority. It was not until a generation *after* 1900 (1921) that they become citizens of the United States with the rights and responsibilities that this entailed. Even then, like other groups such as women and ethic minorities such as Asian or African-Americans, Native Americans still faced discrimination in civil rights, housing, employment, and other aspects of normal life.

Estimates of the decline in Indian tribal populations further underscore the cost that settler genocide, deliberate or not, extracted from the California Indians. According to ethnologists like Shelburne Cook in the 1930s and 40s and numerous others like Robert Heizer, who have come later, the Coastal Miwok population declined from 2,000 in 1800 to 250 in 1851, and to only 60 by 1880.[176]

For better or worse, during the period here examined (from 1850 through 1900), whole new industries, the redwood and Douglas fir logging and lumber industry, the tanbark and railroad tie trade, farming, and fishing began and flourished on the north Mendocino Coast and throughout the Northwest. While in the end it left a twenty-mile swath of still-to-this-day highly polluted land within Ft. Bragg's City Limits, it also created fortunes for a few while supporting thousands of workers and staff members. Hundreds of small saw mills flourished that provided incomes for thousands of new immigrant laborers, while lighting

---

176 See "Bret Harte – Biography and Works, www.online-literature.com/harte/, accessed on the Internet, 2/25/09. Every year since 1992 on the last Saturday in February Wiyot tribal members and their supporters revisit the island and a nearby one to recall and value the lives of those who died there.

the fire under a bubbling, new melting pot on the West Coast. Out of this pot emerged the wondrously diverse multicultural, multiethnic society of today's northern California. Aided by a fleet of schooners and other vessels, the lumber industry was started by many individuals, men like Jerome Ford and Alexander MacPherson, for example, in Mendocino and Fort Bragg. As the nineteenth century waned this industry was further stimulated. During the 1920s, led by C.R. Johnson, MacPherson's company became the Union Lumber Company, one of the most important segments of the nation's economy. Eventually Georgia-Pacific bought out the Union Lumber Company. It shut down in 2002 after creating an as yet unresolved disaster of many acres of polluted waterfront land.

Looking at such developments from the viewpoint of the twenty-first century, one is awed by such a complex and rapidly changing three-dimensional jigsaw puzzle. The desire to examine the past, supposedly a simpler time, is best satisfied by looking directly through the eyes of the indigenous people and the settlers like Etta and Wilder Pullen, Stanley H. Taylor, or Jesse Applegate, who were actually there.

Official Army records on Ft. Bragg are few. However the officer in charge of building the new fort, one of the last to be built by the US Army on the continent, sent a letter on April 22, 1906, from Washington, D.C. (the Mexican War veteran was now a retired Brig. General), addressed to the "Mayor of Ft. Bragg" four days after the earthquake: "I learned with deep regret of the destruction of your city." Enclosed were a check for $5 "which may relieve someone's distress" and an early photo of Fort Bragg.[177]

While the information that comes at us now as "the news of the day" may be repulsive to some, reconstructing the past can be an exciting and enlivening process (if confusing and often challenging). If just one person who reads my work begins to wonder, to probe a little deeper, and is excited and encouraged in the process then I will feel my work has certainly not been in vain. That database of humanity's self-knowledge, to which we add a tiny amount every day of our lives, informs our culture and our posterity.

---

177 See "Letter to Mayor of Ft. Bragg by H.G. Gibson, Brig Gen. USA, Retired, April 22, 1906," *Ft. Bragg Advocate*, May 22, 1906, Noyo Hill House, from letter to author from Sylvia Bartley, Sept. 7, 2007.

APPENDICES

APPENDIX I. GEN. SHERMAN'S VIEW OF HARRY MEIGGS, LUMBERMAN AND MODERN SAN FRANCISCO'S FORGOTTEN FOUNDER

During and after the Mexican War, William Tecumseh Sherman was as-signed by the Army to duty in Northern California. In addition to being here to note events only a few years before the start of the Civil War, in April 1854 Sherman returned once more to San Francisco. He was still a young man, an employee working for Turner & Company, a company sponsored by a St. Louis bank. Although Harry Meiggs did most of his business with the Hamburg Ger-many-based firm Godeffroy & Sillem, by the summer of 1854 Meiggs also owed Sherman's employer $80,000.

One day when Meiggs entered the Turner & Co. building and asked for an additional loan of $20,000, Sherman asked him to repay the debt in cash. Instead of replying, Meiggs asked Sherman to accompany him to the Clay Street offices of Godeffroy & Sillem. According to Sherman's *Memoirs*, "There, in the presence of the principals of the house, he demonstrated as clearly as a proposition in math-ematics that his business at Mendocino was based on calculations that could not fail."

Meiggs explained that the draft was to pay for a propeller for the new steam-er to be built and used to tow the brig and lumber schooners to ship redwood down from his Mendocino mills. As a result of this bit of suave salesmanship, the Hamburg firm agreed to assume Meiggs' outstanding debt of more than fifty thousand dollars. Meiggs was advanced another twenty-five thousand dollars.

And so, while Godeffroy & Sillem made good on most of his debts, Harry Meiggs was starting to plan his October 1854 "Great Escape" departure to South America.

After Meiggs' departure Gen. Sherman commented, "The Hamburg house, which had been humbugged, were heavy losers and failed, I think." A bit later on in his notes, Sherman concluded, "with Meiggs fell all the lumber dealers and many persons dealing in city scrip." It was just one man's brief encounter with business methods in California's first great city. Meiggs' fall also set back but did not stop the development of the north Mendocino coast's lumber industry.

Note: The foregoing quotes come from General William T. Sherman's *Memoirs*, along with interpretation of the events by Nannie Escola. They can be found in her Notebook 76, on file at Kelley House Museum, 45007 Albion St., Mendocino, CA.

APPENDIX II. EXCERPTS FROM THE GEORGE GIBBS JOURNAL

Even though the Smithsonian has labeled the journal 'George Gibbs, Customs Collector, Astoria, Oregon, 1852,' it seems probable to me that Gibbs began writing it while still in the Humboldt Bay area.

1. Business Data from Gibbs' Journal, page 6:

Amt of lumber exported from Humboldt Bay up to December 1, 1852.

Say 50 cargoes piles before custom house was established

3,000,000 feet square timber

4,000,000 do square lumber 1 ¼ inch. 3 inch plank scantling Lc.

Ryan, Duff & Cos mill. Engine &c of Steamer

Sta.[Santa] Clara – 2 Engines of 150 Horse each at Eureka. Has 4 gangs of saws, double lath machines, slab cutter, edger & shingle machine. Run only one engine as yet

40 to 50 saws – can run 75. Went into operation in May 1853.

White's mill. also at Eureka 1 saw

May, Flauoors &c. 2 single saws & edgers. (Not yet at work)

Chesapeake mill – Kingsbury &als. Both power engine 1 gang & 1 edger.

Say 200 men employed as loggers, hower, &c in the L. mills.

Kinds of lumber used – yellow fir or "Oregon" pine – red spruce – Redwoods

Total power of all the mills estimated at 2,000,000 feet per month.

Entries of vessels at Humboldt Bay C.K.

29 from May '51 to Jan. 52.

40 from January '52 to December 52.

A dozen horses round Bucksport– rather more at Eureka.

2. Gibbs' Notes on Northwestern California Tribes, ca. 1850–52.

The following data are from George Gibbs' *Journal of Redick McKee's Expedition Through Northwestern California in 1851*, edited/annotations by Robert F. Heizer, Archeological Research Facility, Dept. of Anthropology, University of California Berkeley, 1972, accessed from "Klamath Bucket Brigade" on line, by author on December 8, 2008.

INDIAN POPULATIONS OF NORTHWESTERN CALIFORNIA				
Tribes	Men	Women	Children	Total
Huta Napo, by count	85	81	29	195
Habe Napo	29	42	13	84
Sahnel				
Yakai				721
Pomo				
Nazu-ta-kaya				
Clear lake and surrounding mountains				1,090
Valley of Sonoma and Russian R. est.				1,200
Road from Ft. Ross south to San Francisco bay, estimated				500
Na-loh, Car-lots-a-po	80	26	19	75
Chow-a-chak, Che-do-chog	25	25	27	77
Chol-ie-eu, Mis-a-lah	34	42	13	89
Ba-cow-a, Tu-wa-nah	28	29	28	80
Sa-min-da, Cach-e-nah	15	25	19	59
[Totals] Betumke, S. fork of Eel river	127	147	106	380
On the Klamath: Writs-pek Wah-sher Kai-petl Morai-uh Noht-scho Men-the Schre-gon Yau-terrh Pec-quah Kau-weh Mauh-teeg Sche-perrh Olyotl Nai-aguth Shaitl Ho-paiuh Rek-qua Whetl-qua				1,500
Klamath river...24) Scott's valley.........7) Shasta valley.........9)	(50 villages, at 60 souls each)			8,000
Trinity Indians				1,500
Grand Total				9,800

(As reported by Redick McKee, U.S. Agent)

3. Pomo Groups

The following is from footnote 4, regarding Pomo groups from R. McKee's letter of Sept. 12, 1851. Big Bend of Eel River from Executive Document 4, 1853, which listed the following estimated populations and locations,

1. Sonoma and the Russian River Valley	1,200
2. Clear Lake and adjacent mountains	1,000
3. First two valleys of south fork of Eel River	1,100
4. Coast, Fort Ross to San Francisco	500
5. Mountains and valleys of south and middle forks of Eel River and Van Duzen's fork and mouth of Eel River	500
6. Mouth of Mad River south to Fort Ross	400
7. Humboldt Bay to mouth of Mad River	300
Total	5,000

4. Five Villages

As Robert F. Heizer (#10) noted, the following five villages were located "near modern Willits." Same tribes noted by S.A. Barrett and by Robert McKee:

Tribe	Men	Women	Children	Total
Na-boh	30	26	19	75
Chou-e-chuck	25	25	27	77
Chor-ti-u	34	42	13	89
Ba-cow-a	23	29	28	80
Sa-mun-da	15	25	19	59
	127	147	106	300

APPENDIX III. A SAMPLING OF POETRY BY BRET HARTE

From *The Poetical Works Of Bret Harte, Complete Edition*, Boston, Houghton, Mifflin and Co., The Riverside Press, Cambridge, 1881.

1. The Babes in the Woods (1871)

Big Pine Flat

"Something characteristic," eh!
      Humph! I reckon you mean by that
Something that happened in our way,
Here at the crossin' of Big Pine Flat.
Times are n't now as they used to be
      When gold was flush and the boys were frisky,
And a man would pull out his battery
      For anything,--may be the price of whiskey.

Nothing of that sort; eh! That's strange,
      Why, I thought you might be diverted,
Hearing how Jones of the Red Rock Range.
      Drawed his "Hints to the Unconverted,"
And saying, "Where will you have it?" shot
      Cherokee Bob at the last Debating!
What was the question? I forgot, --
      But Jones did n't like Bob's way of stating.

Nothing of that kind; eh! You mean
      Something milder? Let's see. Oh, Joe!
Tell to the stranger that little scene
      Out of the "Babes in the Woods." You know
"Babes" was the name we gave 'em, sir,
      Two lean lads, in their teens, and greener
Than even the belt of spruce and fir
      Where they built their nest, and each day grew leaner.

No one know where they came from, None
      Cared to know if they had a mother.
Run-away school boys, may be. One
      Tall and dark as a spruce; the other
Blue and gold in the eyes and hair,
      Soft and low in his speech, but rarely

Talking with us; and we did n't care
    To get at their secret at all unfairly.

For they were so quiet, so sad and shy,
    Content to trust each other solely.
That somehow we'd shut one eye
    And never seem to observe them wholly
As they passed to their work. 'T was a wornout claim
    And it paid their grub. They could live without it,
For the boys had a way of leaving game
    In their tents, and forgetting all about it.

Yet no one asked for their secret. Dumb
    It lay in their big eyes' heavy hollows.
It was understood that no one should come
    To their tent unawares, save the bees and the swallows,
So they lived alone. Until one warm night
    I was sitting so at the tent-door so, sir,
When out of the sunset's rosy light
    Up rode the sheriff of Mariposa.

I knew at once there was something wrong,
    For his hand and his yoke shook just a little,
And there is n't much you can fetch along
    To make the sinews of Jack Hill brittle.
"Go warn the Babes!" he whispered hoarse;
    "Tell them I'm coming,--to get and scurry,
For I've got a story that's bad, and worse,
    I've got a warrant, G—d d—n it, hurry."

Too late! They had seen him cross the hill;
    I ran to their tent and found them lying
Dead in each other's arms, and still
    Clasping the drug they had taken flying.
And there lay their secret, cold and bare,
Their life, their trial, the old, old story!
For the sweet blue eyes and the golden hair,
    Was a woman's shame and a woman's glory.

"Who were they?" Ask no more, or ask
    The sun that visits their grave so lightly;

Ask of the whispering reeds, or task
    The mourning crickets that chirp nightly.
All of their life but its love forgot,
    Everything soft and tender and mystic.
These are our "Babes in the Woods;" you've got,
  Well—human nature—that's characteristic.

2.   FATE

"The sky is clouded, the rocks are bare;
The spray of the tempest is white in air;
The winds are out with the waves at play,
And I shall not tempt the sea to-day.

"The trail is narrow, the wood is dim,
The panther clings to the arching limb;
And the lion's whelps are abroad at play,
And I shall not join in the chase to-day."

But the ship sailed safely over the sea,
And the hunters came from the chase in glee;
And the town that was builded upon a rock
Was swallowed up in the earthquake shock.

TO A SEA-BIRD.

SANTA CRUZ, 1869

Sauntering hither on listless wings,
    Careless vagabond of the sea,
Little thou heedest the surf that sings,
The bar that thunders, the shale that rings,—
Give me to keep thy company.

Little thou hast, old friend, that's new,
    Storms and wrecks are old things to thee,
Sick am I of these things, too;
Little to care for, little to rue,—
I on the shore, and thou on the sea.

All of thy wanderings, far and near,
    Bring thee at last to shore and me;
All of my journeys end them here,
This our tether must be our cheer.--
    I on the shore, and thee on the sea.

Lazily rocking on ocean's breast,
    Something in common, old friend, have we;
Thou on the shingle seek'st thy nest,
I on the waters look for rest,—
    I on the shore, and thou on the sea.

SAN FRANCISCO.

FROM THE SEA.

SERENE, indifferent of Fate,
Thou sittest at the Western Gate;

Upon thy heights so lately won
Still slant the banners of the sun;

Thou seekest the white seas strike their tents,
O Warder of two Continents!

And scornful of the peace that flies
Thy angry winds and sullen skies,

Thou drawest all thing's small or great
To thee, beside the Western Gate.

O lion's whelp, that hidest fast
In jungle growth of spire and mast,

I know thy cunning and thy greed,
Thy hard high lust and willful deed,

And all they glory loves to tell
Of specious gifts material.

Drop down, Oh Fleecy Fog, and hide
Her sceptic sneer, and all her pride!

Wrap her, O Fog, in gown and hood
Of her Franciscan Brotherhood.

Hide me her faults, her sin and blame;
With they gray mantle, hide her shame!

So shall she, cowlèd, sit and pray,
Till morning bears her sins away.

Then rise, O fleecy Fog, and raise
The glory of her coming days;

Be as the clouds that flecks the seas
Above her smoky argosies.

With forms familiar shall give place
To stranger speech and newer face;

With all her throes and anxious fears
Lie hushed in the repose of years;

When Art shall rise and Culture lift
The sensual joys and meaner thrift,

And all fulfilled the vision, we
Who watch and wait will never see,—

Who, in the morning of her race,
Toiled fair or meanly in our place,--

But, yielding to the common lot,
Lie unrecorded and forgot.

APPENDIX IV. DEPOSITIONS RELATING TO SUPERINTENDENT HENLEY'S INVESTIGATION

1.   Deposition of S. (Simmon) P. Storms, Overseer at Nome Cult.

About six months ago a man named Brizentine settled in Eden Valley. When Col. Henley was up here last he said there was a man named Hastings who had a lot of horses, who was looking for a place to take them to. I told him that Eden Valley was a very good place, but that it was nearly all taken up. He told me that if I could buy Brizentine's place for Mr. Hastings to do so. I bought the place in the month of July last [1858], and paid $400.00 for it out of my own funds. Have not yet been refunded this money. Look for repayment in the first instance to [Sic from] Hastings and if he fails to pay it to [Sic from] Col. Henley. This money was not placed in my hands by Col. Henley to buy the claim referred to. I expressed the opinion to Col. Henley that it would be advantageous to the reservation to have Eden Valley settled by some person known to those in charge of the reservation, who would bring stock into it. Eden Valley is a small valley twelve miles distant from Nome Cult. It was at the time [the word that was written but lined out by Storms] I expressed this opinion that Col. Henley informed me that Judge Hastings wanted a place for his horses.

Know Dr. Ames. First saw him when he came over here from Mendocino about three months ago. He said J. R. Browne had made charges in reference to the Mendocino Reservation. Amongst them that the Indians were not furnished with a sufficiency of food. I understood him to say that he had furnished Mr. Browne with the information upon which some of the charges were based. He told me the same thing as he did Dr. Burgess, viz., that when he got food enough to feed the sick Indians under his charge he cured them; and when he did not he turned them loose.

In presence of
Thos. J. Henley   Simmon P. (Péna) Storms[178]

J. Ross Browne

Sworn to and subscribed before me at Nome Cult this 11th day of August, 1858.

2. Supplemental Deposition of John W. Burgess

About three months ago Dr. Ames came over here from the Mendocino reservation; said amongst other things that he had a hospital there; that when the Indians were sick he took them [the word there was written but lined out by Burgess, hatch mark and 'into it' written above] for medical treatment. When he got provisions for them, he

---

178 Deposition of Subagent S.P. Storms, August 11, 1858, *Ibid.* 0303-0304.

said, he cured them, but when they failed to supply him provisions he let them go, as it was not practicable for him to keep them. I inferred from what he said that, that it occasionally happened, as it sometimes [the word will was written and lined out by Burgess] does [added above between the lines], that there was a scarcity of food for the Indians, at the Mendocino reservation.

Since I have been here, have always signed vouchers in blank for my pay. Have not yet drawn any pay except fifty or sixty dollars; because I did not want to use it. Do not know what amount of wages I sign for; that is, what amount is put in the blanks. My pay was fixed by Col. Henley when I first came here at $100 [hatch mark and 'a month' added between the lines]. Afterwards, on the 1st of March last, it was reduced to $1,000 a year. Government owes me all my pay except fifty or sixty above stated. The vouchers were sent over here for me to sign. I did not consider it in the light of a deposit with the Agent. [The word 'complained' written by Burgess and lined out] Stated [was written in above] to Mr. Storms that I thought it was [*Sic.*, a] wrong way of doing business.

J.W. Burgess[179]

In presence of
Thos. J. Henley,
J. Ross Browne

Sworn to and subscribed to before me at Nome Cult, this 11th day of August 1858.

G. Bailey

Special Agt. I. D.

3. Deposition of Charles H. Bourne

Have been living in Round Valley about two years. Saw some of the cattle sent from this valley to Mendocino in October, 1857. The steers were two and three year old apparently Spanish or half-breed cattle. Saw no full blooded American cattle, to my knowledge, among the steers. Saw about six or eight of the steers. They were worth about $50 a head. Did not see any cows in the lot, but was not here when they started. There are about three hundred head of cattle in the valley known as the Wilsey cattle. Do not know what proportion of them is [*Sic.* are] American or what Spanish. If they are American they are poor American; if Spanish good Spanish cattle. Am engaged myself in the stock business in this valley. Know the government brand. Have never seen a Wilsey brand put on top of any other brand. The government brand is a sort of C with a figure inside, which might be taken for a W, but cannot distinctly be made out. In speaking of the government brand, I refer to the brand as the Pont Reyes brand. Know that three hundred head of horses are brought up from below to be left in Eden

---

179 Deposition of Dr. J.W. Burgess, August 11, 1858, *Ibid.,* 0309.

Valley. Was told so by Thomas Henley Jr. Asked him where they were, and his reply was that his father has an interest in them. Said he was going down after them. Do not consider Eden Valley a safe place for stock in consequence of the proximity of wild Indians. Have often expressed that opinion. About a year ago, I sold to Colonel Henley some sixteen head of Americans cows, old and young, for $1,000. Signed the usual government vouchers for them at the time of the sale.

Charles H. Bourne[180]

In presence of
Thos. J. Henley
J. Ross Browne

Sworn to and subscribed before me at Nome Cult this 11th day of August 1858.

G. Bailey
Spec. Agt. I. D.

4. Deposition of Alonzo Kinsley

Was employed in October, 1857 to drive some cattle from Nome Cult to Mendocino. Went with them nearly to Sherwood's Valley. Received no extra compensation for driving them. Was at that time an employee on the reservation. The oxen were good-sized cattle; think there were also some young ones among them but do not recollect how many. Think the steers were worth on average from $150 to $200 a yoke. Think the cows were worth from $75 to $100 at Nome Cult. The bull was an American bull I think. The cattle were driven by George Henley, Thomas Henley, William Fare, [This name is illegible and lined out by author, may be 'Lebrough'] Warren [Francis E. Warren was Overseer at the Cullybull Station on the Mendocino Indian Reservation at this time], and myself. I left at this side of Sherwood's Valley. There were three cows left here; they broke out of the corral and could not be recovered at the time. Do not know how they are branded. They have not been sent over since, to my knowledge.

Alonzo Kinsley[181]

Sworn to and subscribed before me, at Nome Cult, this 11th day of August, 1858.

G. Bailey
Special Agt. Int. Dept. (I. D.)

5. Deposition of Jesse Henley, farmer on the Nome Cult reservation.

---

180 Deposition of Charles H. Bourne, Aug. 11, 1858, *Ibid.* 0311-0312.

181 Deposition of Alonzo Kinsley, Aug. 11, 1858, *Ibid.* 0313.

Was called upon by James Wilsey to make a selection of the cows for the Mendocino reservation. They reserved one cow, and gave me my choice out of the remainder, consisting of over fifty. These were all American cows—some of them of the Durham blood. Am acquainted with stock, and selected ones considered to be the best. Know of a sale of cows by Wilsey from the same brand, to a man named Wright; which both Wilsey and Wright told me were sold at $100 a head. Wilsey gave a bull calf with the bargain. The bull [hatch mark, 'sent to Mendocino' written between the lines—both by J. Henley] was a nice yearling bull, worth about $100. I bought three [the word 'Spanish' written and lined out by author] American bulls to put with the Spanish cattle, and paid for them $83 a head.

When I am paid my salary, I sign the vouchers in blank. All the employees on the reservation sign their vouchers in the same way. They sign receipts with the upper part not filled.

I consider the cows selected by me from the Wilsey cattle as good, if not better, than those bought by Wright. I selected them as if they were for myself.

Came out here last summer [1857]. When I came out I brought with me four Kentucky Jacks [bulls?], two Devonshire bull calves, six Southdown sheep and one Kentucky sheep. Two of the Jacks were for Colonel Henley and two for the government. Bought the Jacks at different places in Kentucky. The Jacks were in good condition when put on board the steamer at New York. No distinction was made between them. They all went together. Had no marks or hands on them. One of them was injured but did not know how it occurred. Thought he was the best Jack. Knew he bred well before I got him. Thought he was in good condition when he arrived here. Observed at Panama that this Jack had been injured; but on his arrival he appeared to be in good condition. Col. Henley asked me to select the two best for the government, and I selected this as one. The cost in Kentucky was as follows: one $810; one $775; one $700 and one $600. The two selected for Government were those which cost $810 and $775. One of the bulls was for Col. Henley, as I understood from him, and one for the Government. The sheep were private property. There was a contract made at Nome Cult with the steamship company by Col. Henley for the passage of this stock to California. I was furnished with a copy. The price paid in [on] the cows from Louisville on all the stock was $208, besides incidental expenses for feeding etc. The price of passage from New York to California was $250 a head for the Jacks, $125 apiece for the bulls, and $50 a head for the sheep. Besides this there was a charge of $100. for shipping the stock at Panama on board the steamer on this side; and $25 a head extra for taking the stock across the Isthmus in the cars; There were other expenses which I do not remember of the two Jacks which belonged to Col. Henley and is here at Bowens in this valley. I think the two Jacks which were selected for the Government would have brought $2000 apiece when they arrived here in one of them. I would have considered them worth $2000 in Kentucky, in another year. I took great pains to buy them cheap; and believe they were bought under the market price.

Am a nephew of Col. Henley. My passage and wages while on the trip were to be added to the cost of the jacks. I never reported to Col. Henley that the Jack at Nome Lackee had been hurt because I thought northing of it.

J.B.M. Henley[182]

Thos. J. Henley
J. Ross Browne

Sworn to and subscribed before me at Nome Cult this 11th day of August 1858.

G. Bailey
Spec. Agt. I.D.

6. Deposition of John P. Simpson.

Was employed from the 1st of January 1857 to the 1st of April 1858, as overseer at Cullybull Station South side of the Noya river on the Mendocino Indian reservation. Was an employee on that reservation from the time of its establishment. Am familiar with the history and condition of the reservation. There is a saw-mill at the mouth of the Noya river on the North side. Have always regarded the land upon which the mill stands as within the limits of the reservation. It was generally understood at the reservation that Hair Creek was the Southern boundary. Was told so by the Agent [H.L. Ford]. Do not recollect that I was ever told so by Col. Henley. The Cullybull station was established upon a claim purchased of [from] W. C. Davis in the fall of 1856. Had the means of knowing what Davis received for his crop and improvements; was one of the appraisers to fix the price. Do not remember accurately what he got for his claim; it was either $350 or $400. he was paid $1,700 or $1,800 for his crop, though I do not remember the precise amount. Crop consisted entirely of potatoes. Do not know the exact amount of the crop: [;] they were to be sold by the pound. The potatoes were sold in the ground and an estimate was made of the probable yield. The crop appeared at that time to be a good one. Do not remember what potatoes were worth at that time. I superintended the digging [harvest] of the potatoes; they turned out as well as the estimate, but they were not weighed. The improvements consisted of a very good hewed-log house [; was lined out, period added]. Davis' general reputation in the neighborhood was good. Do not remember that he ever had any difficulty with the Agent. The reason given by the Agent for buying the claim was to avoid having any white settlers near the reservation. Ever since Davis was bought out the claim has been regularly cultivated.

---

182 Deposition of Jesse B.M. Henley, Aug. 11, 1858, *Ibid.* 0318-0320.

The saw-mill on the north bank of the Noya river is owned by Mr. McPherson. About the time he commenced building, he applied to me [*Sic.* he asked me about] for information in regard to timber and water. The only market of any importance on the Coast for lumber is at San Francisco. There is very little demand in the neighborhood for lumber. Cannot say that it was the general impression in the neighborhood that this mill belonged to Mr. McPherson and Col. Henley, or was a partnership concern, but have heard people say they believed it was. Do not know whether provisions and stores were furnished to the mill hands out of Government stores. Think the Indians were very short of provisions in March and April 1858_Know they were at that time. Sometime during the winter the Indians were very short of provisions. They complained considerably in consequence. Do not know how many white men were employed in erecting the mill there might be more than thirty or there might be less. Do not know whether any of the employees of the reservation were engaged in getting out timber for the mill, except the carpenter who told me he was overseeing the work. The carpenter [Lyman Hinckley] told me he was to receive a certain compensation from McPherson over his wages, but do not remember how much. Understood that Indians were employed in getting out the mill timber, but personally do not know anything about it. Have heard Frank Warren complain that the government feed was eaten up by men employed to haul logs for the mill, and that in consequence his own teams were put in short allowance, or something to that effect. Have heard it said on the reservation that two or three Indians had died during that time of starvation. Never heard of any other cases of death from starvation on the reservation. It is common from Indians even when well fed to complain of starvation. The Indians in my employ frequently complain of a want of food when they are well fed. I place confidence in their claims only when I know the circumstances. Col. Henley frequently urged upon the employees on the reservation to put in all the crops we could, and raise as much food for the Indians as possible. The subsistence of the Indians is supplied in considerable extent from the fisheries in the vicinity. [Here the author wrote 'The salmon fishing in' but then lined it out] The river is the principal source from which the supply is derived. Some fish are caught outside but not a great extent. Did not live at headquarters, but at Cullyb[ull station. Some time last spring a tent was erected on the (End reservation near head-quarters [hatchmark by author- by R.K. Dodge was written in at to of page] in which he kept a store. His stock consisted of miscellaneous articles – know that he had whiskey there; have seen men drink whiskey there; do not know whether any was given or sold to the Indians. Don't know whether liquor was given or sold to the soldiers at the post- never saw any. Have heard it said on the reservation that Col. Henley was interested in the store. Suppose this was a mere suspicion. This store was still in operation when I was there when I was there on the 1st of May last. [Here two words, Before Dodge, were written in but lined out by author] Prior to the establishment of this store, Dodge had been interested in the *Globe* newspaper in San Francisco. Dodge told me so himself. Before he became interested in the paper, he had been a clerk for Tobin and Duncan, ['to' written and lined out] and was afterwards in business for himself for a short time. Know G. Canning Smith, late clerk of the Mendocino reservation- have know him as much as five years. Cannot say what Smith's general reputation for truthfulness is- some say he truthful and some say he is not; his friends speak well of him, his enemies speak ill of him. Have heard Dr. Ames say that he sometimes had to turn away his Indian patients without having cured for want of food, or for want of the right kind of food- do not remember which. Have heard Robert White speak of the Indians at the rancherias as being [hatch mark with word almost written in between the lines] without provisions. during the winter and spring of '57-8. Said they were very hard pushed for something to eat- that they had scarcely anything. My own observation during the same period it was to the same effect. He said Matteo, Chief of the Kineamares, said in front of the head-quarters, about the middle of April, to the Superintendent [Henley] that his people were starving, and that they would be forced to leave the reservation unless they got something to eat. About that time was about the hardest time I have ever known on the reservation. A good many Indians left during the winter- a good many without leave_ some had to leave. The Indians on the South side of the Noya had leave to go. It was the practice to allow Indians to go out from the reservation to gather food in the mountains, whenever it was considered expedient; [I] Think the majority who left the Mendocino reservation never came back. During the acorn season it might be advantageous to let them go out, if they could be depended upon to return. Think I would allow such as I have confidence in to go out during that season.

Thomas J. Henley   J.P. Simpson
J. Ross Browne

Subscribed to and sworn to before me at Long Valley this 12th day of August 1858.

G. Bailey
Spec. Agt. I.D.[183]

7. Deposition of Robert White

Question by Mr. Bailey- If you had been in charge of the reservation at the time Mr. McPherson commenced erecting the mill, would you have felt it your duty to forbid him from doing so?

Answer: Cannot answer the question. Col. Henley informed me that McPherson was going to build a mill there. Was never present during any conversation between Col. Henley and McPherson in reference to the mill, either in San Francisco or at the reservation/ Do not know whether Col. Henley has any interest in the mill. Don't know anything about Col. Henley's affairs. It was generally reported amongst the people on the reservation that Col. Henley was interested with

---

183 Deposition of John P. Simpson, Aug. 12, 1858, Ibid., 0329-0333.

McPherson in the mill. I do not refer to McPherson's men- never heard them speak of it. [There is a sentence written and lined through by the author, appears to say 'Cannot say that I ever heard it said that Col.']

Question by Mr. Bailey. Did you ever hear it said that Col. Henley received a consideration for consenting to the erection of the mill?

Answer: Decline answering the question.

Know that Hinckley was employed in the woods getting out the timber. Hinckley said he received $25 a month from McPherson. There were some of the reservation Indians employed in the woods getting out timber for the mill. There were twelve or fourteen who worked steadily- at the time I saw as many as fifty at this work. Upon that occasion they were working under the direction of one of McPherson's men. He was not working them to the best advantage, and I stopped and told him so. These were wild Indians: the majority [hatch mark- of them] were wild- some were Mission Indians, they were all reservation Indians. We consider all Indians reservation Indians who have ever been upon the reserve. These Indians were in addition to those who worked steadily under Hinckley. Do not know that any of these Indians were paid by McPherson. When I left the reservation on the 12th of April a portion of these Indians had not been paid- a portion of them had been paid in part. Those who were not paid complained. The reason assigned for not paying them was that McPherson had no money at the time. They were to be paid 50 cents a day.

Don't know that any of the government stores were furnished to the Mill hands. Loaned McPherson beef, which was to be returned. On one occasion borrowed a ham and some flour from McPherson for my own use. Borrowed it because I was short of provisions on the reservation-the supplies not having arrived. This was about the middle of March. The rations for the 1st Quarter of 1858 began to give out about the middle of March. The supply furnished is enough to last the quarter through if properly taken care of. ...

Know G. Canning Smith. Don't know whether Smith was at the time the three men were arrested for selling liquor to the Indians, a Justice of the Peace or not. Know the year for which he had been elected was out, but do not know whether under the law, he was authorized to act after that. Cannot say what his general reputation for truthfulness is.

There is a store on the reservation about a half a mile from headquarters kept by R.K. Dodge. It is a canvas tent. Cannot say whether liquor was ever sold there or not. Dodge kept whiskey at his store. [Words written but lined out are Have heard it said on] Kept more than he could use himself. Have seen one barrel there. Have heard it said on the reservation that Col. Henley was interested in the store. Don't know what ground there was for the statement; don't remember who [whom] I heard speak of it. I understood from what McPherson said that James Tobin was the owner of the store. Never saw any government goods in the store.

Question by Mr. Bailey: Did you ever hear of any Indians dying of starvation on the Mendocino reservation in the months of March and April 1858?

Answer: Decline answering the question. My reasons for not wishing to answer the question are 1st Because there are so many rumors: 2 Because a good many of the reports come from sources I cannot rely upon; 3rd Because I was told so by a person whose name I do not wish to give. Do not know that any Indians starved to death on the reservation. At intervals during the winter and spring the Indians suffered from the want of food and were suffering from the same cause in April last. Considered it my duty to protect the food from waste as much as to protect the Indians from suffering. I was then in charge of the storehouse and exercised my own discretion in giving food to the Indians when it was there. During the winter there had arrived on the reservation several shipments of beans and rice. There was not time where there was not some beans in the storehouse....When I issued rations to the working hands I gave each the same quantity, from time to time, as I considered necessary from their support. This was where there were rations on hand and the Indians stood in need of them. Only three issues were made during several months to the tribes; one was a full issue, one a half issue, and one a quarter issue. Some beans sent to the reservation for seed beans were given to the Indians during the period of scarcity. When we found our supply of provisions scarce we were obliged to curtail the number of our working hands. There were about twelve or fourteen hands at work at head quarters during the period when they were curtailed; at Cullybull Station five; at Bald Hill I don't remember- works six or seven when he has work for them. We could have worked a good many more hands.

So far as my observation extended the seeds furnished to the reservation were of good quality. Some seeds belonging to the reservation were sent up in a box of goods to Mr. Dodge. I sent down for them and got them. Suppose they wee put there by mistake. Don't know that Mr. Dodge ever had any seeds to sell in his store. The mill hands had the use of the government boats to bring down timber for Mr. McPherson. They had the boats during the whole time of the building of the mill: they kept the big boat up the river. We could use them whenever we wanted them. The big boat was injured [Sic., damaged] by getting aground with a load in her, by McPherson's men. The Indians during the salmon season [the word the written and lined out by author] catch large quantities of salmon: the rock cod fishing is available all the year round in calm weather, which about one fourth of the time. The Indians get the most food from the salmon fishing.

Recollect seeing the cattle that were sent over from Nome Cult to Mendocino in the fall of '57. Saw the steers. There was one yoke of Spanish cattle; the balance were [sic, was] unbroken American steers- do not what such steers were worth at that time. There were seven American cows with them- don't know what the cows were worth= they were good cows. There was also a young Americans bull- considered him a good bull. Remember sixteen head of work cattle purchased in the fall of 56-7. They were called Texas cattle. They were wild and we had hard work breaking them. Do not know whether at the time I left the reservation, they were obliged to lasso these cattle in order to yoke them or not. George Henley brought the cattle up to the reservation. Don't remember whether George Henley had ever been up to the reservation before- he may have been there once before.

In presence of   Robt. White
Thos. J. Henley
J. Ross Browne

Sworn to and signed before me at Long Valley, this 13th of August, 1858.
                         G. Bailey
                         Special Agt. I.D.[184]

8. Deposition of H. L. Ford, Sub. Agent at the Mendocino Indian Reservation

I have been employed upon that reservation since the 12th of November, 1855. I have been SubAgent since June '56, at which time I presented my official bond. Had previously acted as SubAgent. Am familiar with the history and condition of the reservation. When I came upon the reservation I understood that it consisted of a strip of land three miles wide, extending from the Noya river to some little distance above the Ten Mile River. Took possession of Little Valley in the spring of '57. Little Valley is more than three miles from the Coast. There was no one settled in Little Valley at that time. In the fall of '56, I effected the purchase of Davis' claim; was told by J. Tobin that Col. Henley desired the claim purchased for the reservation; bought it in consequence of what Mr. Tobin said; since that time the land has been occupied as a station; [hatch mark, 'think I' written by author up above the line] paid three hundred dollars for the claim- may have paid three hundred & fifty; - think Davis received $1,700 for his crop, which consisted of oats and potatoes; can't say whether the potatoes were weighed or not- Mr. White received the potatoes and reported that there was a certain number of tons.- think potatoes were worth at that time $3 or $3.50 per hundred.

Knew Davis; the Indians complained that Davis set his dogs on them when they went by – had no cause of complaint against Davis myself. Davis' house was about three-quarters of a mile from the river. Never heard that Davis had paid any clerk or Agent [*sic* capitalized in original] of Col. Henley, or any Government employee $250 or any other sum for effecting the sale of the said claim or crop. After the purchase was effected I considered that Hair creek was the Southern boundary of the Reservation and claimed and took possession accordingly. Davis' claim extended to Hair creek.

---

184 Deposition of Robert White, at Long Valley, Aug. 13, 1858, *Ibid.*, 0321-0328.

Considered it my duty to prevent settlements being made within the limits of the Reservation, and would prevent them under would have felt it my duty to prevent its erection, if McPherson had not received permission to build it. Think the establishment of the mill a benefit to the reservation, and frequently recommended to Col. Henley the erection of the saw mill on the Noya. My reasons were that the facilities for obtaining supplies would be increased, and employment afforded at good wages to those Indians for whom we had no use on the farm. -and therefore urged Col. Henley to permit a mill to be erected. Was acquainted with McPherson; introduced him to Col Henley and recommended that permission should be given him to build a mill. ...

There was a man by the name of C.L. Wolf and General Estill had talked a great deal with me about building a mill on the Noya, and I remarked to Col. Henley that McPherson would be a better person to erect a mill on the reservation than either of those two. Prior to my coming on the reservation, Wolf had bought the machinery for the Government or made arrangements that he could use it himself. I told him I would not purchase the machinery [hatch mark, 'except' written above by author]\by order, and [the two words 'could not' written in but lined out by author] [hatch mark, 'had no authority to' written above by author] give him permission to build the mill. Wolf wanted to build on the site of Hazzeineyer's [Hegenmeyer's] old mill. Cannot say whether the woodcutters settlement is within the limits of the reservation or not: the lines have never been marked out. If that settlement is less than three miles from the Coast it is within what the limits of the reservation as I understand them. In May 1858, Col. Henley instructed me that when 1st Lieut. Gibson should commence surveying the reservation, the line should run up the Noya to the garden; thence in a line so as to include Bald Hill and Little Valley, thence across to Ten Mile river. These boundaries would not include the wood-cutter's boundaries on the banks of the river, above the garden. In my conversations with Col. Henley at different times prior to and at this time, he stated that it was his wish to include [here the word 'all' written but scratched through by author] the fishing station and all the good land within three miles of the Coast. The settlement of the wood-cutter's is [the word 'upon' written but lined through by author] [hatch mark, 'a continuation of' written above] the same flat upon which the garden is made. [Here the word 'twelve' written and lined through].

Nine of the reservation Indian work- hands were employed for three months getting out timbers for the mill; three others were also employed at the same work for two-thirds of that time. These Indians did not receive rations from the Government at that time. They were retained by McPherson. I loaned provisions to Mr. McPherson to ration these Indians. Think this was in December and January last [1857]-might have extended into November. McPherson was to pay these Indians fifty cents a day. He paid them up in April; he had previously given them some clothing, on account. He got some clothing from me for that purpose at the completion of the payment in April; it was Reservation blankets borrowed to be replaced. None of McPherson's white employees ever received rations from the Government. McPherson borrowed provisions from me at different times to supply them. A small portion of these were rationed in April- the balance in May. In the month of March, I borrowed a few sacks of flour and half a barrel of pork from McPherson for the white employees on the reservation; it was borrowed in my name during my absence to the Mattole [the Mattole River] station.

The crop on the reservation was short at that time, and I had heard complaints that the wheat crop was short elsewhere. The weather was very rough during the spring of '58 and it was difficult to get supplies up. In December and January [Dec., 1857 and Jan., 1858] last government feed (sheaf-oats) was furnished to Mr. McPherson's teamster. This was replaced by baled hay from San Francisco. McPherson's teams continued to feed on the baled hay after it was stored in the barn, but I considered that a sufficient quantity had been returned to pay for the sheaf-outs consumed, and allow for the baled hay subsequently used. McPherson did not use any government oxen to my knowledge and I never heard of any being used. Hinckley was employed in supervising the Indians who were getting out the lumber for the mill; did all the carpenter work that I required to be done on the reservation. I persuaded him to remain, and stated to him that the difference was made up to him [the difference between what he might earn working as a carpenter in the settler's community vs. what he was being paid for the same work on the reservation].

Had an understanding with McPherson that he would refund to the government a portion of Hinckley's wages. The arrangement was this-Hinckley was to receive $75 per month from the government and $25 from McPherson. McPherson was to refund to the government such portion of $75 paid to Hinckley as had not been earned by [*sic* at] Government work. Besides the nine and twelve work Indians [or twenty one Native Americans] before mentioned, there were employed from time to time in getting out for the mill, a number of other Indians belonging to the reservation. These Indians were to receive rations from McPherson in addition to their pay. When McPherson borrowed provisions from me to ration his Indians, he borrowed enough to ration all that he employed. The understanding between McPherson and myself was that these borrowed provisions were to be returned by McPherson the first opportunity of getting supplies up. McPherson and myself never made up a written contract in respect to furnishing lumber for the reservation. Don't know whether Col. Henley received any compensation from McPherson for consenting to the erection of the mill- have heard rumors to that effect, but have been assured by McPherson that no one had any interest [or share] in the mill [any proportion of the ownership] but himself.

An understanding was had with McPherson in the presence of Col. Henley that the white men employed upon the mill were to be discharged if they Interfered with the Indians in any manner. I have had no complaints made since that understanding. At one point during the erection of the mill, the services of Wm. Ray, the reservation fisherman, who understood fishing and net-making, were exchanged for those of an Italian fisherman who understood fishing and net-making better than Ray, and whose wages were paid by McPherson. Do not know whether Col Henley has any direct or indirect interest in Dodge's store- was never advised by Col. Henley to purchase any goods from Dodge, but was advised by him [hatch mark, 'by him' written in above by SubAgent Ford] to make my purchases, as far as practicable, in San Francisco; which I do, and never buy of Dodge unless I am short of some article. Don't know if Dodge keeps liquor in his store or not, think he does not; never heard of his selling any liquor to [here] 'anybody' was written in but lined out] Indians, but Lieut. Gibson complained that the [here the word and fragment 'last sold...' were written in and lined out] soldiers at the Post had obtained liquor at Dodge's store.

Know the twenty steers that were sent over from Nome Cult to this reservation in October, 1857. Most of them were American steers-some were half-breeds. Two yoke were broken, the rest had to be broken. Think they were worth on an average from fifty to sixty dollars a head in the market. Remember the seven cows that were brought over at the same time. They were American cows. I consider them very fine cows; they are now on the reservation. Think they were worth $100 a piece [*sic* sp. apiece] at that time. Remember the bull that came over with the same lot- thought when he came he was not worth more than $50; Consider him now worth $150. As soon as I could communicate with Col. Henley after seeing the steers, I reported to him that they were not suited to the purposes for which they had been purchased; and about the 1st of April last [April 1, 1858] a new lot of oxen came [hatch mark, 'to the reservation' written in above by SubAgent Ford] from below, from which Col. Henley directed me to select such as would fill the contract. The oxen selected were worth from $175 to $200 a yoke. Remember sixteen head of Texas cattle brought here in 1856. They had been worked but some of them were very wild. Never considered them worth any more than they would fetch for beef- that would depend upon their weight. Think beef was selling at that time in the markets on the hoof at 12 ½ cents a pound- some beef, I think, was sold at Big River at 15 cents a pound. These steers would average seven hundred pounds.

Have heard rumors that Indians died on this reservation of starvation; the facts never were reported to me, and I do not believe them. The Indians were very short of provisions on this reservation this spring, and suffered from hunger, but not so much as the Indians back in the Valleys who never were on the reservation. Did not have a sufficient supply of provisions to give them all that they wanted. They suffered most in the months of February and March. It was during these months that I loaned provisions to McPherson. [here SubAgent Ford wrote, 'they were fed notwithstanding employees' and lined it all out] I believe they were fed to the Indians in his employ, and not to his white laborers. Did not see the provisions distributed, and do not know whether the white laborers received these rations from the same supply or not. Loaned these provisions to McPherson on my own responsibility- a portion of them with the knowledge of Col. Henley, who stated that he saw no objection to it if they should be returned in due time.

If my crop turns out as well as I expect, I shall be able to feed four hundred & twenty-one Indians from the 1st of September next till the 30th of June- allowing each Indian three pounds of provisions per day. By reducing the amount of the rations and compelling the Indians to subsist in part upon the natural resources of the place, double the number of Indians can be subsisted during the same period. The above is a rough estimate, not designed to be strictly accurate.

H. L. Ford

In presence of
Thos. J. Henley
J. Ross Browne

Subscribed and Sworn to before me at the Mendocino Reservation, this 16 day of August 1858

G. Bailey
Special Agent, I.D. [185]

9. Deposition of T. [Thaddeus] M. Ames, Physician on the Mendocino Indian Reservation

[I] Have been employed as Physician upon this reservation for about seventeen months. There was a time last March [March 1858] when provisions were short on the reservation, and during that period, I had to discharge some of the patients under my charge to let them go out after clover. Did not discharge more than four or five on this account, there are about thirty patients there drawing rations in the hospital and the rancherias.

They could obtain plenty of mussels at that time, but I preferred to let them go after clover in consequence of the nature of their disease which was gonorrhea. There was [sic. were] beans in store but the rice was out.

Consider the erection of the saw mill beneficial to the reservation. Think the Indians are better contented when they are kept at work; some of my patients now go away against my orders to procure work at the mill.

We have always had difficulty in consequence of the intercourse of white men with the Indian women in giving them disease; but do not know whether any of the white hands employed in the mill have interfered with the Indians. Know that orders have been given in case any of the mill hands were found interfering with the women to report to McPherson, and he would discharge them. Have had no cause to

185 Deposition of Subagent H.L Ford, Aug. 16, 1858, *Ibid.*, 0335-0344.

report such interference. There has been a gradual increase of venereal among the wild Indians for the past eight or nine months; I attribute this in great measure, to their having become acquainted with the Christian [Christian was another term for Mission] Indians.

T. (Thaddeus) M. Ames, MD

In presence of
Thos. J. Henley
J. Ross Browne

Subscribed to and Sworn to before me at this Mendocino Reservation this 16th day of August 1858.

G. Bailey
Special Agt. I.D.[186]

10. Deposition of L. (Lyman) F. Hinckley, Carpenter on the Mendocino Indian Reservation.

Have been employed since the 20th of September 1855 on this reservation; as carpenter. Was paid at the rate of $100 a month, up to January '58, when my pay was reduced to $75 a month. When my pay was reduced made up my mind to leave the reservation, but was induced to stay upon the understanding that that I was to be placed in charge of Indians getting out lumber for Mr. McPherson and to receive from him $25 a month in addition. Was paid by McPherson during the months of January, February, and March [1858]. Was employed in superintending of the cutting of lumber for McPherson's mill from the 16th of October to the 7th of February. During the same period did all the work that was required to be done on the reservation. Draw my rations from government as usual during [here the word 'the' written but lined out] that period, and received pay from the government at the rate of $100 a month up to the 4th of January. The number of Indians employed under my supervision ranged from ten to thirty- but usually there was an average of about twelve. These were selected on account of being good choppers; there were fifty others on the reservation as good choppers, work hands. Heard of no complaints of a want of farm hands during that time; when they wanted any of those under my charge they took them.

Know nothing of any liquor being sold or given to any of the Indians on the Reservation by Mr. Dodge. Never heard Dr. Ames complain that he had been obliged to turn Indians out of his hospital because he could not get proper food for them. Do not know whether a contract was ever made by Mr. McPherson with any person on this reservation of $500 or any other amount for getting out the timber for his mill. Cannot say what the lumber got out by the Indians under my care was worth.

---

186 Deposition of Dr. T. (Thaddeus) M. Ames, Mendocino Reservation Physician, Aug.16, 1858, *Ibid.* 0349.

Whilst working those Indians I employed eight or nine white men, who were paid by Mr. McPherson. Some of these men were paid by [*sic.* on] orders on J. L. Hill at Big River, signed by H.L. Ford. The orders were redeemed, as I was informed by Mr. Hill, when McPherson came up, some time in April. Mr. McPherson borrowed money from myself and Hegenmeyer, amounting to about a thousand dollars to take them up. McPherson had the use of our boats about six days; one of them got jammed by one man at Big River, McPherson's men [repaired it; the repairs they did to our boat were worth more than the 'services,' so that in point of fact the use of [here the word 'the' was written but lined out and the word 'our' was written in above] boat by McPherson was a benefit to the reservation. We are using one of McPherson's boats now at this time. Have used it for over two months. Think the mill is a benefit to the reservation in that it furnishes work for the Indians, when not otherwise employed. When we used Indians who are at work in the mill we go and take them, which we have done on several occasions.

My orders from Captain Ford are to allow no Indians to work there, who are wanted on the reservation; it is a general order. [Illegible word, possibly 'The'] farmers I know [the preceding phrase was written but lined out by author] The provisions which I borrowed for McPherson's men at work in the [here the word 'mill' was written but lined out and the word 'woods' was written in above] were returned. The provisions were borrowed for white men and Indians. Do not know whether any other provisions were loaned to McPherson. The Indians in the rancherias made no complaint to me of suffering from hunger; those under my charge were well fed during the winter; did not visit the rancherias ten times a year that I know of.

Lyman F. Hinckley

In presence of
Thos. J. Henley
J. Ross Browne

Subscribed and Sworn to before me, at the Mendocino Reservation this 16th day of August 1858.

G. Bailey
Special Agt. I.D.[187]

11. Deposition of William H. Ray, in charge of the fishing station at the Mendocino Indian Reservation.

Have been employed on this reservation about two years. The Indians have generally been well supplied with food since I [the two words, 'have been,' written in by Mr. Ray here but lined through, one word, 'came' written in above] here- sometimes they have been short. Think the amount of fish and shellfish which the Indians could procure for themselves would be equal to about half their subsistence.

---

187 Deposition of Lyman Hinckley, April 16, 1858, *Ibid.* 0356-0357.

Think the rock cod that could be caught outside would be equal to one half the salmon and small fish that could be caught in the river [the Noyo River]. The logging in the river has not had any effect upon the fishing that I have observed. There has been no salmon fishing since the logging commenced, but the amount of small fish has been the same. Am not apprehensive that the logging will disturb the salmon fishing; on the Albion and Big River, it has been no injurious effect. The Noya river is not so large as Big river, think it is larger than the Albion. There was a Company on Big River last season, who [sic, that] caught the salmon below the mill; never saw any seines hauled in the Albion. Fisherman tell me they [here the word 'salmon' was written in above] are very plenty there [or 'fishermen tell me that the salmon is very plentiful there']; do not know whether they caught their fish below the mouth or above it. Have known quantities of right [? or 'night'] cod and pozies [?] to be caught in the Noya [Noyo] river since the boom was extended across it for logging purposes, which were never caught inside the river before to my knowledge. Think the logs and boom kept them in the river. Believe fish have been caught that would not have been caught if the boom and logs had not been there. Believe the establishment of the boom and logs on the Noya has been benefit to the fishing so far. [Here the author wrote and lined out the following four words, 'McPherson and his men'] Have a surf boat; a yawl and a [here the word 'skiff' was written in and lined out by author] dingy belonging to the reservation. McPherson and his men borrowed the boats for fetching down shingles and boards. He never had them when I needed them. He injured me [or, possibly, he impaired the progress of my fishing] by leaving it [the skiff?] loaded with shingles; it was strained [sic, it was damaged], and leaked when the tide went out. McPherson has had one boat [hatch mark: illegible word, possibly 'for' his men] since the first of April; has had other boats since. Borrowed his boat when they were repairing our boat; have borrowed his boats since to go fishing; have had one of his boats for two months at a time for crossing the river. Have had his boats a great deal more than he has had ours. Know of liquor having been brought ashore in bottles; by Captains [sic, captains] of vessels- never saw any barrels of liquor brought ashore; have written orders from Captain Ford to allow no liquor to cross in the boat.

The Chief Matteo at a table in front of the head-quarters in April last [April 1858], which was interpreted into Spanish by an Indian and into English by myself, told the Superintendent [Supt. Henley] that his people would [here the two words, "were starving," were written and lined out with a hatch mark and the two words, "would starve," written in above] and asked leave to take them back to Bodega where they came from. He was afraid everybody would starve on the reservation. He subsequently told me as a reason for his making this request at that time that he was told by a white man that [here Mr. Ray wrote and lined out 'there would never be'] no more vessels with food coming to the reservation, and there would never be any more food sent here. He said to Col. Henley at the same talk 'if you doubt my word come down to my rancheria and see the condition of my people for yourself.' I inquired of him, a few days or less than a month, after the talk who told him to speak of starving, and he said he was afraid to tell- that the white man would kill him. Matteo has several times in my presence expressed his good feeling towards Capt. Ford for giving him food; he said Captain Ford always gave him food when there was any to give him.

In presence of   Wm. H. Ray
Thos. J. Henley
J. Ross Browne

Subscribed and Sworn to before me at the Mendocino Indian Reservation this 16th day of August 1858.
G. Bailey
Special Agt. I.D.[188]

Supplemental deposition of Wm. H. Ray

Am acquainted with G. Canning Smith. Have heard him say in the office that he had the dead-wood on Col. Henley; that Col. Henley had promised to get him an office and had not done it and now had promised him again, and he (Smith) [parentheses those of Mr. Ray] was not going to take promises any more; but would see that he did do it, and when he had got all the influence he could out of him; he would twist him out of his boots; the damned old shit. This was a few days after Mr. Browne had left for San Francisco in April last [April 1858]. Shortly after this conversation, Smith left the reservation and went down to the City. He had been up here all the winter and spring up to that time.

In presence of   Wm. H. Ray
Thos. J. Henley
J. Ross Browne

Subscribed and Sworn to before me at the Mendocino Indian Reservation this 17th day of August 1858.
G. Bailey
Special Agt. I. D.[189]

12. Deposition of W.A. Wilsey, Farmer on the Mendocino Indian Reservation

Have been an employee on this reservation since 15th or 10th of March last [1858]. Was engaged in the States with Col. Henley in the business of stock-raising, but prior to leaving the States bought him en-

---

188 Deposition of William H. Ray, Head Fisherman at Mendocino Reservation, August 16, 1858, *Ibid.*, 0358-0359.

189 Supplemental deposition of William (Bill) Ray, Aug. 17, 1858, *Ibid.* 0362-0363.

tirely out. Have had business connections with Col. Henley since. Have sold him some stock since I came to California, and have sold him other things. Col. Henley supplied me with a few cattle, since that date [March 15 or 19, 1858], to be kept on joint account. [hatch mark by author here, the following sentence was written in between the lines, 'Have no business connection with Col. Henley now.']

Question by Mr. Bailey- Did not Col. Henley have a lot of cattle on a ranch in San Mateo County and did you not take care of them on shares?

Answer- Decline answering the question.

Question by Mr. Bailey- Were you not interested in taking care for Col. Henley of five hundred head of cattle now in Nome Cult Valley?

Answer- Decline answering any such question.

Question by Col. Henley- Do you have any particular reason for declining to answer?

Answer- Yes, if I answer the question I wish to answer correctly, and that I am not prepared to do at this present time.

Question by Col. Henley- Have you any additional reasons for declining to answer and if so, state them!

Answer- One reason would be because the stock belonged to different men.

Question by Col. Henley- Is there any other reason?

Answer- Don't remember any other reason at this time.

Question by Mr. Browne- Do you own cattle in partnership with Col. Henley now?

Answer- I decline answering.

W. A. Wilsey

In Presence of
Thos. J. Henley
J. Ross Browne

Subscribed and Sworn to before me at the Mendocino Indian Reservation this 16th day of August, 1858.

G. Bailey
Special Agt. I.D. [190]

---

190 Deposition of W.A. Wilsey, Aug. 16, 1858, *Ibid.* 0359-0360.

13. Deposition of G. Canning Smith

Was an employee on the Mendocino reservation from sometime in the fall of 1856 to some time in April 1858. [Mr. Bailey here showed papers to interpret. These papers are correct copies of the originals which I furnished to Mr. J. Ross Browne, except that I think the wages paid to Hinckley as Carpenter of the reservation were set down as an additional item, in the original account. The "account" was made out from the books of the reservation: the facts made in the memorial are true to the best of my knowledge and belief.

Question by Mr. Browne- Did you not furnish me with a separate memorandum, in reference to Hinckley's wages?

Answer- I may have done so, but do not distinctly remember. it [sic, It] was my intention to put it in the account. The memorial was prepared some time during the month of February 1958.

Did not furnish a copy to Col. Henley. A copy of the original was taken from my desk about two weeks before Mr. Browne came up to Mendocino. ["Heard after my return from San..." ,written but lined out by Mr. Smith] While in San Francisco, soon after Mr. Browne visited the reservation, I was told by Dr. Ames that a copy was in Col. Henley's possession. Never informed Col Henley of my intention to make these charges, I received a communication in reference to them. Capt. H.L. Ford prepared to sue on the part of Col. Henley that I should retract the charges that I had made, and that if I would do so, Col. Henley would use his influence to obtain me the post of Inspector of Customs at the Big River. I did not accept the proposition.

Question by Col. Henley: Did Capt. Ford state to you that he was authorized by me to make this proposition?

Answer. Captain Ford came to me and told me that he had had a conversation with Col. Henley and that his (Col Henley's) wish was that I should retract these statements I had made, and sign a document to that effect, [written in above, 'that'] he [hatch-mark- 'Col. Henley' written in above] would secure me an appointment at Big River, and provide for me, in the meantime, till that came on.

Question by Col. Henley. [One word, 'Objected,' written and lined out, probably by Mr. Smith.] Will you reply categorically yes or no?

Answer. I will not.

Question by Col. Henley: Then you did remember [here the word 'that' written in but lined through by Mr. Smith and a single word 'whether' written in between the lines] he did say that he was authorized [sic. ?].

Answer: He did not say in so many words that he was authorized, but did say it was his (Col. Henley's) wish.

Question by Col. Henley: Did you ask him or did he say whether it was my wish.[?]

Answer: Both.

Question by Col. Henley: Did he say that he had it from me, that it was my wish.[?]\

Answer: He did not say in so many words that he had it from him, (Col. Henley) but he did say that it was his (Col. Henley's) wish.

Question by Col. Henley: Did you ask him whether he had any authority?

Answer: I did not ask him that question.

Question by Col. Henley: Did you not think a matter of some importance to know whether he was authorized by me.[?]

Answer: If I had wished to acceed [sic. sp. accede] to such a proposition. I should have been more minute [precise] in my inquiries; [here the word 'though' was written in but lined through by the Head Clerk Smith].

Question by Col. Henley: Had you any purpose at that time of making [hatch mark, 'any' written above] use of this proposition?

Answer: No.

Question: by Mr. Browne: Did Col Henley a day or two after you arrived in San Francisco in April, go with you into the office of the Collector of Customs. [B.F. Washington] and recommend you for the appointment of Inspector at Big River?

Answer: He did.

Question by Col. Henley: When were you elected Justice of the Peace at Big River?

Answer: In the fall of 1854, I was elected for one year. Was not commissioned the first year. Did not act as Justice of the Peace, that year. Was re-elected the next year, (1855 [no period] Was elected and commissioned for one year; or until another Justice of the Peace was elected and commissioned.

Question by Col. Henley: Does your commission read in that way?

Answer: I object to answering the question.

Question by Col. Henley: Do you remember how your commission reads?

Answer: Doubtful. I do not remember.

Question by Col. Henley: If you do not remember, why did you state and how do your successor was elected. [?]

Answer: Because I believe I was right in making such a statement.

Question by Col. Henley: What ground had you for believing s[?]

Answer: [here the words 'Objected to the question' were written and lined through someone] Decline answering the question.

Question: [here it does not state who asked this question, probably Col. Henley] During the time you were Justice Of the Peace at Big River, did you impose any fines?

Answer: I object to answering the question.

Question: Was your time expired before you went to the reservation?

Answer: I object to answering the question.

Question: Were some persons arrested-Big Charley and some others at Mendocino reservation and brought before you for selling liquor to the Indians?

Answer: Objected to.

Question: Did you ever pay over into the Treasury, to the credit of the proper funds, any fines collected by you while acting as Justice of the Peace.[?]

Answer: Object to the question.

Question by Mr. Browne: Will you state why you object to answering these questions?

Answer: I don't consider it any of Col. Henley's business. Consider it my business.

Question by Col. Henley: Did you ever tell Mr. McPherson, Mr. Wm. Ray or any other persons that you had obtained information that you intended to use for your interest in getting that appointment of Inspector at Big River. [?]

Answer: I did not, but that Col. Henley wished me to go to San Francisco, and he would obtain the appointment for me.

Question by Col. Henley: Did you ever tell Bill Ray that you had the deadwood on Col. Henley?

Answer: No.

Question by Col. Henley: Do you state positively that I told you that if you would go down to San Francisco, I would get you that office.[?]

Answer: I state this, that Col. Henley told me that if I would go down to San Francisco, he would use all his influence to obtain this appointment for me, and said, that if I would down with him there [at the time he and Mr. Browne were on the reservation] [the preceding was in the original] that he thought and felt sure there would be no trouble in obtaining it for me, as he had been under a understanding heretofore in regard to my being an applicant for the office.

Question [probably by Col. Henley] Did I not tell you that I thought it exceedingly doubtful whether such an appointment would be made or not.[?]

Answer: You did not, [;] I went down expressly on your promise.

G. Canning Smith

In the presence of,
Thos. J. Henley
Subscribed and Sworn to before me, at [Illegible, presumably 'Men Res' i.e., "Mendocino Reservation"], this 29th day of August, 1858.

G Bailey
Special Agent I.D.[191]

14. Deposition of Horace Maloon

I reside in San Francisco. Am acquainted with G. Canning Smith formerly Clerk at the Mendocino Reservation. He called upon me on the 27th of April last [April 27, 1858] and stated his object in coming to the city at that time. Capt. Sprague [Capt. Sprague, US Army, was the commander of the federal troops at Fort Bragg or at Mendocino Reservation near this time.] had told him (Mr. Smith) that he (Mr. Smith) ought to have a better place, and advised him to ask J. Ross Browne to procure him the post of Inspector at Big River. Smith told me that he had spoken to Brown [Special Agent J. Ross Browne] on the subject at Mendocino Reservation, and that Browne had promised to use his influence for him when he (Browne) returned to San Francisco, and had advised him to come down. He further stated that he had called on Browne and that Browne had promised to go with him to Mr. Washington if he would call the next day. He did call the next day and Brown asked him if Col. Henley had said any thing to him in reference to the papers he (Smith) had furnished him (Browne) at Mendocino. Smith said no, and Browne remarked that was very singular. Brown advised Smith to get Col. Henley to go to Col. Washington with him. Smith told me that he had done so. At the time Brown gave Smith this advice he repeated his promise to use his influence in his Smith's behalf.

After this Smith told me that he never could get to Mr. Brown, tho [although] he had appointments with him and he thought he (Browne) was acting singular. He said he thought Brown kept out of his way on purpose. He thought Brown was acting in bad faith with him. Smith said that it had cost him a great deal of money to come down here; that

191 Deposition of G. Canning Smith. Aug. 29, 1858, Ibid. 0362-0363.

he would not have come unless he had expected to get the place, and that he thought Ross Brown might have done better by him. He said he had not been getting more than fifty or seventy five dollars a month on the reservation, but that there was a better place there, worth $150 per month, and he believed he would go back there and make old Henley give it to him. This $150 place was one that Col. Henley's son had formerly filled. He made threats against Col. Henley about that time & said Henley was in his power. That he [Smith] could compel him (Henley) to do what he wanted thro [through] certain information he had obtained at the reservation. He got [the reservation information] partly from men who were employed on the reservation.

I had no previous acquaintance with Smith. I believe his statements. Have had no correspondence with Smith since. I am an employee at the Mint.

H.H. Maloon[192]

In the presence of Thos. J. Henley

Subscribed to and sworn to before me at San Francisco this 3rd day of September 1858.

G. Bailey

15. Deposition of James Tobin

I was formerly engaged in business in San Francisco. Mr. R.K. Dodge was at one time employed by me as a clerk, and was afterwards a partner with me. After the dissolution of the firm of Dodge, Edouard & Co. Mr. Dodge and myself continued to have business transactions on joint a/c [account]. Some two years ago I remarked to Col. Henley that I was out of business and that Dodge had very little to do in the Globe office, that we were both familiar with the market and if he needed any assistance in purchasing goods we would cheerfully furnish it gratuitously. [Here the word 'This' was written but lined out by Mr. Tobin] Col. Henley accepted our services and we furnished goods occasionally, sometimes on the order of Col. Henley, and sometimes on the order of the Agents, from that time until [hatch mark, one word 'towards' written in between the lines] the latter part of 1857. The greater portion of the goods were [sic., was] furnished on the orders from the Agents of the reservations. I was specially [Sic. sp, especially] instructed by Col. Henley to buy at the lowest cash rates, and I agreed to do so, & did so. I was particularly instructed to buy only articles of the best quality; I remember that on one occasion a bale of blankets of inferior quality were sent out to Mendocino and they were returned on my hands. A bale of blankets [hatch mark, 'of fine quality' written in between the lines] was sent up to replace them for which no charge was ever made to the U.S. The damaged blankets were distributed to the Indians at Mendocino.

---

192 Deposition of Horace Maloon, San Francisco, Sept. 3, 1858, *Ibid.* 0404-0405.

Question by Mr. Bailey- How is it that the receipts of the merchants from whom the goods were purchased, are not filed as sub vouchers, to those signed by R.K. Dodge? Ans. R.K. Dodge and I were independent merchants, on our own a/c [account], and bought and sold to all the world. I know G. Canning Smith. He told me when he was down here in April last [April 1858], that Col. Henley could have got Lansing's place for him if he had chosen to do so, and he (Smith) would be revenged on him. I have [hatch mark- one word 'previously' added above] heard him use similar language more than twenty times. He said he would do his utmost to be revenged. I prefer not to use his exact language as it not fit for ears polite.

I know Robt. White, have known him a great many years: have known him intimately.

I know him to be the greatest liar in the country; the greatest in fact I ever heard of in any country. That is his reputation wherever he is known.

Jas. Tobin[193]

In presence of
Thos. J. Henley

Subscribed to and Sworn to before me this 3rd day of September 1858
G. Bailey
Special Agt. I. D.

16. Deposition of John H. Wise

I am acquainted with Capt. Charles Sprague [Capt. Sprague commanded of the Army's troops at Ft. Bragg near the Mendocino Reservation]. I had a conversation with him soon after his return from his visit to the reservation at Mendocino last Spring [Spring of 1858]. He said he had been there with Mr. Browne. He told me that he furnished Col. Henley with a copy of Mr. Smith's charges and remarked that they were very strong. That he (or Mr. Browne, I forget which) had seen Henley's reply, and that Browne had said "Either I or Henley must go overboard." I don't remember that exact date of this conversation.

John H. Wise

In presence of
Thos. J. Henley

Subscribed to and Sworn to before me at San Francisco this 3rd day of September 1858.
G. Bailey
Special Agt. I. D.[194]

---

193 Deposition of James Tobin, San Francisco, Sept. 3, 1858, *Ibid.* 0410-0411.

194 Deposition of John H. Wise, San Francisco Sept. 3, 1858, *Ibid.* 0412.

APPENDIX V. "DOGHOLE" SCHOONERS

Barney Hakkala, whose work focused attention on West Coast ships, estimated that forty-five schooners were built in Mendocino's many shipyards. The following list of ships were cited by Walter A. Jackson, in *The Doghole Schooners*, originally published 1969, republished 1977, Bear & Stebbins, Mendocino Lithograpers, Fort Bragg. CA.

Two-masted sailing schooners built by the Peterson brothers:

1864- COLUMBIA, San Francisco.
1865- LIME POINT, San Francisco.
1865- VANDERBILT, Little River.
1869- PHIL SHERIDAN, Little River.
1869- LITTLE RIVER, Little River.
1872- NAPA CITY, Little River.
1873- SEA FOAM, Mendocino River.
1873- UNCLE SAM, Mendocino River.
1874- EMMA and LOUISE, Little River.
1874- ALICE KIMBALL, Little River.
1874- W. H. PRESCOTT, Little River.
1874- SILAS COMBS, Little River.
1875- ELECTRA, Little River.
1876- JOHANNA M. BLOCK, Little River.
1876- S.M. COOMBS, Little River.
1878- ORION, Eureka.
1878- GEORGIA R. HIGGINS, Eureka.
1879- MARY D. POMEROY, Little River.
1881- HELEN KIMBALL, Cuffey's Cove, Mendocino County.
1882- ROSE SPARKS, Whitesboro, Mendocino County.
1883- GENERAL BANNING, Navarro River, Mendocino County.
1884- ELSIE IVERSON, Whitesboro, Mendocino County.

Three Masts

1866- SUE MERRILL, Russian Gulch, Mendocino County.
1876- JAMES TOWNSEND, Noyo River, Mendocino County.
1879- PEERLESS, Umpqua River, Oregon.

Four Masts

1887- ZAMPA, Port Madison, Washington.

1887- TRANSIT, Salmon Bay, Washington.
  Five Masts
date? SHERLIND.

The SHERLIND was the first five-masted schooner. William Peterson also built two so-called "steam schooners," the LAKME, at Port Madison, Oregon and the LUELLA, at Florence, Oregon. Finally three tug boats also built by Peterson were the C.J. BRENHAM, STINSON, and DISCOVERY.

Other schooners and their builders, built in Mendocino County before 1900:

1860– GOLDEN RULE, Point Arena, John Ross,
1861- CHARLOTTE, Point Arena, John Ross.
1864- HELEN, Point Arena, W & R.
1865- LIZZIE WILDER, Point Arena, ?.
1866- MAGGIE JOHNSON, Navarro River, Crawford.
1868- MARIE G. ATKINS, Point Arena, John Ross.
1869- LIZZIE WYLDE, Point Arena, Reimers.
1874- HINDA, Point Arena, H. C. Wright.
?- INO, Navarro River, Fletcher & Bryant.
?- JOHN A. HAMILTON, Point Arena, W & R.
?- JOHN HUNTER, Point Arena, Walworth.
?- KINGFISHER, Navarro River, Fletcher.
?- NAVARRO, Navarro River, Fletcher.
?- NETTIE P, Point Arena, W & R.
?- OCEAN PEARL, Navarro River, F & K.
?- OCEAN SPRAY, Navarro River, Bryant.
? - WM. SYMONDS, Point Arena.
1875- VENUS, Point Arena, Whitehurst.
1888- LILA and MATTIE, Albion, John A. Peterson.

W&R was Walworth and Reimers.
F&K was Fletcher and his son-in-law Kennedy.

Possibly the most famous single shipbuilder on the West Coast was Hans D. (Ditley) Bendixsen, a native of Thisted, Norway. As a youth he began building ships at shipyards in Aalborg, Norway and Copenhagen. Soon after moving to the San Francisco Bay Area, he worked in San Francisco for Matt Turner, another famous shipbuilder. Bendixsen moved to Eureka where in 1862 he produced his first schooner, the two-masted FAIRY QUEEN. By the time he retired (1900) he had built over one hundred schooners. Up until 1900 Eureka was one of the most active ports on the West Coast for ship-building. He passed away in 1902. On the day of his funeral nearly every business in Eureka closed and ships all along the West Coast flew flags at half mast.

So many of the "doghole" schooner captains happened to hail from Sweden, Norway or Denmark they were often referred to as the 'Scandinavian Navy.' Most captains worked at least as hard as any of their crewmen did. Therefore most of their orders were immediately obeyed and rarely questioned. They had to be hard-fisted, scrupulously honest men who understood human nature and who sensed times to be most frugal and time to loosen up a bit. Many were part-owners of the ships they operated, yet few, if any, ever made enough money to be termed wealthy.

APPENDIX VI. EARLY LITTLE RIVER FAMILIES

The Early Pullen Family
Charles Pullen 1814 (Maine)–1884 (Little River, California)
m. Sybil Dudley (1814-1857) in 1835
    m. Elizabeth Coombs (1822–1917) in 1859
Children of Charles Pullen & (1) Sybil Dudley
Loren
James (1846–1923)
 m. Elvira Randlett
Amelia
    Mary Adelaide 1881–1948
    Arthur Jewell (Jaspar) 1882–1952
    Howard Walter 1884–1950
    Gladys Delight 1893-?

Wilder Start (1848–1925)
 m. Emily Etta Stevens (1849–1898)
William
Samuel (1850–1898)
m. Cornelia Long   m. Mary Larsen
Charles
Augustin (1852–1931)
m. Lizzie Norton
Tryphenin (Phene) (1844-1934)
m Hiram Long (1844-1924

Children of Charles Pullen & (2) Elizabeth Coombs
Sybil Imogene   Katie   Annie
1861–1917   1863–1864 1867–1948
m. Jaspar Perkins   d. age 14 mo. m. Lyman Babcock

   Early Stevens Family

   Isaiah Stevens 1809 (Maine) – 1885 (Little River, California)
1. m. Mary V. Hall (1816-1859)
2. m Rebecca Coombs 1830 (Maine) — 1898 (Little River, California)

 Children of Isaiah Stevens & (1) Mary Hall
Ellen Hall   m. William White
Rachel Francena (1846–1911)
   m. Eugene Grant Sampson
Lydia Goddard m. Isaac S. Davis
Emily Etta (1849–1937) m. Wilder Start Pullen
Steven Gifford   Mary Rosilla
1844–1904   1865–1932
      m. Helen E. Moore   m. Mark Dana Gray

   Children of Rachel Francena & Eugene Sampson
      May 1870–1951
      Eugene 1875–1901
         Hazel 1881–1896

   Children of Mary Rosilla Stevens & Mark Dana Gray
      Mark Dana, Jr. 1879–1974

SOURCES

INTERVIEWS

Mr. Patrick Renick, Usal Pomo, (Sinkyone), at the Black Bart Casino, Willits, CA, Aug. 28, 2008.

Mrs. Harriet Rhoades, Pomo, 130 N. Noyo Pt., Fr. Bragg, CA. Mother of Lucy Cooper.

Mr. Bruce Levene, local Indian expert, Kelley House Museum, summer, 2007.

PUBLISHED SOURCES:

Applegate, Jesse, "Recollections of My Childhood," Roseburg, Oregon, Press of Review Publishers, Co., 1914, Southern Oregon Digital Archives (SODA), accessed January 8, 2008.

Bear, Dorothy, copyeditor," The First Steam Powered Saw mill," Vol. IV, No. 2, The *Mendocino Historical Review*, Mendocino Historical Research, Inc. 1974.

_____ , and David Houghton, "The Chinese on the Mendocino Coast," Winter/Spring, 1990– #91, Mendocino Historical Research, Inc.

_____ , "William Henry Kelley," *Mendocino Historical Review*, Vol. II, No. 2, Spring, 1975, pp. 3-5.

_____ , and Stebbins, Beth, *Members Bonus Edition, Mendocino Historical Review*, Volumes III and IV, Number 4 and 1, Winter, 1976, 76 pp.

Bidwell, John, "The First Emigrant Train to California," reprinted 1973 by the Parks and Recreation Department, State of California, *The Century Magazine*, Echoes of the Past, Nov., 1890, Dec., 1890, and Jan. 1891.

Brodie, Fawn M., *Thomas Jefferson, An Intimate History*, New York, W. W. Norton & Co., 1974.

J. Ross Browne, *Crusoe's Island: A Ramble In The Footsteps Of Alexander Selkirk With Sketches Of Adventure In California And Washoe*, New York, Harper's Brothers, Publishers, Franklin

Square, 1871, The Scholarly Publishing Office, The University Of Michigan, University Library.

Buffum, Edward Gould, "Six Months in the Gold Mine," *Mexican Days to the Gold Rush for the Memoirs of James Wilson Marshall and Edward G. Buffum Who Grew Up* with California, Doyce B. Nunis, Jr. Editor, Donnelley & Sons Co., Christmas, 1993.

Browne, J. Ross, "The Coast Rangers, A Chronicle of Adventures in California", reprinted from *Harper's New Monthly Magazine*, Vols. 23-24, 1861-62, Balboa Island, CA, Paisano Press, 1959.

Calhoon, F.D., *Coolies, Kanakas, and Cousin Jacks And Eleven Other Ethnic Groups Who Populated the West During the Gold Rush Years* Sacramento, Cal-Con Publishers, 1986.

Coan, C.F., (State University of New Mexico), "The Adoption of the Reservation Policy in the Pacific Northwest," *The Quarterly* of the Oregon Historical Society, Vol. XXIII, March, 1922, No. 1, accessed via the Internet, *SODA, (Southern Oregon* Digital Archives), Dec., 23, 2006- Jan. 15, 2007.

Chu, Daniel and Samuel, *Passages to the Golden Gate*, New York, Doubleday, 1967.

Cornford, Daniel A., Workers and Dissent in the Redwood Empire, Philadelphia, Temple University Press, 1987.

Dillon, Richard H., J. Ross Browne: Confidential Agent in the Old West Norman, University of Oklahoma Press, 1965.

Dickinson, A. Bray, *Tomales Township- A History*, Kathie Nuckols Lawson and Lois Randle Parks, Coeditors, who also added materials, Tomales, CA, Tomales History Center, 1993.

Gapp, Bonni, "Footprints, An Early History of Ft. Bragg, California and the Pomo Indians," self-published pamphlet, 1967.

Guinn, J.M., History of the State of California and Biological Record of Coast Counties CALIFORNIA, Chicago, Chapman Publishing Company, 1904.

Harte, Bret, *The Poetical Works Of Bret Harte, Complete Works*, Boston, Houghton, Mifflin and Co., The Riverside Press, 1881.

Herman, Arthur, How the Scots Invented the Modern World, The True Story *Of How Western Europe's Poorest Nation Created the Modern* World and Everything In It, New York, Crown Publishers, 2001.

Holmes, Alice and Wilbur Lawson, co-editors, *Mills of Mendocino County*, A Record of the Lumber Industry 1852-1996, Mendocino County Historical Society, 1996.

Hoopes, Alban W., Indian Affairs and their Administration, New York, University of Pennsylvania Press, 1932, Kargus Reprint Co., 1972.

Hunt, Aurora, The Army of the Pacific, Its Operations in California, Texas, Arizona, New Mexico, Etc. 1860–1866. Glendale California, Arthur Clark Co., 1951.

Hyman, Frank J., HISTORIC WRITINGS, REMINISCENCE, Biography of *My Activities*, Ft. Bragg, Mendocino Lithographers Printer, 1973.

Jackson, Walter A., *The Doghole Schooners*, originally published 1969, Republished by Beth Stebbins, Ft. Bragg, Mendocino Lithographers, 1977.

Jennings, Francis, *The Founders (Indians) of America*, New York and London, W. W. Norton & Company, 1991, 457 pp.

Jones, Evan, CITADEL in the WILDERNESS The Story of Fort Snelling and the Northwest Frontier, New York, Coward-McCann, Inc., 1966.

Layton, Thomas N., *Gifts from the Celestial Kingdom*, Stanford, California, Stanford University Press, 2002.

_____, The Voyage of the Frolic New England Merchants and the Opium Trade, Stanford, California, Stanford University Press, 1997.

Levene, Bruce and Tahja, Katy, *Perley Maxwell's MENDOCINO*, Introduction by Bruce Levene and Katy Tahja, Mendocino, CA, Kelley House Museum, 2008.

McLeod, Norman, *Distant Voices, Different Drums, An anthology of true stories chosen from annals of Northern California and the State of Nevada*, Historically dated from 1805 to 1915. Newcastle, California, Goldridge, CA, 1990.

McNairn, Jack & Mac Mullen, *Ships of the Redwood Coast*. Stanford, California, Stanford University Press, 1945.

Mann, Charles C., *1491, New Revelations of the Americans Before Columbus*. New York, Vintage Book Division of Random House Inc., 2006.

Olmsted, Roger R., C.A. *Thayer & the Pacific Lumber Schooners*, Los Angeles?, San Francisco?, Ward Ritchie Press, 1972.

Owens, Thomas C., *The YOKAIA, A History of the Ukiah Valley Indians, 1579-1979*, Ukiah, A Publication of the Mendocino Historical Society, 1980.

Palmer, Lyman L., Historian, *History of Mendocino County, California*, San Francisco, Alley, Bowen & Co., Publishers, 1880.

Phillips, George Harwood, *Indians and Indian Agents, The Origins of the Reservation System*, Norman, Oklahoma, University of Oklahoma Press, 1971.

Pitt, Leonard, *The Decline of the Californios A Social History of the Spanish-Speaking Californians, 1846-1890*. Berkeley, Los Angeles and London, University of California Press, 1966.

Raphael, Ray, *Little White Father, Redick McKee on the California Frontier*, Eureka, California, Humboldt County Historical Society, 1993.

Rogers, Fred B., "Bear Flag Lieutenant," (H.L. Ford), *California Historical* Society Quarterly, XXX (June, 1951), pp. 157-175.

_____, "Early Military Posts of Mendocino County," *California* Historical Society Quarterly, XXVII (September, 1948), pp. 215-228.

Smith, Elbert, *The Presidency of James Buchanan*, Lawrence, Kansas, University of Kansas Press, 1975.

Stewart, George R., *The California Trail 1849-1859*, @ 1962, New York, McGraw-Hill Book Company, 1971.

Stillmon, Dorothy, *The Long Trail*, Mendocino Historical Society, 1967.

Supplemental Estimates for Indian Service on the Pacific Coast and in Remote Territories Upon either Side of the Rocky Mountains, 35th Congress, 1st Sess., House Document 93, Vol. 11, March 26, 1858, Series Set no. 957, Accessed on the Internet Dec. 26, 2006, Indian-White Relationships in Northern California 1849-1920 in The Congressional Set of United States Documents, compiled by Norris A. Bleyhl, Regional Service, California State University, Chico, 1978.

Taylor, Stanley Howard, Letters of Stanley H. Taylor, Oregon Bound 1853 to the *Watertown, Wisconsin Chronicle*, republished in *The Quarterly of the Oregon Historical Society*, edited by Frederick George Young, Vol. XXII (March, 1921- December, 1921), pp. 159-160,

Document #129, *SODA* (Southern Oregon Digital Archives) accessed December 2006 to February 2007.

Trafzer, Clifford, *California Indians and the Gold Rush*, Sacramento, Sierra Oaks Publishing Co., 1989.

Vernon, Lawrence, "A Bottle of Beer and a Bag of Durham," unpublished article, date not recorded, -ca. 1980s, Noyo Hill House, Ft. Bragg, August, 2008.

"What Became of the Little Red Schoolhouse? Tales and Photos of Early Mendocino County Schools," Ft. Bragg, The Mendocino Coast Genealogical Society, 1987.

Wilcox, Del, *VOYAGERS TO CALIFORNIA*, Elk, CA, Sea Rock Press, 1991.

Winn, Robert, "The Mendocino Indian Reservation," Vol. XII (Fall/Winter, 1986) Mendocino, California, *Mendocino Historical* Review, 1986.

"Godard Bailey-the Abramoff of 1860, Part 2: The Congressional Investigation," at historysleuth@yahoo.com/godard 2.html, accessed Nov. 30, 2006.

"The End of an Era," *A Special Section of The Mendocino Beacon and Fort Bragg Advocate-News*, Nov. 7, 2002, 24 pages, mailed to author, courtesy of Mrs. Sylvia Bartley, Noyo Hill House, Ft. Bragg, CA.

UNPUBLISHED SOURCES:

George Gibbs "Journal, Astoria and Oregon Territory, 1850–1853," Smithsonian Institution Archives, Capital Gallery Building, 600 Maryland Avenue SW, Suite 3000, Washington, D.C.

Rachel Francena Stevens Sampson's Diary.

Emily Etta Stevens Pullens' Diary.

Two 1865 Diaries: Rachel F. Stevens Sampson and Eugene Grant Sampson. Transcribed as written by Ronnie James, Little River, December, 2007.

Love Letters file, "Eugene & Rachel Verbatim." Courtesy of Mr. Ronnie James, December, 2008.

GOVERNMENT DOCUMENTS:

National Archives of the United States, MICROFILM PUBLICATIONS, Microcopy 234, "Letters Received by the Office of Indian Affairs, from 1855 through 1861, File 234, Rolls #33 thru #38 (seven rolls), CALIFORNIA SUPERINTENDENCY, 1849- 1880, 1858," National Archives and Records Service, General Services Administration.

National Archives of the United States, MICROFILM PUBLICATIONS, Microcopy 617, roll #1467, "Post Returns of Fort Wright, Round Valley, Dec. 16, 1862 to April 28, 1863," National Archives and Records Service, General Services Administration,=.

The Eighteen Unratified Treaties Of 1851-1852 Between The California Indians And The United States Government, George Heizer, Archaeological Research Facility, University of California Berkeley, CA 94720, 1972, Facsimile Reprint by COYOTE PRESS, P.O. BOX 3377, Salinas, CA, 93912

Coyote Press.com, 101 pages.

INDEX

A

Acapulco, Mexico, 147
Alabama (Confederate cruiser), 146-147
Albany, New York, 183
Albion
    Grant, 30, 155
    Lumber Mill, 153-155, 166, 168
    River, 30, 70-71, 121-124, 132-133, 141, 153-155, 159, 166, 168, 213
    tugboat, 157, 159
Alderpoint, 173
Aleut Indian tribe, 12
American Exchange Hotel (San Francisco), 156
Ames, Thaddeus, MD, 96, 106, 110-114, 197, 203, 211, 216
Anderson Valley, 147, 150, 152
Andes Mountains, 71
Applegate, Jesse, 19-20, 28, 45, 180, 186, 227
Armstrong, George Parker, 49, 54, 56
Arra-Arra, villages, 40
Aspinwall,
    Hotel, 73
    Panama, 73, 147
Astoria, Oregon, 12, 24-25, 33-35, 197, 230
Augusta (Maine), 146

B

Ba-tem-da-kai, 58
Bailey, Goddard, Special Agent, 101, 105, 108, 117-120, 198, 201, 206, 210, 219
Bald Hill Station, Mendocino Res., 94-95, 205, 207
Baptist Church (Caspar), 75, 149
Bark
    Arthur Pickering, 144
    Tarquin, 39
Barks
Beale, George, 21
Bear
    Butte, 61
    Mountains, 85
Bell Springs Mtn., 179
Bidarkas, 12
Big Gulch (Little River), 143, 152, 154, 156-157, 170
Bing, Ah, 124
Black,
    Hills, 83, 85, 88
    James, 31
Blair, Samuel, 75
Blucher Rancho Grant, 30
Blue Jacket, 36
Boise River, Idaho, 23

Bourne, Charles H., 106, 198-199
Bow Wah, 125
Boxer, George, 127
Breton, Ed, 151
Briceland, 15
Buchanan, Pres. James, 120, 229
Buck, Davis A., 36
Bucksport, 35-36, 189
Buldam (Big River), 49, 66, 68
Bull Don River, 66
Burgess, Dr. John W., 106, 111, 197-199

C

Cahto, 107
Calopooia Mountain Range (OR), 24
Carson, William, 140
Caspar Lumber Company, 125, 128
Caspari, 93
Caw tribe, Missouri, 19-20
Cedar Rapids (Iowa), 81
Charbonneau, Toussaint, 9
Charleston, South Carolina, 144
Chastee Valley, 90
Cherbourg (France), 147
Chief
    Halo, 27-28
    (Kinemares tribe), 107, 113-114, 203, 213
    Lassik, 173, 177
Chimney Rock, 82
China trade, 121
Chinese immigrants, 48-49, 103, 121, 123-127, 139, 227
Cider from manzanita berries, 40
Clear Lake, 11, 15-16, 18, 53-55, 59, 190-191
Coast Guard station, Ft. Bragg, 122
Columbia River, 3-4, 9, 12, 24-25, 33
Coombs,
    Rebecca, 146, 225
    Richard, 151
    Silas, 146-148
Cooper brothers, murder of, 38, 87, 136, 138, 227
Cottonwood, Oregon, 89
Council Bluffs, Iowa, 79-80
Cow Creek, 12
Cox, Dr., 157
Cullybull Indian Station, 95, 107, 199, 201, 205
Cushing, Horatio, 34

D

Daily Alta Californian, 48
Dallas, Alexander Grant, 155
Dancing Bill, 38
Davis, W.C., 107, 201
Deutcher, First Mate, 48
Devil's backbone, 22
Dobbins, Bill, 178
Dock, Charlie, 124
Dodge, R. K., 100, 108, 118, 202, 204, 220-221
Don Quixote, 30
Donner party, 83
Dougherty, M/C., 95
Dry Sandy Creek (Wyoming), 84
Duncan & Hendy Ranch, Ft. Ross, 69
Dupern, Norman, 34

E

East, John, 19-20
Eddy, Bill, 160
Eel River Rangers, militia, 116
Eli,
    Su Wang, 126
    Tia Key, 126
Ellsworth, George W., 34
Escola, Nannie (local historian), 124, 131-136, 181, 184, 188
Estill, Gen., 110
Euniou, 36
Eureka, 33, 35-39, 54, 62, 98, 183, 189, 222-224, 229

F

Farmingdale (Maine), 145
Farnham, Emily, 35
Faucon, Capt., Edward H., 47-49
Fillmore, Pres. Millard, 51
Finney, James ("Old Virginny"), 89
Fitch's Mountain, Healdsburg, 54
Fletcher & Bryant, 132, 223
Foo, Charles Li, 123
Fook, Choy Yan, 124
Ford,
    Henry or H. L., Agent, 98-101, 109-112, 116, 184, 201, 206

Jerome, 30, 49, 63-64, 66-68, 71-74, 76-78, 122, 127, 148, 152, 184, 186
Martha, 74, 171
Forts
Baker, 175-176
Bragg, 1, 13, 35-36, 68, 75-76, 90, 93, 97-98, 102, 107, 112, 117, 119, 121, 127, 129, 131-132, 134-138, 141, 151, 156, 184-186, 219, 222, 228, 230
Bridger, 20, 24
Clatsop, 7, 9
Kearny, 79
Laramie, 24, 82-84
Ross, 11-14, 48, 54, 67, 69, 135, 191
Seward, 177, 179, 181
Walla Walla, 12, 23-24
Fremont, John C., 22, 96

G

Garberville, 15
Garcia
Rancho, 67, 69
River, 14, 124
Gibbs, George, 1, 10, 29, 32-41, 44-45, 53, 55, 57, 60-61, 127, 189, 197, 230
Gibson, Horatio, 122
Glen Blair Lumber, 75
Godeffrey brothers, 71
Gold Bluff, 37, 39
Golden Gate, 29, 66, 69, 147, 164, 228
Gonzales (MacPherson), Petrita, 122
Graham, Major, 36
Grant, Gen. Ulysses S., 137
Gray,
Bay, 4
Mark Dana, 158, 225
Great Father speech, 58
Green River (Wyoming), 84, 86-87
Greenwood, Frank, 68
Griggs, Josiah, 36
Gualala
Railroad Logging Company, 124
(Walhala), 13, 67, 70, 124, 131, 141
Guest House Museum, 1, 97, 132, 137
Gunther's Island, 183

H

Hadley Friend, 80-81
Hallowell, Maine, 145, 149
Harmony Mission (Missouri), 20

Hayfork (branch of Trinity River), 180
Hays, Col. Jack, 117
Heard, Augustine, 121
Hegeler, Henry, 48
Hegenmeyer brothers (John, George, Gebhardt), 68, 71-72, 112, 207, 212
Heinzelman, CA Sen., 108
Helvetia Grant, 30
Henley,
Jesse, 107, 200
Supt. Thomas J., 93-102, 105-110, 113-119, 213
Higgins, Capt., 166
Hinckley, Lyman F., 112, 211-212
Hoe, Tom, 121, 124, 141
Homestead Act, 155
Hong Kong, 48, 119, 121
Hoopa, 60, 62, 95, 177
Hopah (Hoopa) Reservation, map of, 60, 62, 95, 177
Horn, Maggie, 139
Hudson Bay Company, 11-12, 17, 23
Huesti, A. J., 38
Humboldt Bay, 18, 29, 33-38, 40, 44, 54, 57-61, 90, 103, 133, 141, 183, 189, 191, 197
Hunter, James, 136, 138
Hyampom, South Fork of, 180
Hyman, Frank, 228

I

Independence Rock, 84

J

Jacksonville, Oregon, 79, 86
James,
George, 68
R. Whitney, 35
Jarboe, Capt. Walter J., 174
Jardine,
Matheson & Company, 47, 111
William, 47
John, Lee Sing, 125
Johnson, Charles Russell (CR), 136

K

Kanesville (Omaha), Nebraska, 88

Kaston, William, 68
Kelley, William, 72, 74-75, 123, 171
Kelsey, Benjamin, 35-36
Kendall, Jerome, 76-77
Kibbe, Gen. William C., 90
Kibesillah Mill, 152
Kinsley, Alonzo, 107, 199, 201
Klamath Reservation, 60
Knight, Dr., 65
Knights of Labor, 140
Kostromitinoff, Capt. Peter, 11, 13
Kye (or Ky), Lee Sing (Eli Tia), 125-126

L

Lagoda, 9
Landsbury, W. L., 34
Lansing, Capt. David, 66
Larocque, S. L., 14
Lassik Peak, 173, 176
Leidy, Dr. Joseph, 45
Lewis, Joel, 114
Liscom, Charles, 35-36
Look, Eli, 126
Lundsbury, W. L., 36

M

Mackerricher, Duncan, 128
Mackey, 7-8
Madd River, 35-36, 173-174, 177
Mal Paso, 67
Maloon, Horace, 117, 219-220
Manger, Dr., 163
Manifest Destiny, 3, 32, 79, 97
Marshall, James, 32
Matheson, James, 47, 109, 111, 121, 123
Mattole River, 11, 14, 183, 208
Mayacama Mountains, 53, 57-58, 116
McCallum, Alexander, 75
McClellan, Gen. George, 32-33
McCormick, Dr., 164
McDonald, Walter, 34
McDuffie, James V., 119
McKee,
    Eliza, 52
    John, 53

Redick, 1, 18, 33, 35, 51-54, 59, 62-63, 183, 185, 189-190, 229
McKinney, F. N., 34
McMullen, Rock, 139
Measles, 148, 160
Meewok, Miwok or Liicatuit tribe, 29, 31
Meiggs, Henry (Harry), 64
Melindy, Dr., 160
Mendocino
    Lumber Company, 65-66, 70-71, 75-77, 93, 123, 184
    Reservation, 1, 68, 78, 93-101, 105-108, 110-111, 113-114, 116-117, 119, 125, 127-128, 183-185, 197-198, 200, 203, 205, 210-212, 214, 216, 218-219, 221
    War, 174
Michelle, deputy of John Work, 13, 15-16
Milton, Mr., 148
Mittom Pomo, 14, 48
Monrovia (West Africa), 145
Moore,
    C. D., 34
    Dr., 163
Mormon Island, 32
Morrison, A. G., 45
Mosher, Dr., 159
Muir Woods, 30
Muley Jack, 127-128
Murdock, A. K., 34
Murphy, Edith V. K., 174

N

Navarro
    Ridge School, 151-152
    School Library, 169
Navata Navarro House, 67
Nelson,
    Capt. Henry, 153
    Laura, schoolteacher, 125
Noble, Alexander, 31
Nome
    Cult Farm Indian Reservation, (see also Round Valley Reservation), 62, 97-99, 105, 107, 115-117, 127-128, 184, 197-201, 205, 209, 215
    Lackee Reservation, 94, 97
Nordheimer, Bernardo, 35, 37
North Star newspaper, 73
Northern Railroad Commission, 33
Noyo Hill House Museum, 1, 13, 17, 64, 127, 129, 138, 140, 184, 189, 230

O

O'Farrell, Jasper, 64, 156
Ontario, ship, 66
Oroville, 174

P

Palace Hotel (San Francisco), 163
Palmer, Joel, 94
Pawnee country, Pea Vine (Frog Ranch), 81
Peters, George, 34
Peterson,
 Capt., 135
 John, 132
 Thomas Henry, 132
 William, 133, 223
Pillar Rock, 4
Pinole, 55
Pit River Indians, 174
Platte River, 81
Point
 Arena, 13, 124, 132, 135-136, 223
 Cabrillo, 48, 63
Poison Rock, 180
Pollard, Thomas, 138
Pomo tribes, 2, 10, 12, 14-15, 48, 53, 55-56, 63, 68, 127, 185, 190-191, 227-228
Pullen,
 Charles, 143, 151-152, 161, 224-225
 Etta Stevens, 2, 143-152, 154-155, 159-161, 164, 170-171, 186, 224-225
 Phene (Tryphenia), 224
 Wilder, 143-144, 160, 171, 186

R

Railroad Crossing (Maine), 145
Raphael, Ray, 52-54, 59, 62, 229
Ray, William (Bill), 113, 212, 214-215, 218
Read, I. L., 34
Red Bluff, 94, 116, 174
Redwood Valley, 16-17, 105
Richardson, William, 29, 122
Robinson House (Jacksonville, Oregon), 87
Ross, Rev. John Simpson, 149
Round Valley, 58, 62, 90, 97, 99-100, 105-107,
110, 114, 116-118, 127-128, 160, 174, 177, 180, 198, 230
Rowe, Theodore F., 34
Rundall, Captain, 93
Rundle, Richard, 125
Russell, Waddell & Majors, 119, 122

S

Sacagawea, 9
Sah-nel, 55
Salmon
 Creek Mill, 160-161, 166-167
 River, 37, 71, 123
Sampson,
 Eugene (Gene) Stevens, 144, 147, 153, 156, 230
 Hazel, 225
 Lane (Gordan Lane), Little River, 151
 May, 153, 225
San Francisco Chronicle, 154
San Hendrick, 74
Sanitary Ball, 149
Sausalito Rancho, 30
Schooners,
 Abraham Lincoln, 134, 150, 157
 Barbara, 136, 150, 157
 Electra, 134
 Golden West, 157
 Joanna, 158
 Laura Virginia, 36
 Little River, 36, 132, 134, 150-151, 157-158
 Mendocino, 136
 Phil Sheridan, 150
Scott's
 bar, 36
 Bluff (Nebraska), 82
Scruwauk yellow butterfly spirit, 44
Sebring, Charles, guide, 34-36, 56-59
Serrazoin Trail, 38
Severance Hotel (Shannon), 152
Sherwood Valley, 99, 127
Shipbuilders, 74, 131-132, 223
Sierra Nevada, 36
Silem (Sillem), Wilhelm, financier, 71, 73
Simpson, J. P., 94, 203
Sing Chong Company, 126
Skinner, Mrs. Alonzo A., 45
Smallpox, 51, 85
Smith,
 C. G., 66

Capt. Stephen, 30
G. (George) Canning, 99, 105-106, 108,
   114-118, 203-204, 214, 216, 219, 221
Jedediah, 58
John, 8
Maj. Albert, 45
Snake
   Indians, 22
   River (Kansas) , 22, 88
South
   Fork Mountains, 177
   Pass (Wyoming), 83-84
Southard, Jonas, 36
Squeaky Charlie (Hi-sho-na-ma), 127
St. Louis (Missouri), 9-11, 84, 187
Steamer Rocker, 157, 167
Stevens,
   Etta (see Pullen, Etta), 154
   Isaiah, 145-147, 149-150, 225
   Rachel, 144
   Rebecca, 151
   Russell, 124
Stewart,
   Calvin Cooper, 136, 138
   George R., 79, 229
Stickney,
   Barbara, 135
   Vandalia, 150
Stillwell Gulch, 155
Stinson Beach (Marin County), 30
Storms, Simmon Pena, Subagent, 97-98, 105-
   106, 111, 128, 133, 153, 158, 185, 194, 197-198
Stout, Dr. Arthur B., 45
Strawberry Ranch, 165
Suniyowhiynoof, 26-27
Susan Wardler (ship), 35
Sutter, John, 32
Sweetwater River (Wyoming), 22, 87
Sy, Ah, 123

T

Taggert, George W., 37
Taklit Indians, 49
Talbot, Lt. Theodore, 45
Taylor,
   Clarissa, 82
   Stanley H. (S.H.), 80
Tejon Indian Reservation (Kern County), 98
Ten Mile
   River, 68, 94, 136, 152, 206-207

Station (Mendocino Reservation), 114
Thompson,
   Capt., 93
   W.N., 71
Thomson Party, 69
Tillamook Head, 7
Tobin, James, 94, 117, 204, 220-221
Tolowot Wiyot Indian village, Gunther's
   Island, 183
Tompkins Ferry, 39-40
Tongs (San Francisco Chinese-American
   gang), 126-127
Trinidad, 34-37, 39-40
Trinity River, 35, 37-38, 44, 180
Truesdale, 36
Twain, Mark, 57, 156

U

Ukiah Valley, 49, 56, 229
Umpqua Valley (Southern Oregon), 24, 26-
   28, 222
Uncle Sam, Schooner, 156
Union
   Hotel (Sonoma), 66
   Lumber Company, 70, 76, 97, 121, 129-
   130, 132, 137, 171, 186

V

Valentine, John "Kanaka John", 131, 133
Van Duzen River, 38, 173, 175, 191
Vance, 37
Vioget, Jean Jacques, 30
Virginia Works, Knox & McKee, 52
Vischer, Edward, 95-96

W

W & R (Walworth & Reimer), 132
Wailaki, Indian tribe, 174
Walhalah (Gualala), 13, 67, 70, 124, 131, 141
Warren, Frank, 128, 202
Washilton, 8
Waterman & Hyatt, 66
Watt, Sam, 93

Weaverville (Trinity County), 177
Weller, John B.,Governor and US Army General, 90, 95
Wessels, Maj. Henry M., 45
Wetherbee, Henry (MacPherson & Wetherbee Lumber Co.), 111, 121, 123, 137, 155, 160-161, 165
Whaley, John W., 36
Wheeling, Virginia (West Virginia), 52
White,
    L. E., Lumber Company, 124
    Robert, 93-94, 107-108, 203, 210
Whitesboro, 167, 222
Willamette Valley (Oregon), 19, 24, 26, 33
Williams, E. C., 64, 66, 69, 71-73, 75, 93, 152, 184
Williamson, Lt. R. S., 45
Wilson, Isaac, 36
Wind River, 84

Wise, John H., 118, 221
Wiyot tribe, 183, 185
Wolf's Bar, 36
Wood Creek (Nebraska), 82
Wood, Thomas, "Tom Vaquero" , 30
Woolley's creek, 40
Writspek ranches, 37-38

Y

Yangoler tribe, 26-27
Yerba Buena (San Francisco), 30
Yoncalla Valley, 24
Young,
    Lucy, 173-174, 181
    Sam, 174, 180
Yuki tribe, 10, 15, 55, 174, 185